Robert L. Drury
Legal Counsel,
Ohio Education Association

Kenneth C. Ray
Ohio University

P-21
P
②
F.C.
990-s/wht

ESSENTIALS OF
SCHOOL LAW

New York
APPLETON-CENTURY-CROFTS
Division of Meredith Publishing Company

Preface

Although the more esoteric legal aspects of education require long-term study and are properly the concern of the specialist, a basic knowledge of school law is essential to the personal security and professional confidence of every classroom teacher and administrator. Indeed anyone, including school employees, parents, and the general public, concerned with our schools, should be alert to the legal rights, duties, privileges, and responsibilities entailed in the educational enterprise.

Essentials of School Law is a condensation of the authors' more in-depth treatment of the subject in their *Principles of School Law*. Its purpose is to present the minimum essentials of school law in such a way that the reader will be able to obtain both a general understanding of the processes of law as they affect American education and also important specific information. Obviously the authors have had to be selective in their choice of materials and cases. The basis of selection has been primarily the importance of the material to the role of the teacher and the general applicability of the principles involved.

Although it may well be useful in graduate school courses in which the instructor prefers to rely less heavily on organized textbook material than is usual, this concise presentation of school law and actual cases is intended primarily for student teachers, in-service teachers, and beginning administrators. It is hoped that its very conciseness, along with its attention to the basically significant aspects of school law, will contribute to its use as collateral reading in those relevant education courses in which the legal rights and responsibilities of school personnel are presently too sketchily covered or even ignored. It is the authors' conviction that a basic knowledge of school law is indeed essential to the professional and personal well-being of all such personnel, and this from the very first moment of employment.

R. L. D.
K. C. R.

iii

Table of Contents

VI. TORT LIABILITY

Court Cases and Principles

United States Supreme Court Cases Review

Appendixes

General
Legal Principles

I

Public School Structure

1.1. Historical Source of Public School System

The term *public schools* is used synonymously with *common schools,* and is meant to include schools created by law and maintained at public expense, which are open to the children of all the inhabitants alike. They are supported by general taxation and are generally under the control of the applicable law-making body. The terms *common* or *public schools* are likewise used to indicate the character of education found therein and are generally meant to include schools that begin with the rudimentary elements of an education as contradistinguished from academies and universities devoted exclusively to teaching advanced pupils in the classics and in all the higher branches of study usually included in the curriculum of the colleges. A school that is carried on under a church organization could not be held to properly come within the ordinary meaning of *common schools.*

The idea that a person, without reference to any special, practical end, should be educated so as to better fit him for the ordinary duties of life seems to have occurred first to the Greeks; but it was not until the post-Reformation era that the thought that every man's intellect should be trained so as to enable him to be able to read, inquire, think, and act for himself became more prevalent.

Within the period of the so-called "Dark Ages," however, two monarchs, whose names are familiar to all historical students, stand forth in bold relief. Charlemagne, while incapable of writing, himself, invited men of letters abroad to come and reside at his court schools in various cities of his empire. Alfred the Great, of England, made similar efforts, but his successors were not so much impressed with its importance, or were too much occupied with warfare to continue the educational work that he had begun.

3

In 1616 the Scottish Parliament adopted measures for establishing and supporting a public school in each parish at the expense of the land-owners and proprietors. This legislation was repealed in the administration of Charles II, but was re-enacted by the Scottish Parliament in 1696.

In reference to the effect of this educational movement in Scotland, Lord Macauley said:

By this memorable law it was, in the Scotch phrase, statuted and ordained that every parish in the realm should provide a commodious school house and should pay a moderate stipend to a schoolmaster. The effect could not be im-mediately felt, but, before one generation had passed away, it began to be evident that the common people of Scotland were superior in intelligence to the common people of any other country in Europe.

To whatever land the Scotchman might wander, to whatever calling he might betake himself, in America or in India, in trade or in war, the advantages which he derived from his early training raised him above his competitors. If he was taken into a warehouse as a porter, he soon became foreman. If he enlisted in the army he soon became a sergeant. Scotland, meanwhile, in spite of the bar-renness of her soil and the severity of her climate, made such progress in agri-culture, in manufactures, in commerce, in letters, in science, in all that con-stitutes civilization, as the Old World has never seen equalled, and as even the New World has scarcely seen surpassed.

This wonderful change is to be attributed, not indeed solely, but principally to the national system of education.

At the present time every great power of the civilized world has adopted some system of public schools. Some are not upon the high plane or basis that would suit an American, but all show an advance in the world's thought upon this question. In the United States the earliest schools were established in the towns, and this, no doubt, occurred because the town government was better able to furnish such school facilities and because the country settlements were sparsely inhabited.

The New England communities were the first to go on record in this matter, and the origin of these schools may properly be traced to Boston, Dorchester, Salem, Hartford, New Haven, and other of the older settle-ments. There is some evidence that prior to the time when the town ordered the establishment of schools, the people had by voluntary agree-ments and associations employed teachers to instruct their children.

The vote or order of the colonial government generally followed that of the town organizations. In the Massachusetts colony there was a seven-year interval, and in New Haven, three.

In 1642 and 1647 the colony of Massachusetts passed laws in reference to the education of children which, it may be said, have been the basis of succeeding requirements concerning education. In 1642 it was enacted that certain persons in each town should take account of the employment of children and especially of their ability to read and understand the capital laws.

The Act of 1647 required every town containing fifty householders to appoint a teacher to teach all such children as shall resort to it to write and read, and every town containing one hundred householders to set up a grammar school whose teacher should be able to instruct the youth so far as they be fitted for the university. They did not leave this matter to voluntary enforcement, but provided a penalty for noncompliance. At first the penalty was five pounds. In 1671 it was doubled; in 1683 it was again doubled; and afterwards it was increased still further.

The Connecticut colonists were not far behind those of Massachusetts, for within three years after the first log house was built at New Haven, they opened a public grammar school. Even previously there had been established a more elementary school.

In 1672, four county grammar schools were established and endowed with 600 acres of land. Before the middle of the first century of its settlement every colony in New England, with the exception of Plymouth, had made education compulsory. The other colonies of the United States were much slower in establishing a general plan of education than the New England colonies.

Virginia for three generations after its settlement suffered a neglected system of education. The rulers of that colony certainly did not encourage such matters, for in 1671 Sir William Berkeley, the governor for thirty-six years, wrote in reply to a question of the English Commissioners, "I thank God there are no free schools nor printing, and I hope we shall not have, these hundred years; for learning has brought disobedience and heresy and sects into the world; and printing has divulged them from libels against the best government; God keep us from both." But Governor Berkeley could not impede the onward march of civilization, and within five years after the above was written, a citizen bequeathed six hundred acres, together with ten cows and one breeding mare, for the maintenance of a free school forever.

The colony of New Amsterdam, afterwards known as New York, was as slow to take up this matter as Virginia. The first schools there seem to have been under the control of the church.

In promoting education Pennsylvania was more in accord with New England than New York; and it has been said that before the pines had been cleared from the ground, William Penn and his comrades began to establish schools and set up printing presses. The first school was opened during the initial year of the colony, and in six years a free academy was established in Philadelphia. In various other settlements the system of education developed along different lines, but there has been a general progress and improvement until the present time. The fifty years following the Revolutionary War found the common schools much better supported by law and public opinion than previously.

The South progressed considerably more slowly in this matter than the North, due largely, no doubt, to the system of slavery.

In 1844, Governor Hammond of South Carolina, said, "The free school system has failed. Its failure is owing to the fact that it does not suit our people, our government, our institutions. The paupers for whose children it is intended, need them at home to work."

The condition of affairs in the South following the Civil War changed radically, and all the southern states readily established a system of public school education.

While at first only education of an elementary and secondary character was included within the free school system, now that of a higher class is frequently included; and the tendency today is to bring education of a manual nature within the provisions of the public school system as well. Normal schools were likewise established for the training of teachers in many states.

A law passed in Massachusetts in 1827 appears to be the first legislative attempt to provide for a public high school. The first public high school had, however, previously been established in Boston around 1821.

The Massachusetts law, which was followed subsequently by similar laws in several other states, prescribed that in every town having five hundred families or more a high school should be established. Courses in algebra, United States history, surveying, and geometry were to be provided. Each town having four thousand or more inhabitants was also to provide in the high school courses in history, Latin, Greek, logic, and rhetoric. Penalties were provided by law against the towns which refused or failed to provide a high school.

In 1874, the Supreme Court of Michigan, in a case commonly called the Kalamazoo Case, decided an issue about the authority of a school district to establish a high school, as well as to employ a superintendent. In Michigan the state legislature had given school districts permissive authority in such connection. A taxpayer claimed such powers were contrary to the state constitution; but the court held otherwise.

This case had considerable impact on the establishment of high schools in the country, especially in respect to many boards which had been reluctant to do so, on the ground that the legal authority to establish high schools as a part of a public school system was doubtful. Between the years 1870 and 1890, the number of high schools in the country increased significantly. Since 1890, the establishment of high schools has continued, and the public high schools are now firmly established as a part of the American public school system.

1.2. Legal Source of Public School System

The United States Constitution is silent on the matter of education. It would seem that by the passage of the Tenth Amendment in 1791, it was the implied intent of such Amendment to reserve to the states matters of education. Such Amendment states "The powers not delegated to the United States by the Constitution, nor prohibited by it to the states, are reserved to the states respectively, or to the people."

Nevertheless, there are limitations provided by the United States Constitution which are applied to the exercise of public education in the various states. The courts have ruled that both the First Amendment and the Fourteenth Amendment may be applied to the public schools. The Fourteenth Amendment reads as follows: "No state shall make or enforce any law which shall abrogate the privileges or immunities of citizens of the United States; nor shall any state deprive any person of life, liberty or property without due process of law; nor deny to any person within its jurisdiction the equal protection of the laws."

The First Amendment reads as follows: "Congress shall make no law respecting an establishment of religion or prohibiting the free exercise thereof; or abridge the freedom of speech or of the press; or the right of the people peaceably to assemble and to petition the government for a redress of grievances." While it is not a settled issue as to the extent to which the federal government should go in supporting education in the states, the courts have ruled that Congress may enact laws under the "general welfare" clause of the Constitution to support education in the United States.

It has been established by many court cases that education is a function of the state government, and each state in its constitution provides for a system of state-supported schools. Generally, under the constitutional provisions, the state legislature is made responsible for the creation, operation, management, and maintenance of the public school system. The state legislature is considered by the courts to have plenary control over educational matters within the state, subject to whatever constitutional provisions may affect the exercise of the legislative authority. Each state legislature has provided for a central state educational agency, usually referred to as the State Department of Education.

School districts are established in each state pursuant to legislative authority, and state statutes have been passed providing for the election or appointment of school board members to exercise management and control of the school affairs of the districts. However, since the school districts are created by the state they are considered to be state agencies, as are the boards of education that are elected or appointed to operate the school districts. As a general rule of law, a board of education has only such legal authority as may be found in the various statutory provisions or which may be necessarily implied from such express statutes. Such boards of education, however, are ordinarily given certain areas in which they have the right to use their discretion and judgment, such as in the adoption of rules and regulations.

While public education is considered a state function and not a function of the Federal Government, the state legislature must exercise its responsibilities for public education in such a manner as to be consistent with the provisions of the state and Federal constitutions. The administration of public education in a state, however, is to be kept separate from other local or municipal functions, and a local subdivision has no inherent right as a part of local self-government to provide for a system of public education within its boundaries.

II

Administrative Government and Officers

2.1. Generally

While the administration and management of public school systems, like their creation, are essentially matters of concern to the state, and while the state legislature has the authority to pass such legislation as it considers advisable or necessary for the proper management and administration of the public schools, it has been the general practice for state legislatures to provide for the creation of boards of education to be in immediate charge of the public schools of the various school districts. Having created such managing boards, the legislature further implements the authority of such boards by enacting laws prescribing their powers, duties, and responsibilities. It is fundamental that such boards of education have no inherent authority, but are lawfully authorized to take such action only as is expressly granted by statutory enactments, or such action as may be necessarily implied from the express authorization. The composition of a school board, the nature and eligibility requirements of board members, are regulated in the various states by statutory provisions.

As a governing board, created by the state, such board is considered an agency of the state, although in many states the school districts are considered political subdivisions of the state; while for some purposes, in some cases, the members of a board of education have been held to be county, municipal, or town officers. Various courts have also held such members to be state officers. Consistently, however, they have been held to be public officers, holding a fiduciary relationship to the school district. A board of education in the eyes of the law is considered to be a continuing body and its authority does not change because of changes in the membership.

Matters pertaining to qualifications or eligibility, terms of office, vacancies, the holding of regular or special meetings, and the extent of the authority of a board of education as a corporate body are usually regulated by statutory provisions.

2.2. De Facto Officers

A de facto school officer is a person who has entered into possession of his office under color of title and who has assumed to exercise the functions of his office on the basis of an appointment or procedure which is irregular or invalid. If a person officially acts as a de facto officer and performs acts which a de jure officer would be authorized to perform, and if such acts are executed in a lawful manner, the acts of the de facto officer are as binding on third persons and the public as are the acts of de jure officers, and the authority of the de facto officer to act may not be questioned collaterally. However, the acts of a person who is not under any consideration a de facto officer are regarded by the law as completely void.

2.3. Right to Office—Vacancies

The general rule is that an action of quo warranto is the appropriate action to be taken to ascertain the validity of a person's legal right to a public office. Courts of equity, however, will not interfere by injunction for the purpose of settling questions concerning the proper appointment or election of persons as school board members, as such questions are of a legal nature and subject to determination by courts of law only.

The general rules of law that apply to public offices, usually, in the holding of more than one office at the same time apply with equal effect to school officers. Under the common law rule of incompatibility, public offices are considered incompatible when one is subordinate to or in any way a check upon the other, or when it is physically impossible for one person to discharge the duties of both. In many states there are various statutes which expressly prescribe that a person being elected to one specific office may not lawfully hold any other public offices. However, unless there is in existence a state statute which expressly prohibits a school board member from holding another public office, or engaging in other public employment, or unless a school board member accepts another kind of public office or public employment concerning which the legislature has prescribed that the holders of it, likewise, are not permitted to hold other public office or employment, then the common law rule would have to be applied in determining whether or not the offices are compatible. While ordinarily there is no rule that prohibits a person from becoming a candidate for or being voted for at the same election for two incompatible offices, if elected to both offices which are incompatible, he would be required to make a choice as to which he would accept. If a school board member accepts another public office under conditions which are identified as incompatible, then the rule of law is that in his act of accepting the second office, he, therefore, forfeits his first office.

For the most part, matters pertaining to vacancies in school boards are the subject of statutory regulation. Commonly, a vacancy in any board of education may be caused by death, non-residence, resignation, removal from office, failure of a person elected or appointed to qualify, removal from the district, and absence from board meetings for a prolonged period of time. Ordinarily, where school officers are elected for a fixed term, they cannot be removed without notice and without a hearing on the charges brought against them.

2.4. School Board Meetings

As a general rule, a board of education may only lawfully transact business when it is convened together as a body for such purpose, particularly in the cases where a board takes action involving the exercise of its discretion. Individual members of the board may not act to bind the district where board action is required. A school board is an entity which may act and speak as such. The separate and independent acts and decisions of the board members, even though they be in complete agreement with each other, have no legal effect. The board members must be assembled and act as a board.

Ordinarily, a board of education may transact business only at a meeting open to the public. Unless prevented by statute, a board may go into executive session and exclude the public, or decide who may be present other than the board members. While the board members at such executive session may discuss matters or receive information, ordinarily, a board has no legal authority to adopt motions or resolutions, as does the board of education of the district. Necessarily, such motions or resolutions are to be adopted at the public meetings of the board. If the board retires into executive sessions, and an agreement or conspiracy is made at such executive or secret meeting as to how each individual board member will vote on a certain matter, such agreement is illegal, and any so-called binding agreement would be unenforceable. As a matter of law, if such an agreement were made and the board members then went into public session for the purpose of officially voting on a certain matter, pursuant to the agreement made, the court on being satisfied as to the truth of the matter would have a sound basis to invalidate the action taken at the board meeting. It is not legally permissible for individual board members to make any agreements among themselves or with others by which their public action is to be restricted or bound. The courts have held that the public for whom the board acts, has the right to the exercise of the best judgment of the board members after free and full discussion among themselves, and upon the public matters entrusted to them in the public session provided them by law. Such course cannot be assured when the members by some form of agreement or prearrangement are bound to take a certain line of action.

While a board of education must take action as a body in the exercise of its judgment, and cannot delegate its discretionary powers to one of its members, a board employee, or a committee of the board, it may delegate its ministerial functions to persons authorized to perform such functions by the board.

While the courts have generally held that a board of education may only lawfully transact business at a legal board meeting held for such purpose, when the board members act together as a body, there have been situations recognized by the courts, where because of an extreme emergency necessitating speedy action, the law has not required that the board meet as a unit before taking action. Where the courts in a few cases have justified the departure from the original procedure, it has only been in cases of extreme emergency requiring that immediate action be taken by the school authorities for the safety of the school buildings or pupils, or because of some peril that was immediately threatening such safety.

In order for a school board meeting to be approved by the court in the case where a question arises, the facts must substantiate specific requirements, namely: that the meeting was properly called, legally held, and that the action taken by the board was in conformity with the requirements of law. In many states the statutory provisions authorize regular board meetings and special meetings. In some cases the statutes provide some restrictions, as to when the regular meetings shall be held, and quite often grant authority to the school boards to establish the date of the regular meetings in accordance with the time schedule established by law. Notice of both regular and special meetings must be given to the board members. In the cases where the time of the regular meetings is set by the law, or by action taken by the board of education itself, all of its members are presumed to have notice of the time of the regular meetings. As a general rule, if a regular meeting is adjourned, the board members are not required to receive individually written notification of the time and place of the adjourned meeting. The original meeting should, however, have been a legal one, and the minutes should show the time and place at which the adjourned meeting is to be held. The members present at the original meeting are then presumed to have knowledge of the adjourned meeting. However, if certain members at the original meeting were absent, and were not given notice as to the adjourned meeting, such could be declared illegally held.

As a general rule in respect to special meetings, notices must be given to each individual board member. This requirement must be strictly observed in order for the special meeting to be legally held. Individual board members could not enter into any agreement specifying that no special notice would be required. On the other hand, even in the absence of the required notice of a special meeting, if all the members are convened together at the special meeting, those not receiving notice may agree to waive the notice, and if all the members make the waiver, so long as all members of the board are present at the special meeting, the meeting may be legally held. The only purpose of a notice of a special meeting is that all members of the board may be informed of such a meeting. Such requirement is dispensed with by the presence of all members at the meeting. It is fundamental, however, that all the members must be present and all agree to act without the requirement of notice having been given. If one member is not given notice, or he refuses to waive notice, then the special meeting would be a nullity.

It has even been held that although a reasonable notice is necessary to require attendance at a special meeting, or at least the notice required by law, if all the members of the board should come together with no prior agreed intention of holding a meeting or transacting business, it would still be competent for the board members, upon suggestion and by mutual agreement, to hold a meeting and transact any official business they might deem necessary, except that required to be transacted only at a regular meeting.

In some states the statutes provide that the notices of the special meetings shall set forth a purpose for which the meeting was called. Unless the statutes so specifically provide, however, the notices are not required to specify the purpose of the special meeting. Any business that a board of education is authorized to exercise may be transacted at a special meeting, unless the statutes require that certain action of a board of education may be taken only at a regular meeting. Some jurisdictions expressly provide that certain things may be done by a board of education only at a regular board meeting.

Time and Place of Holding Meetings. The general rule of law is that unless a specific statute requires otherwise for a board of education, such board has the judgment to select its meeting place even though the meeting may be outside the district. Where the law requires that the meeting of the board be held in the district or at a specific place, the statute prevails and a meeting held at any other place would be illegal.

While the board has the discretion, unless restricted by statute, to select the place of holding a meeting, if a particular board is in the practice of ordinarily holding its meetings at a regularly designated place within the district, and if the board members should conspire together to hold a secret meeting away from their regular place for the purpose of

denying the public the right to be present, then in an appropriate lawsuit the court could conceivably hold such a meeting illegal.

So long as the actions of the board are reasonable it may hold its meetings at any time it decides to do so, in the absence of a statute to the
contrary. Where, however, a particular statute sets the date of holding
a board meeting, the statute controls. Whether or not such type of statute
is directory or mandatory is not a completely settled question. The better
rule would seem to be that the statute is directory and if a board of
education acts in good faith and holds a meeting within a reasonable
time to that designated in the statute, it should still be considered a legal
meeting.

Board Quorum. While, ordinarily, all board members must receive
notice of a board meeting, which notice depending on the statutes involved may be either actual or constructive, it is not required that all the
board members be present in order to make the meeting a legal one. It
is an established principle of law, however, that a quorum must be
present. As a general rule, if there is a quorum present, there is a sufficient number present to justify the legality of the meeting, and the authorization of the transaction of such business as may be permitted in
the absence of a statute requiring that particular types of board transactions shall be approved by at least a majority of the full membership
of the board. As a general rule, a majority of a quorum may legally transact board business, unless a statute provides otherwise.

In some jurisdictions the statutes mandate the number of board members required to be present to constitute a quorum. Under such a
situation, the statute must be strictly complied with in order for the
meeting to be a legal one. If a statute is silent on the matter, the courts
consistently apply the common law rule that stipulates a quorum as being
a simple majority of the full membership. In the absence of a statute, the
common law rule prevails and a board of education is without legal
authority to prescribe its own definition of a quorum.

Conduct of Board Meeting. Ordinarily, it is not required that a board
meeting be strictly conducted in accordance with the technical niceties of
parliamentary law. The courts recognize the fact that most school boards
are composed of laymen who have but little training in parliamentary
procedure. For this reason, if there are minor irregularities occurring
during a board meeting which are contrary to strict parliamentary practice, the courts will not invalidate the action taken. In the absence of
unfairness, fraud, or arbitrary action, the courts are generally inclined
to uphold actions taken, even though there were minor irregularities, so
long as a fair consideration is given to the business before the board and
each board member has the opportunity to participate in the action
taken. In a case where a chairman failed to follow the technical requirements of parliamentary procedure, such was not considered adequate

reason for declaring the action illegal, where there was no evidence to doubt that the sense of the board members on the subject was ascertained, and where the evidence did not show that a different result would have been reached if the irregularities had not occurred. Particularly, in the transaction of board business if the will of the required majority on a particular board transaction is fairly and accurately ascertained, then slight irregularities in the conduct of the board meeting in such connection will not invalidate the action taken by the majority.

In some cases because of the informality of board actions, a motion for adjournment may have been made and approved, when, with all board members present, the board considers some item of business and votes on it. Under such circumstances, the courts, ordinarily, hold such action is legal if it was taken before the members who were originally present left the meeting place. The courts have held that an adjournment as a matter of law is an act and not a declaration. It is an act of separation and departure and until such takes place the adjournment is not complete. On the other hand, after the board has adjourned and some of the members depart, it would not then be legal for the remaining members present in the board room to transact any board business.

It has been previously noted that if a legal quorum is present at a board meeting which, ordinarily, consists of a simple majority, it would be legal for a majority of a quorum to transact business, unless by statute, the nature of the business transacted requires a unanimous vote of at least a majority of the full membership of the board. If such be a five-member board, then a simple majority would be three members, and unanimous approval of the three members would be necessary to approve a motion or resolution introduced, in respect to a particular transaction, which by law requires a majority vote of at least three members. The courts, however, will insist on strict compliance with the appropriate statutes and any action taken contrary to them in the matter of voting would be illegal.

Where there is a quorum present mere refusal to vote on the part of some members will not defeat the action of those actually voting. It is the duty of all members present to vote, and if they fail to do their duty, they will be considered as assenting to what those who do vote determine. Those who wish to defeat a measure must vote against it, for inaction will not accomplish their purpose. In a situation where all seven board members were present at a board meeting a contract was considered, and on a motion to adopt it three members voted "aye," two voted "no," and two did not vote; the court held the contract legally approved on the theory that the two members who refused to vote gave their assent to the action taken by a majority of those voting. In a comparable situation where there are nine members on a board, five constitute a quorum, and if on some board business, three of the five vote "aye," two vote "no," and two abstain from voting, the action would be legally approved. If the members present desire to defeat a measure, they must vote against it. Their refusal to vote is in effect a declaration that they consent that the majority of the quorum may act for the body of them as members. In effect, those that remain silent are regarded as voting "aye" with the majority.

One important thing to remember regarding what has been said heretofore in reference to voting, is that silence will not be considered as voting with the majority or acquiescence under all circumstances. Where the law requires affirmative action by a majority of the full membership of the board, the measure under consideration must be supported positively by the required majority. Under such circumstances, a failure to vote amounts to a negative vote.

In the case where the president is presiding at a board meeting, it is not illegal for such president to vote on a proposed motion or resolution. Where a statute sets forth the manner of voting such as specifying that the "yea" and "nay" votes must be taken and recorded in the board's minutes, courts agree that failure to follow the statutes invalidates any action taken. Where a statute requires that on the employment of a teacher the clerk shall publicly take the roll of the members and record individually how each member votes, any action taken contrary to such statute would invalidate the teacher's contract of employment.

2.5. Board Minutes

As a general rule, based for the most part on statutory provisions, written minutes or a written record of proceedings are required to be kept in respect to a board of education. A board of education speaks only through and by its record of what was done when acting as a body in a corporate meeting. In some jurisdictions statutory provisions requiring the keeping of records are mandatory, so that the failure to follow the law is fatal, and the want or insufficiency of the record of proceedings invalidates the board's actions and results in nullification of the attempted action.

On the other hand, in some states the laws with respect to the keeping of records are directory, so that failure to keep accurate records of the board's proceedings does not affect the validity of the action taken, or affect rights accruing to third persons in such action. It has been held, therefore, that the actions of a board of education are not impeachable for lack of record unless the action attacked is one of the actions enumerated in the statute which requires such record. In any case, the burden is on the person claiming the right to act under an order of the board, to establish its legality where the minutes are not kept as prescribed by statute.

Quite frequently, records kept in reference to school board meetings are the only evidence of its actions, or at least such records are the best evidence. Generally, the minutes or the records of the board's proceedings must be prepared and kept in such fashion as to show what was done by the board, and that it acted in accordance with the requirements of law. Nevertheless, the courts will not require that the keeper of the records comply strictly with the statutes that define the nature of the record required to be kept. Ordinarily, the courts will approve a record that is in substantial compliance with the law, and technical correctness is not requisite. Irregularities or informalities in the keeping of the minutes do not legally affect their sufficiency where the meaning clearly appears. The courts have held that overly strict rules should not be established with reference to records of the proceedings of school boards. Such records are usually kept by persons not versed in the law and are generally somewhat informal in character. If they show the action in fact taken although not conventionally or formally expressed, they should be held sufficient.

Quite often, it is not precisely clear as to what constitutes the official record of the board. It has been held that maintaining records on pieces of paper, even of varied sizes, complies with the requirement that the proceedings of the school board meetings should be kept in record books. Records which contain only the gist of the action taken by the board, such as the approval of motions, but which omit any reference to the names of the board members making or seconding the motion, as well as the final votes or the methods of taking them, have been held to comply with the requirements of law. Thus, it may be noted that courts are inclined to be generally liberal when they rule on the adequacy of board proceedings. Nevertheless, the board minutes should reflect a record of what actually transpired.

Ordinarily, the official records of the board proceedings speak for themselves, import verity, and are considered conclusive as to the matters set forth therein, except where fraud or mistake is shown. Parol or oral evidence is usually not permitted to be introduced to disapprove, impeach, or contradict the written record. As a general rule, however, the fact that a particular action does not appear in the minutes is not conclusive that it was not taken, and while the board proceedings are the best evidence of the official acts of the board and usually the only proper evidence thereof, parol evidence is held admissible where facts are omitted or not truly stated by the record to show what was actually done. In order to supply omissions to the records or to explain or clarify them, the courts will permit parol evidence to be introduced. Parol evidence is receivable unless the law expressly and imperatively requires all matters to appear of record and makes the record the only evidence. In case of a conflict between the minutes and an original resolution on file with the clerk of the board, the minutes cannot be held conclusive as to the action taken by the board, and the resolution prevails. A board of education's approval of false minutes of a prior meeting cannot validate action thereby shown to have been taken.

Board minutes or a record of its proceedings may be amended at any time by a board of education to make the records state the facts and to show all of the proceedings taken, but may not, otherwise, be amended. It is axiomatic that a record must speak the truth. When it does not do so through any adversity or mistake, those who have the authority and power may correct the record to make it conform to the truth. Such authority, however, is not unlimited in character. The power to amend records cannot be exercised in such fashion as to prejudice the rights of third persons who had heretofore taken action based upon what they thought was a correct record.

2.6. Rules and Regulations

In discharging duties imposed upon them by law, school boards have the power to make rules and regulations pertaining to the schools and pupils, which are considered administrative provisions. The right to enact such regulations for the purpose of its existence is inherent in every corporation. In some jurisdictions the laws specifically empower a board of education to adopt such rules and regulations as are necessary for its government and the government of its employees and the pupils of the schools.

Such regulations must be suitably adapted to the purpose of the existence of the board and must be designed for the proper management and efficiency of the school system or the discipline and training of the children. Such rules and regulations must not be inconsistent with law, unreasonable, or oppressive, and must apply equally to all pupils regardless of race, color, or creed. The courts will not attempt to interfere with rules established by a board, revise them, or intervene to prevent their being made effective unless such rules are unreasonable, a clear abuse of discretion, or a violation of law. So disinclined to interfere with regulations adopted by school boards are the courts, that they usually will not consider whether the regulations are wise or expedient, but merely whether they are a reasonable exercise of the power and discretion of the board. A school board may not, under its rule-making power, attempt to confer upon itself further jurisdiction beyond the provisions of law.

In their review of board rules, the courts consistently apply the test of reasonableness. The courts, however, will not substitute their judgment for that of the board of education. A board regulation is not reasonable or unreasonable per se; its reasonableness is determined by the facts in each particular case. Acting reasonably within the powers conferred, the board of education has within its province the responsibilities to determine what things are necessary for the successful management, good order, and discipline of the schools and to adopt legislation to regulate or control such conditions. The presumption is always in favor of the reasonableness and propriety of a rule or regulation sensibly made. A school regulation, however, must be not only reasonable in itself, but its enforcement must also be reasonable in the light of existing circumstances.

It should be pointed out that it is not required that *all* the rules, orders, and regulations for the discipline, government, and management of the schools be made a matter of record by the school board, or that *every* act, order, or direction affecting the conduct of such schools, be authorized or confirmed by a formal vote. It is recognized that no system of rules, however carefully prepared, can provide for every emergency or meet every requirement. Consequently, much must necessarily be left to the administrative officers of a school system and to the teachers in the several schools. It follows that any reasonable rule adopted by a superintendent or a teacher, not inconsistent with some statute or some other rule prescribed by higher authority, is binding on the pupils.

In respect to pupils, a board of education may adopt rules regulating the dress and personal appearance of pupils, require pupils to pursue particular subjects, establish health regulations, require pupils to be vaccinated, and make such a condition of school attendance, require pupils to pay laboratory or breakage fees, describe reasons why a child may be disciplined or excused from school, forbid pupils to leave the school premises during the noon hour, forbid pupils to patronize a public restaurant during the noon hour, regulate the use of automobiles and bicycles to and from school and while school is in session or during the noon hour, provide grounds for suspension or expulsion from school, provide rules as to absence or tardiness of pupils, provide rules for detention of pupils after school hours, adopt rules prohibiting pupils from wearing metal heel plates, adopt rules regarding pupils to wear caps and gowns at graduation exercises. A board of education may also adopt rules relating to the extracurricular, recreational, and social activities of pupils which are designed to promote proper discipline and training of the pupils and to direct the time and interest of pupils toward their schoolwork. A school board may also adopt regulations prohibiting a married or pregnant pupil from participating in athletics or extracurricular activities.

On the other hand, the courts will intervene to prevent the enforcement of a rule if the authority of the board of education has been illegally or unreasonably exercised, and the courts will interfere if the rule deprives a child of rights to which the law entitles him, or which tends to

alienate the pupil from proper parental authority, or which exceeds the
school board's powers, or its sphere of action, and in no way relates to
the management or successful operation of the school. Thus, rules have
been held unreasonable which deprive a child of school privileges, except
as a punishment for a breach of discipline or an offense against good
morals; rules which require school pupils to pay for school property
which they carelessly damage unless done wilfully or maliciously; rules
seeking to monopolize the school trade for the particular school by forbidding pupils to purchase supplies elsewhere; rules which attempt to
regulate the extracurricular activities of students for the particular benefit of a certain group of citizens; rules which attempt to require pupils
to act as student patrols to protect the younger pupils at dangerous street
intersections on their way to and from school; rules which require a pupil
to devote certain fixed evening hours at home to study; a rule that during the school term no pupil should attend a social party; or a rule which
requires pupils to participate in a flag salute ceremony contrary to their
religious beliefs.

It is generally recognized that any conduct of the pupils which either
directly or indirectly affects or may affect the interest of the pupils in
their relation to the teachers, principals, superintendents, or their fellow
pupils with respect to their schoolwork and which may be reflected in
the schoolroom during school hours, is a proper subject for regulation
by rules promulgated by the board of education, and if such acts are
detrimental to good order and the best interests of the pupils or the
schools, they may be entirely forbidden. Such rules, of course, are limited
in that they must be reasonable and not arbitrary, capricious, or contrary
to law.

The authority of the school officials extends into the twilight zone
between the school and the home and includes the enforcement of reasonable rules and requirements while the pupils are on their way home or
on their way to school. The misconduct of pupils is properly within the
scope of the power of the board of education, and the conduct of pupils
outside school hours and school property which directly relates to and
affects the management of the school and its efficiency is within the regulation of the board of education.

While as noted there is no question about the authority of the school
to regulate the conduct of pupils to and from home, there is substantial
authority to the effect that the power of school authorities over pupils
does not cease absolutely when the pupils leave the school premises or
even after they arrive at home.

Generally, the conduct of school pupils outside of school hours and
away from school property may subject a pupil to school discipline if
his conduct directly affects the good order and welfare of the school, the
respect that is due a teacher, or the proper discipline and training to

school pupils. However, the connection between the prohibited acts and the discipline and welfare of the school and its teachers must be direct and immediate, not remote or indirect.

The following regulations in reference to conduct off the school premises have been held valid: requiring the pupil to take home schoolwork, work on it, and bring the work back the next day; limiting the participation of pupils in social activities which interfere with their school work; prohibiting the organization of fraternities or sororities in connection with the public school system and forbidding students from becoming members; rules pertaining to proper moral conduct; rules regulating participation or conduct of pupils in athletic or extracurricular activities in connection with the school, even though such activities may occur at times off school property; and a rule regulating the use of automobiles and bicycles to and from school.

Within the broad authority reposed in a board to adopt rules providing for the government of the pupils, it may provide by rule for the corporal punishment of any pupil violating a proper rule adopted by the board, or for being disobedient to a proper order of a school teacher, principal, or superintendent, or for any improper conduct on the part of the pupil. By long practice and custom, however, the discipline of pupils in a school system is largely reposed in the teachers and the principal in each school. A board of education may provide by regulation, however, the procedure to be followed in the administration of corporal punishment and may even prohibit the use of corporal punishment in the school system. Even though a board of education may authorize the use of corporal punishment, the punishment must be reasonable, done without malice, and confined within the bounds of moderation. The instrument to be used must be suitable and proper for the purpose, and the punishment must be proportioned to the gravity of the offense, the motive and disposition of the offender, the influence of his example and conduct on others, and the age, size, sex, and physical strength or structure of the offender. A board of education may never lawfully authorize the use of punishment that is cruel, actuated by malice, or excessive. A board of education by regulation may prescribe the methods of discipline that may be properly exercised by its employees, such as detention.

It would seem, however, that even in the absence of board regulations on the matter of discipline, the school teachers would have the inherent or implied right to prescribe the methods of discipline and to use such method as might seem appropriate to the teacher. It should be pointed out, however, that a board of education may, if it so desires, exercise its discretion in such connection and regulate the use of disciplinary measures to be used in the school system.

A board of education has the right to supervise and control the activities of groups, organizations, athletic teams, and student associations within the pupil population of a school. The activities of such groups necessarily consume portions of the pupils' time and such activities may reach into the classroom and affect the pupils' schoolwork in one way or another. If not properly regulated by a board of education, such activities may displace to some extent the pupils' interest in their regular schoolwork, or prevent a school from efficiently administering the regular courses of instruction in the classrooms. In the light of such facts, there is no doubt as to the authority of each board of education to adopt rules and regulations providing for the proper supervision and control, or the establishment or suspension of such activities. A board of education may provide that designated school officers, personnel, or others may manage, control, or supervise such activities, subject to the primary control of a board to authorize or permit the carrying on of such pupil activity programs. No school employee or officer, nor any private association has any legal right to establish, operate, or supervise such pupil activity programs, contrary to any authority that a board of education may exercise in such connection.

In the functioning of such pupil groups and programs, including fund-raising programs by school classes or school groups, substantial amounts of money may be collected and disbursed. Such pupil activity programs are generally an integral part of the broad educational program, and the activities are generally subsidized in part through the use of board-owned facilities and the labor and services of school personnel; therefore, the proper collection and disbursement of moneys involved in such programs hold sufficient public interest to authorize a board in the exercise of its discretion to adopt rules providing for the proper management, handling, and disposition of any moneys collected by such pupil groups or activities carried on in the schools under the auspices of school personnel.

In a broad sense, moneys collected and disbursed through the medium of student activity programs are trust funds, and the persons who act in respect to such moneys in administrative capacities would appear to be charged with the duty of seeing that such moneys are properly handled and used for the purposes for which they are collected. It is fundamental that school facilities and the services of students cannot be used or exploited for the personal gain of school officials or private organizations, insofar as the pupil activities relate to the conduct of an enterprise on school property, or in connection with the school facilities or school curriculum. While there is little legal authority in respect to the right of a school board to regulate student activity programs, there appears to be no question of the right of a board of education, even in the absence of a specific statute, to adopt reasonable regulations providing for the proper conduct of the pupils, the control and management of the pupil activity programs, and to provide for the proper management and handling of any moneys collected or disbursed in connection with such programs.

Reference is made to the chapter on School Funds for additional comments relative to student activity funds.

2.7. General Authority of a School Board to Contract

A board of education has no inherent authority to enter into a contract, but in such connection has only such powers as may have been expressly granted to it by state statutes, or which may be necessarily implied from such statutes. If a contract is not authorized by law, even though the board of education were to execute one, it is void. The persons who enter into purported contracts with the board of education, are presumed by law to be aware of the board's contracting authority, and even though a contract may be entered into, if such contract exceeds the board's authority, generally, the contracting party will not be permitted to recover even though the contract has been performed and the board may profit by the merchandise delivered. On the other hand, there is some authority to the effect that even though the contract may have been invalid, if it has been performed and the contracting party has been paid a sum of money by the board of education for benefits which the board has received, a court of equity in a lawsuit will leave the parties where it finds them. In good conscience, it would not be right for the board to receive the benefits of the contract, such as having a building built, while seeking to recover from the contractor the amount that had been paid for such building.

Where a school board is authorized to contract, it must necessarily act in its corporate capacity and actually enter into the contract in order for the contract to be binding. It may not delegate to the superintendent or another school employee or to one or more of its members the authority to enter into the contract. Such is according to the legal principle that where a board of education has been conferred with the power of discretion by the legislature, it may not delegate such power to any other person or unit. It may, on the other hand, delegate a ministerial function. Accordingly, where a board in its corporate capacity has agreed upon a contract or authorized the execution of one, it may delegate to a person the reduction of the agreement into the form of a contract, or authorize some person to sign the contract in behalf of the board.

Board of education contracts are required to conform to the general rules of law governing contracts. It should be remembered, however, that a public contract is different from a private contract in that every statutory provision having a valid connection with the subject matter of the contract, or the extent of the board's capacity, is by implication made a part of the contract as though expressly written therein.

In order for a contract to be legally binding it must be executed by parties possessing the legal capacity to contract. A second principle to remember is that there must be a meeting of the minds of the parties to the contract, together with a definite offer and acceptance. As a general rule, the passage of a resolution by the board to the effect that an offer has been accepted does not constitute a contract; at any time prior to the acceptance of an offer, the offer may be withdrawn. Ordinarily, a board may rescind its action at any time before its acceptance of an offer has been officially communicated to the other party.

A contract must be definite enough in its provisions as to be understandable. If the language is so ambiguous that the intent of the parties cannot be ascertained, the contract would be held unenforceable. For a contract to be valid it must also be based upon a proper consideration. A contract which violates the law, likewise, will not be enforceable.

In the interpretation of a written contract, a court of law first looks to the written language in the contract. Parol evidence may not be introduced to change, subtract from, or add to the contract. Although there may have been negotiation, discussion between the contracting parties, and possibly verbal understanding, the court will look at the written language of the contract, and not to such other extraneous matters. Parol evidence may be admitted, however, for the purpose of assisting in a proper interpretation of the written contract, particularly if the language of the contract is somewhat uncertain, or if some language in the contract is intended to be used in a technical sense. Parol evidence cannot be introduced, however, to create rights or responsibilities not set forth in the written contract.

Where the statutes prescribe a method for a board of education to enter into a contract, such procedure must be strictly followed. Where the statute prescribes, for example, that the employment of a teacher shall be at a public board meeting where the roll shall be publicly called and the individual vote of each board member recorded, any other procedure is void, and a contract entered into that does not follow a mandatory requirement of the law would be void. Where a statute specifically requires particular types of contracts to be in writing, or to be authorized pursuant to a prescribed method, the particular manner of a board's capacity to execute a contract is the measure of its power, and such procedure must be followed to create a valid contract. It should also be pointed out that when a board of education enters into a contract it does so as a corporate body and not by individual members of the board acting separately or as a committee. Even though the board may appoint a committee to discuss matters relative to the possible execution of a contract, such committee can make no agreements or commitments which bind the board. It is only when the board is convened together for the transaction of business, in accordance with the law, that it may act as a corporate unit to make a contract, and the members of the board acting individually, as a committee, or separately, cannot make a contract or obligate the board.

In some jurisdictions a board of education may not lawfully enter into a contract, unless a prior act has been performed by such person. Where the prior step is not taken, a contract entered into by the board would be void. As an example, in some states the law provides that the board may employ a teacher only on the recommendation or nomination of its superintendent of schools. If the superintendent fails to make a nomination or recommendation, a contract entered into by the board with a teacher not nominated or recommended would be unenforceable. Where the act of the other party, by law, is a condition precedent to the execution of a contract, the execution of such act after the board has attempted to contract would not meet the requirements of law. In the case where a superintendent is required by law to nominate a teacher prior to the board's employment of such teacher, the act of the board in first employing the teacher and obtaining thereafter the ratification or approval of the superintendent would not meet the requirements of law.

As heretofore indicated, the majority rule is that contracts entered into by a school board without legal authorization are absolutely void and unenforceable. Under such rulings, the board is not liable, even though the contract has been fully performed by the other party, and the board retains the benefits thereof. Under such rulings, payments that have been made by the board can be recovered, and payments that have not been made can be enjoined. The reasoning of the courts is that the persons who deal with the board are charged with knowledge of the law, and if they are in error or ignorant of the authority of the board the consequences ought to be borne by such parties. Under such court holdings, since the board has no authority to contract, the other party would have no legal right even in a court of equity to recover on quantum meruit for the value of the goods or services delivered or performed by him. On the other hand, where a board of education has the authority to contract, but a particular contract entered into by it may be considered illegal because of some irregularity or other technicality, the general rule of law is that where there is a mere irregularity in connection with entering into a contract, a board of education will be held liable to pay on quantum meruit for the value of the benefits realized by the board under such contract.

While, as heretofore noted, the general rule is that contracts that a board has no authority to make are void and may not be recovered upon by the contracting party, even though he has delivered the merchandise or performed the work, the minority view is that school boards should not be permitted, in good conscience, to enjoy the benefits of illegal contracts, without paying the actual value of the goods or services. Some courts in reference to executed contracts will leave the parties where they

find them, and will not permit recovery by the board or a taxpayer for
the payments made under an illegal contract. Some courts adhere to the
doctrine that where a political subdivision receives benefits under a contract, even though such contract is illegal because not made in conformity with the law, such political subdivision will be held at least
liable on an implied contract for the reasonable value of the benefits
which it may have received. While such contracts are void and no recovery for board payments is permitted thereon, the courts hold that common honesty and fair dealing require that the political subdivision
should not be permitted to receive the benefit of money, property, or
services without paying just compensation therefor.

It is legally possible for a board of education in some situations to
ratify a contract which was not valid at the time it was first entered into.
The contracts may not first be valid because of irregularities, or because
the person purporting to enter into the contract was not lawfully authorized to do so. While a board of education cannot ratify a contract
that it would have no legal authority to enter into, the courts consistently
hold that a board of education may ratify a contract, if the board had
the legal authority to make it in the first instance. The board of education may ratify the contract by adopting a resolution for such purpose;
or, where the board of education, with full knowledge of all the facts,
takes such action as leads to the reasonable supposition that it intended
to ratify the contract, the courts may find that a legal ratification has
actually taken place. While the mere acceptance and use of merchandise
by a school district which was delivered under an invalid contract will
not always indicate an intention to ratify, if the school board has full
knowledge of all the facts, and so acts to approve or authorize the taking
or use of the goods or merchandise, the courts will probably hold that
ratification had taken place. It is legally possible for the courts to consider that the conduct of a board of education has given rise to implied
authorization to do certain things, and by implication, particular contracts that have been impliedly authorized may be ratified.

2.8. Pupil Transportation

The matter of pupil transportation is largely regulated in each state
by statutory law. While the constitutionality of laws providing for transportation has been raised in a number of cases, the courts have consistently upheld the constitutionality of the law. The fact that all pupils
are not transported by a board of education does not establish by law
discriminatory action on the part of the board. Neither are there any
violations about uniform operation of laws because a child who is in
attendance at a public school may be eligible for transportation if he
meets the standards prescribed by law.

The courts have ordinarily held that in the absence of statutory authority to transport pupils, authority to do so may not be implied. As a general rule of law, where there are mandatory statutes requiring pupils to be transported, the courts have held that the statutes should be construed reasonably in order that no child who is entitled to transportation will be barred from being transported. Where the state legislature has expressed the restrictions or conditions under which a school child should be transported, no discretion is conferred upon a board of education to expand the specific authority granted.

On the other hand, the fact that a considerable expense item may be involved in the transportation of children required to be transported is of no legal consequence in excusing the board from its statutory duty. Even though a child may live in an isolated area, if the law requires his transportation under the standards or provisions of state law, such pupil must be transported even though considerable expense may be involved. Where the law establishes a distance criterion in that children living beyond a certain distance from school shall be transported, no area of discretion in such connection is conferred upon a school board. Where the state statute, on the other hand, permits areas of discretion to be exercised by a board of education in the transportation of pupils, such power must be reasonably exercised by a board of education and, if abused, a court may intervene. Where a state statute may require that a child who does not reside within reasonable walking distance of the school shall have transportation provided for him, the courts may consider factors other than the distance of the child's home from the school to which he is assigned. Where certain hazards exist regarding the route used by the pupils, presenting a possible peril to pedestrians (for example, if it has neither sidewalks nor an adequate berm, and is a route that is heavily traveled by vehicles), such factors may be considered more decisive than the particular distance involved. Where the law requires a child to be transported beyond a designated mileage distance from the school to which he is assigned, such distance ordinarily is to be measured along the usual public highway from the child's home to the school.

Transportation of Parochial Pupils. The United States Supreme Court has upheld the constitutionality of a New Jersey state law which provides for the transportation of parochial school pupils at public expense. The court held that the state law did not violate either the Fourteenth Amendment of the Constitution or the First Amendment in providing for the transportation of parochial pupils at public expense. Such expenditures or transportation, in the opinion of the court, did not constitute the conduct, establishment, or support of religion. Whether or not a parochial pupil may be transported at public expense in the respective states depends largely on the constitutional or statutory laws of each state. It would seem that if the constitutional or statutory laws of a state authorize a board of education to transport parochial pupils, or permit transportation of parochial pupils at public expense, such would not be in violation of the U. S. Constitution. Most states have constitutional provisions prohibiting the expenditure of public funds for religious purposes. In spite of such provision some courts have upheld the expenditure of public funds on the theory that such expenditure is not directly for the benefit of sectarian schools, but more directly for the benefit primarily of pupils who happen to attend parochial schools. The legal extent to which such theory may be constitutionally applied in the disbursement of public funds for transportation or so-called auxiliary services in relation to the operation of schools remains somewhat unsettled.

Liability of School Board. The general rule of tort liability of a board of education, discussed elsewhere, would, likewise, apply to the question of the liability of a school board for an injury to a pupil or person occasioned through the operation of a school bus. In most states a board of education is free from tort liability and is not legally responsible in damages for the negligence of its bus drivers. Ordinarily, in the absence of a specific law authorizing a suit to be brought against a school board for the negligence of its employee, such suit may not lawfully be brought.

On the other hand, in a very small minority of states, either through judicial decree or enabling legislation, the tort immunity of a board of education has been dissolved and such board may be suable in tort for the negligence of any of its employees which would, of course, include persons employed by a board of education to drive school buses. In California, New York, and Washington specific statutes have been enacted by the legislatures which abrogate the common law rule of tort immunity resulting in making school boards liable for injuries sustained as a result of the negligence of school employees. In the states of Wisconsin, Arizona, Minnesota, and Illinois the courts by judicial decree have abrogated the foregoing common law rule and held that a board of education is suable in tort for the negligence of its employees in the absence of a statutory or constitutional provision prohibiting a board from being sued. However, as heretofore noted, in most states the tort immunity of a school district, or its board as an agency of the state, remains unchanged, thus protecting the board from liability because of the negligence of its bus drivers; and in some states the constitutions expressly provide that neither the state nor a state agency, which would include a board of education, is suable in tort in the absence of express authorization granted by the state legislature.

On the other hand, there is some authority to the effect that while a school board as a corporate unit is immune from tort liability for the negligent acts of its employees, individual members of the board may be held liable for damages individually if malicious action on their part is established from the evidence. It has even been held that individual members of a school board may be personally liable for the death of a child caused by the reckless driving of the bus driver where the evidence clearly established that the school board members knew at the time he was hired that such person was reckless and unfit for the position of a school bus driver.

Liability of the Driver. The driver of a school bus, unlike a school board, ordinarily is not protected from personal liability because of injuries through the operation of a school bus. The courts have consistently held that the bus driver is not clothed with governmental immunity because he is merely an employee of the school board, acting in an individual capacity, and assumes personal liability for his own actionable negligence.

As a general rule of law, because of the extreme hazards involved, the driver of a school bus is expected to exercise more than merely ordinary care in the operation of the bus. The courts have consistently ruled that extreme care is to be exercised by the driver in order to relieve him from personal liability because of injuries. He is required to operate the bus with the highest degree of care consistent with practical operation of the school bus. While the driver of a school bus is expected to exercise high care in the way he drives or operates a school bus, he is personally liable for injuries resulting proximately from his want of care, is also legally responsible for properly supervising the children on the school bus, and may be held liable for want of proper supervision if a child is injured by the bus driver's failure to exercise proper control of the children. A bus driver may also be liable for want of care if a pupil is injured after he has left the bus. In a situation where the law requires a school bus driver not to start his bus until a child has crossed the highway in safety, where the evidence disclosed that the bus driver had violated such law, he was held personally liable for injuries to a child who was hit by the driver of another automobile free of negligence, who struck the child before he reached the place of safety.

In some states in order to afford a method of protection to a driver of a school bus the state legislatures have enacted enabling legislation permitting school boards to expend public funds for the purpose of insuring the driver of a school bus against claims for injuries sustained through his operation of a school bus.

2.9. Religious Exercises

Sectarian instruction in a public school system, or the expenditure of public funds in support of sectarian instruction, is unlawful. The mere wearing of religious garb by public school teachers does not constitute sectarian instruction. Ordinarily, boards of education may permit school buildings to be used as places of worship, subject to board regulations, so long as such use does not conflict with the primary purpose of using school buildings as places of instruction. Religious groups, however, cannot enter upon public school property while school is being conducted, and give religious instruction to the pupils. On the other hand, the pupils in a public school during the school day, may be permitted to be released to attend religious exercises conducted off the school premises, presuming that public funds are not used for such purposes.

The practices of selecting and reading verses of the Bible and recitation of The Lord's Prayer by students in unison, at the opening of the day in public schools are religious in character, and the laws that required such exercises are unconstitutional under the First Amendment of the Federal Constitution as applied to the states by the Fourteenth Amendment. On the other hand, study of the Bible for its literary and historic qualities and study of religion, when presented objectively as a part of the secular program of education, are not legally improper.

III

Pupil Admission and Attendance

3.1. Generally

As a general rule, it is well-established policy in each state of the union to permit all qualified children of school age to attend, at least, an elementary and a secondary school. In most states, it is considered to be the duty of the state government to provide a system of public education.

The admission of pupils to public schools, to receive a free education, is of a civil nature. It is not a right guaranteed by the Federal Constitution, but is rather a political privilege. No parent has a vested right to have his child admitted to a public school merely because he is a citizen.

For the most part, the statutes that establish a public system of education also provide for the expense of operating such schools by taxation of the inhabitants thereof. Thus, as a general proposition, it seems to be the policy of the state to impose upon the residents of the district, particularly those who own real property, the expense of educating the children of the inhabitants, with the assistance of the state government.

3.2. School Residence

Ordinarily, since the taxpayers of a school district are charged with the duty of paying the operational expenses of their public schools, the privilege of receiving an education at public expense in the district is made available only to those children who are bona fide residents of the district. For the most part, this means children or wards of persons who are actually residing in the school district.

The term *residence* is given a liberal construction. While the courts are not always in agreement, the general rule does not require that there be a legal domicile, a permanent residence, or suffrage rights, but rather that the adult is, in part, residing in the district with apparently no present purpose of removal. Even though the residence be temporary, such fact alone will not deny the child the privilege of attending the public schools, so long as the residence was not established for the sole purpose of attending the public schools, combined with the intention of leaving as soon as the school year is over. A parent going temporarily into a school district during a school year for the primary purpose of sending his children to the schools in that district is not a bona fide school resident in that district.

Generally, it is not required that children reside with their parents in a particular school district in order to qualify for free schooling. If the child resides with persons other than his parent or guardian, under conditions whereby the person with whom he resides stands in loco parentis to him, such child may attend school in the district where those persons are actual residents *free of charge.*

Generally, a minor whose parents are living has no capacity to select his own place of residence with respect to his right to attend school. However, a child who has been emancipated and is earning his own living is entitled to free schooling in the district where he lives, regardless of his parents' residence. While the usual rule is that while a child's father is alive, the child's residence is that of the father, the courts recognize that facts may exist to establish the child's actual residence with the mother or other persons who may be in charge of him.

Whether a person is an actual resident of a school district, so as to entitle him to a free education, depends largely on the facts of each particular case. Even though the parent may own property in the school district and pay taxes in such district in which he does not reside, these circumstances do not entitle him to send his children to the schools of that district free of tuition.

3.3. Non-Residence

Generally, except as expressly authorized by statute, school children whose parents are not residents of a school district may not attend schools in such district. Under some statutes, however, children whose parents are non-residents of a particular school district may attend school in such district with the consent of the school authorities of the district in which the school is located.

The constitutional provision for the establishment of a system of public education does not contemplate that facilities provided in a district by means of taxes imposed on the inhabitants thereof shall be available to pupils of other districts without charge. Thus, many statutes require that if a child is educated in a non-resident district, the cost of tuition is to be paid by the district in which the parents reside, or require payments to be made directly by the parents to the district in which their children attend school. The constitutionality of legislation of this nature has been upheld.

As a general rule, a non-resident child committed to the custody of a charitable organization or institution does not thereby become a resident of the district in which the institution is located, but remains a resident of the district of school residence at the time of commitment. On the other hand, an orphan or a child who has no home other than an institution in which he resides therein for an indefinite period of time, may be entitled to free schooling in the district where the home is located.

3.4. Eligibility

Each state has the right to determine who shall be entitled to attend the public schools, and in order for a child to be eligible to attend a public school he must meet the requirements prescribed by law and the rules of the board of education. The authority of a school board to exclude children is very broad, but it must be exercised in the best interests of the pupils and the schools. The right or privilege to attend public schools is subject to such regulations as are not unreasonable or inconsistent with law. The classification and assignment of school children are purely administrative functions inherent in school authorities.

Courts have upheld board regulations which, as a condition for admission, prescribed scholastic qualifications, or which excluded children because of moral character, general health, physical condition, membership in fraternities or sororities, impairing the efficiency of the school, or endangering the health of other pupils. Under such conditions, admission may be denied even though there is no wrongful conduct on the part of the people.

On the other hand, rules have been held unreasonable which excluded a child on the sole ground that he was married, which makes admission dependent on the child's parents paying his assessed taxes, or which imposed a matriculation fee.

3.5. Age

Ordinarily, eligibility in reference to age is regulated by state statute. In the absence of state law, a board of education is authorized to fix the age limits. It is not uncommon for school boards to adopt rules which restrict the admission of pupils to certain times during the school year. Occasionally, such regulation operates to postpone the admission of a child beyond the time when he reaches school age. Such rule is generally held reasonable. Thus, a regulation which excluded pupils under a certain age unless they entered during the first month of the fall term was deemed a proper one. Where the school authorities have consistently, over a period of considerable time, admitted certain persons regardless of age, and have admitted a child to a particular school knowing that he will be qualified before his first year is completed, they are then estopped to deny his right to attend school on the ground that he is over school age.

3.6. Compulsory Attendance

The constitutionality of statutes making the education of children compulsory has been firmly established, for the natural rights of parents to custody and control of their children are subordinate to the power of the state to provide for the education of infant children. Laws providing for the education of children are for the protection of the state itself. The primary purpose of the maintenance of a school system is to promote the general intelligence of the people constituting the body politic, and thereby to increase the usefulness and efficiency of its citizens, on which the government of society depends.

One of the most important natural duties of the parent is the education of his child. This duty he owes also to the state. Thus, if a parent neglects to perform such civil obligation, or wilfully refuses to do so, he may be required by the law to execute it. However, free schooling granted by the state is not so much a right granted to the pupils as it is a duty imposed on them for the public good.

Generally, compulsory attendance laws do not require that children be sent exclusively to public schools. Statutes requiring the attendance of children at public schools ordinarily except from these provisions children who are otherwise educated for like periods in subjects comparable to those prescribed in public schools. Sending a child to a private, parochial, or denominational school which meets the standards expected of public schools is, ordinarily, in complete compliance with the compulsory attendance laws.

3.7. Classification and Assignment

In the exercise of its broad authority, especially in the field of discretionary powers, a school board may assign pupils to board-selected schools, such as grade schools, high schools, special schools; and, where in the exercise of such powers the assignments made are such as will afford all eligible children an opportunity to receive the benefits of proper instruction, such orders will be undisturbed by the courts, except in instances of clear abuse. In some jurisdictions the power of assignment is given expressly to the superintendent of schools.

In the exercise of its powers, school authorities may refuse to permit children who have been provided with a proper school, to enter another school which is overcrowded.

The school authorities may adopt any reasonable method to determine a child's fitness for admission to a particular grade or class, or to a particular branch of study. Classification based on the scholastic regulations of the school which the pupil attended previously, recommendations about the pupil's ability, and inferior examination results have been held to be proper. A board of education may require classification with respect to the physical or mental capacity of children, their proficiency, or their degree of advancement, and may make rules governing methods of schoolwork. Parents have no right to interfere with the board's exercise of its discretion or to demand for their children instruction in certain classes or grades against the judgment of the school authorities. It is not the duty of school authorities to segregate mentally retarded pupils in special classes.

In some states, the legislatures have enacted statutes by which they establish the criteria for the assignment of pupils to particular schools. If such standards are not discriminatory, not based on color, race, or religion, the courts usually hold such statutes constitutional. Likewise, the same general rules of law apply to local school authorities in the placement of school pupils.

In some jurisdictions, the neighborhood concept of pupil assignment is being attacked on the ground that it perpetuates de facto segregation. As of the present moment, such issue has not been finally resolved by judicial interpretation.

3.8. Out-of-District Pupils

Generally, if adequate school facilities are available in the district in which a child resides, he is expected to attend school in such district. The child has no vested right to attend school in another district at the cost of his home district.

In many states, the statutes permit the attendance of a child in a non-resident district, or the transfer of the child from his home district to another district. Frequently, attendance in a district other than his own is based on express statutory law, and is often processed on an agreement between the two school districts involved. Under such law, the district of attendance is often granted a discretion as to whether it will admit a non-resident agreement. Where admitted, the tuition cost is generally paid either by the parent or the sending board. Where the burden of tuition is placed on the sending district, the law is generally that the tuition is to be based on a statutory-prescribed tuition formula, which is most often the actual per capita cost of instruction.

As a general rule, a district is without authority to admit non-resident students unless it is granted statutory authority to do so, and then generally on the payment of tuition, either by the district of school residence or the parent. As a general rule, the district of attendance has no legal right to waive the payment of tuition, unless expressly permitted to do so by statute. The responsibility of the latter district for the payment of tuition is confined to the attendance of children of the compulsory age limitation. It has been held that where a district is unable to furnish schooling to an eligible child who attends school elsewhere, the district of residence is legally bound to pay tuition charges for such attendance, so long as such attendance is at a public school.

In a case where transfer of a student from one district to another is involved, such is usually regulated by statute. Often, such attendance is limited to cases where it would be more convenient for a child to attend a school outside his district, particularly if it would work a hardship for him to attend a school in his own district because of the remote distance of the school, or the lack of adequate bus transportation. Often such transfers are confined to pupils who attend a high school outside the district because their home district lacks one.

While school boards possess broad discretionary authority in sending their pupils to other districts (which is often pursuant to an arrangement between the involved boards of education), their actions are subject to court review; and if an abuse of discretion is established, the boards' actions could be reversed.

Once a transfer is lawfully consummated, or attendance is permitted in a district other than the one of school residence, the pupil comes under the administrative control of the receiving district and its employees.

Ordinarily, where a school district is under legal duty to furnish high school instruction to all eligible residents, and where there is no high school in the district, such district is liable for the tuition charges of such pupils as have complied with its requirements in a high school in another school district. State laws which provide for the admission of high school pupils in one district into high schools of another district, and for the payment of schooling costs therein, are generally valid; but where they fix a maximum charge for tuition which may be less than the actual cost thereof, such statutes may be invalid.

Where the law imposes an obligation on the sending district to pay the costs of schooling to the district of attendance, failure to pay such costs may be enforced by appropriate legal action.

3.9. Curriculum

The state has the legal right to require that designated studies essential to good citizenship be taught and that nothing be taught which is contrary to the public welfare. Generally, while the state has the power to prescribe studies and the curriculum in the public schools in the absence of state regulations, each local board has the discretion to provide for the teaching of such studies as it deems advisable. State laws which spell out the requirements that certain courses be given or certain subjects be taught are mandatory on school boards, but such statutes must be given an interpretation which serves their purpose.

When a local school board has the discretion in the development of the studies and curriculum, such discretion may extend to such areas as the board determines reasonably advisable, including the teaching of music, drawing, physical education, dancing, dramatics, and other extracurricular activities, thrift by means of a savings deposit in a bank, and the teaching of such languages as the board deems advisable. However, certain state laws which prohibit the teaching of any modern languages but English to any pupil who has not passed the eighth grade have been held unconstitutional by the United States Supreme Court.

While the board, subject to state law, has the right to generally establish the curriculum, the law contemplates that general methods of instruction are within the control of professionally trained teachers, principals, and superintendents and not the members of the school board. The public school system should be maintained in reference to the curriculum, so as to keep abreast of progress generally, and to meet the needs of the times. To this end, it is the administrative function of school authorities to create new courses and to rearrange the curriculum in proper cases.

While school authorities, subject to state law, have the right to define the school curriculum, parents may make reasonable selections from the prescribed studies for their children, provided that the selections do not interfere with the method of instruction in the particular school. A parent cannot insist that his child be taught subjects not in the prescribed course in the school. A parent cannot insist that his child be permitted to use a textbook different from that adopted or school methods of study which interfere with others in their studies.

In the development of the school curriculum, care should be taken to the end that in state-supported schools the curriculum be non-partisan, non-sectarian, and the use of denominational or sectarian materials or the conduct of sectarian, religious exercises be forbidden. This extends to deny school authorities the right to enforce religious worship on children even in the faith of their parents. Morning devotional exercises, the reading of religious books and the Bible, may be prohibited by regulation of the school authorities, and decisions to such effect by the school board are final.

3.10. Transportation

In the absence of specific statutory provision, school authorities are not required to furnish free transportation to pupils. Under the statutes permitting transportation of pupils the right to use school funds has been upheld. In some states, however, statutes which permit the furnishing of free transportation at public expense for pupils attending a parochial school have been held to violate the constitutional provision forbidding the use of public funds or grants of aid to any sectarian school.

The discretion of school authorities in providing transportation is largely subject to state regulation. Unless the terms of a particular statute are mandatory, it is ordinarily interpreted to vest school authorities with discretionary powers. The discretion to be exercised by the school authorities is to be exercised in accordance with the appropriate statutory provisions, with due consideration given to the interests of the public in the operation of the public school system, as well as to the lawful privileges granted to the individual.

Under rights which provide for the transportation of students living more than a designated distance from the school building, the distance to be measured should include that from the yard of the student's home in a direct line to the public highway. The words *nearest route* in a statute requiring transportation when a school is not maintained within a certain distance of the residence of the child by the *nearest route,* means the nearest public route or one that has been duly authorized by law.

Where a distance is to be measured by the nearest traveled highway, such includes a public highway leading to the child's home. Under many statutes, the local board has discretionary power to determine how near a bus transporting the pupils may pass the residence or private driveway of such pupil. A board of education may authorize its school buses to leave a public highway and to use a privately owned road for the purpose of transporting school children who reside in homes abutting same. In the computation of the distance in the case where a statute says, for instance, that transportation for children who live more than two miles must be provided, such distance must be computed by the most direct public route. Under such statute such distance must be measured from the school to the nearest portion of the yard around the house in which such pupil lives. If, however, such yard is not situated upon a public highway, but, rather upon a lane, the distance from the yard, down the lane, to the public highway must be included, as well as the distance along such public highway from the lane to the school house.

In the case where the law provides for transportation of school children to and from school, such laws are interpreted to give the school board reasonable discretion as to the sufficiency and type of transportation provided. In some cases, state laws permit boards of education to designate places as depots from which to gather children for transportation. In such cases the school board has reasonable discretion to decide where the depots shall be located.

As a general rule, in the cases where authority is conferred upon a school board to provide for the transportation of pupils, the school board cannot contract for transportation without statutory authority. The failure of the school board to comply with express statutory provisions may defeat the right of recovery upon a contract for the transportation of school children. In accordance with the general rule of law, that delegated authority cannot be further delegated. A board of education may not delegate to a member or a group of members the powers to contract with reference to the general method of transporting pupils. Where the matter of providing transportation is discretionary with the school authorities, mandamus will not be issued to compel the transportation; but where a mandatory statutory duty is imposed for the transportation of pupils such obligation may be enforced by mandamus or other appropriate remedy. In some cases, where a school board is lax in its duty to transport, a parent may have a remedy to recover the cost of transportation provided by him.

IV

Pupil Discipline

4.1. Pupil Discipline and Control

In the field of pupil discipline many law suits have been tried in the United States in which teachers have been the defendants in either criminal or civil actions. Many teachers have been charged with assault and battery in reference to disciplinary actions, but for the most part such teachers have been able to present adequate defenses. This is due, in part, to the fact that teachers have quite a bit of legal protection in the performance of disciplinary actions. When a teacher is charged with assault and battery in reference to a pupil, his defense may go beyond the general law of assault and battery.

Generally, so much of the authority of a parent is impliedly delegated by law to a teacher as is necessary for the proper control, supervision, and discipline of a child. The teacher stands in loco parentis to children under his supervision and may exercise such powers of control and discipline as are reasonably necessary for him to properly perform his duties as a teacher and to accomplish the purposes of education.

So long as his directions are reasonable, the teacher has the legal right to direct each pupil as to how he shall attend to his duties and how he shall conduct himself, not only at the school during school hours but in the classroom or in the assembly hall. The teachers' duties go beyond technical teaching or instruction, but involve the preservation of order and matters relating to the morals, health, and safety of the pupils.

As a general rule, a school board which is charged with the management and operation of the public schools has the legal right to adopt reasonable rules for the discipline and management of such schools. The rules of a board of education are final in such respect, and the courts will not interfere unless the board acts unreasonably or in violation of law.

A court will not substitute its judgment for that of a school board regarding the wisdom or logic of the rules. A court, however, will interfere if a board acts arbitrarily, violates the law, deprives the pupils of rights granted by law, alienates the pupil from proper parental control, or acts in a manner which is completely unrelated to the proper efficiency or conduct of the school system, or the control, training, or discipline of the pupils.

While a school board has the right to adopt appropriate rules for the management and discipline of the pupils, it is also recognized that the teachers and administrators have the legal right to adopt reasonable rules, particularly in reference to methods of discipline, because of their professional competence and training in such matters. Such rules must be reasonable under all conditions, and in their enforcement due regard shall be given to the health, age, comfort, and welfare of the pupil. In some cases the weather, physical conditions of the child, and other similar factors may call for a relaxation of enforcement.

While many state statutes expressly grant to a board of education the right to make and enforce rules which govern the conduct of pupils, in the absence of statutory grant such boards have the inherent power to make rules and regulations for the discipline, government, and management of the school and pupils within the district.

While ordinarily a governing group may delegate to a subordinate officer or employee only administrative or ministerial duties not involving a great degree of judgment, a school board, except in the cases where the legislature clearly intended otherwise, may refer to its administrators the power to establish rules regulating pupil conduct.

While one court has held that members of the professional staff of a school have exclusive jurisdiction over the control of pupils, the more acceptable view is that school employees may set forth reasonable rules connected with the area of their responsibility and which are not in conflict with law or the rules and regulations promulgated by the board of education.

It is appreciated that certain authority must be granted to administrators and teachers to enact rules for and to regulate the conduct of pupils. No set of rules adopted by a board can provide for every emergency, or meet every requirement, and any reasonable rule adopted by the superintendent or a teacher, merely not inconsistent with statute or some other rule prescribed by higher authority, is binding upon the pupil. A school employee, however, would have no power to enforce any requirements which the school board cannot lawfully impose. For illustration, a superintendent or teacher cannot compel a child to take part in a flag salute ceremony which conflicts with his religious belief.

School rules have been upheld, in some cases adopted by the school boards, and in other cases adjusted by the administrators or teachers, regarding the following situations: regulating dress and personal appearance of pupils; requiring pupils to pursue certain subjects; requiring pupils to be vaccinated; establishing health regulations; requiring pupils to pay laboratory or breakage fees; prescribing reasons for which a child may be excused from school; regulating the conduct of pupils and the use of automobiles and bicycles by pupils to and from school and during the noon hour; providing grounds for suspension or expulsion from school; operating extracurricular, recreational, and social activities; prohibiting or regulating high school fraternities, sororities, or social clubs; prohibiting married pupils from participating in athletics or extracurricular activities; prohibiting a child from being diverted from his schoolwork; forbidding students to leave the school grounds during school hours, even though the effect is to prevent pupils from taking their mid-day meals under the supervision of their parents or eating in a public restaurant across the street from the school grounds; regulating absence or tardiness of pupils, or detention after school hours; prohibiting pupils from wearing metal heel plates; requiring pupils to wear caps and gowns at graduation exercises; requiring children to go directly home from school; providing for safety measures; requiring pupils to perform specified school assignments at home; and prohibiting offensive personal habits of pupils.

On the other hand, the following regulations have been held unreasonable in specific court cases: rules requiring children to pay for school property carelessly damaged, unless done wilfully or maliciously; those requiring a pupil to devote certain fixed hours and evenings at home to study rules; requiring pupils to wear official uniforms during the school session; suspending or expelling a student on the sole ground of marriage; seeking to monopolize trade for the school by forbidding pupils to purchase supplies elsewhere; requiring children to serve on school patrols; requiring children to participate in a flag salute ceremony contrary to their religious beliefs; prohibiting a child from attending any social party during the school term; and attempting to regulate the extracurricular activities of pupils for the benefit of various private groups.

4.2. Out-of-School Activities

Generally, school authorities have no concern with the conduct of pupils wholly outside the schoolroom and school grounds when they are presumed to be under the control of their parents. It has been said that when the child enters the school premises the authority of the parent ceases and that of the teacher begins; when the pupil is sent to his home, the authority of the teacher ends, and that of the parent is resumed.

On the other hand, it is good law that the authority of the school does not terminate absolutely when the children leave the school premises. Conduct of pupils away from the school premises and outside of school hours is subject to school discipline and regulation, if it directly affects the good order and welfare of the school, its proper management and efficiency, and the discipline and training of the pupils. This authority extends not only in respect to the behavior of the pupils to and from school, but also extends to conduct of a pupil after he has returned home, or conduct off school premises and outside of school hours, where such acts have a direct and immediate tendency to influence the conduct of other pupils while in the schoolroom, to set at naught correct discipline, to impair the authority of the school and its teachers, and to bring the school authorities into ridicule and contempt. The connection between the acts, however, and the discipline and welfare of the school must be direct and immediate, not remote or indirect. The school may prohibit by regulation such acts of misbehavior as it deems subject to reasonable regulation, and the school authorities may punish an offending pupil when he returns to school, or may suspend or expel him.

Thus a pupil may be punished, suspended, or expelled for misconduct on the school premises or away from the school subversive to the discipline or welfare of the school or its pupils, for disrespect towards school authorities, for drinking, smoking in public, using profanity, immorality, or for other improper conduct, although guilty of no reprehensible conduct on school premises.

4.3. Violation of Rules

Generally, a teacher is permitted to disarm a child, to detain him after school hours, to remove a child from the room, to inflict such reasonable punishment as he deems necessary for the enforcement of school policies and the good discipline of the school, and even for misbehavior in respect to which no formal rules have been adopted. However, a teacher has no right to search children on mere suspicion or to inflict cruel and unusual punishment. The punishment must be for some specific offense for which the pupil knows he is being punished, must be commensurate with the offense committed by the child and not unreasonable, and must be a reasonable ground for the punishment and not administered maliciously.

A method of enforcing discipline which has been upheld by the courts is known as detention. Such consists of keeping a pupil for a time after the rest of the class has been dismissed or the school has closed, as a penalty for misbehavior. If such penalty is inflicted in good faith without wanton or malicious motives, it does not constitute forced imprisonment even though a teacher may be mistaken in his judgment as to the justice or propriety of detaining a pupil.

4.4. Corporal Punishment

Generally, a teacher stands in place of the parent, and so much of the authority of a parent over his child is impliedly delegated to a teacher as may be reasonably necessary for the discipline and efficiency of the school and the supervision, control, and discipline of the pupil. Accordingly, a teacher may inflict reasonable corporal punishment on a pupil for insubordination, disobedience, or other misbehavior.

While school officials, including superintendents, principals, and teachers, are vested with broad discretionary authority in the infliction of corporal punishment, the punishment must be reasonable and within the bounds of moderation; it cannot be cruel or excessive, and the official administering punishment must not act maliciously or wantonly.

The law lays down no precise or exact rule as to what is excessive or unreasonable punishment. It is a question to be determined by the circumstance in each case. In the determination of whether the punishment is reasonable, the courts have held, however, that consideration must be given to the age, sex, and size of the pupil, his apparent physical strength and structure; that the type of instrument used should be one suitable and proper for the purposes; and that the punishment should be proportioned to the offense, the apparent motive and disposition of the offender, and the influence of his example and conduct on others. A legitimate object of punishment by forceful means is to not only cause pain, but the degradation which it implies. Merely because pain or bruises are produced does not of itself imply that the chastisement is either cruel or excessive. Teachers act within the limits of their authority when they produce temporary pain or injuries; they exceed such limits when they inflict permanent injuries.

It has been held that punishment is not necessarily excessive because a pupil suffers pain or bruises. The fact that a child appears unresponsive does not in itself justify the continuation of the punishment. Corporal punishment may be inflicted for misconduct out of school or on the school premises, and a teacher's right to inflict corporal punishment is not always limited to pupils in his own classroom.

Regarding the criminal or civil liability of a teacher who inflicts corporal punishment, certain general rules are important. In a civil action against a teacher for damages caused by improper punishment of a pupil, the burden of proof rests on the plaintiff to satisfy the jury that the teacher unlawfully beat and injured the child and that damages resulted therefrom. Whether the punishment was unreasonable or excessive and whether there was an injury are questions of fact for a jury to determine in a civil lawsuit.

As heretofore noted, a teacher stands in loco parentis and acts in a quasi-judicial capacity in the administration of corporal punishment. In a teacher's administration of such punishment to a pupil under his control there is a presumption of the correctness of his acts and that he acts in good faith. It has been recognized by the courts that a teacher's immunity from civil liability for reasonable corporal punishment administrated to a pupil is based on the fact that the teacher stands in loco parentis and shares, so far as matters relating to discipline are concerned, the parents' right to use moderate force to obtain a child's obedience.

On the question of a criminal liability it has been held that moderate and reasonable correction by a teacher with a proper instrument is not a criminal offense. Mere immoderate and excessive force does not constitute a crime unless it is of such a nature as to produce or threaten lasting or permanent injury and is accompanied by express or implied malice. If a teacher in administering correction or punishment to pupils uses his authority as a cover for malice, he is subject to the criminal laws; and the same holds true if he is actuated by revenge, spite, or evil passion.

In conclusion, it has been judicially recognized that the discipline of pupils is a matter committed for the most part to teachers. The authority of the teachers in such respect, however, may be controlled or regulated by rules and regulations adopted by a board of education or by statutory law. In two places, the District of Columbia and New Jersey, statutory enactments prohibit corporal punishment in the schools.

4.5. Suspension and Expulsion

The enjoyment of the right or privilege to attend public schools is conditioned by the pupils' compliance with the reasonable regulations and requirements of the school, violations of which may be punished by suspension or expulsion. A suspension under the law is usually for a short time, or until the pupil meets conditions established by the school authorities. Expulsion is ordinarily permanent, or for a substantial period of time. While the element of time is usually one factor in the distinction between an expulsion and a suspension, it has been judicially recognized that expulsion is of a more severe character, and should be used only as a means of preserving good order and discipline in the schools.

As a general rule, the power of suspension or expulsion is granted to a board of education, unless a particular statute provides otherwise. The courts have held, however, that there are times under urgent situations where a teacher, principal, or superintendent would be justified in suspending a pupil pending submission of the case to the board of education. It has been held that a teacher has the inherent right to suspend a pupil pending board action where the interests of the school require it. However, where a state statute expressly designates who has the power to suspend or expel a pupil, such takes away the right to exercise such power by any other person or officer.

Subject to the limitation that their actions must be based on reasonable rules and regulations, school authorities may suspend or expel pupils for any insubordination or misbehavior subversive to the good order and discipline of the schools. The discretion vested by law in the appropriate school authorities is broad, and the grounds on which a pupil may be expelled are ordinarily a matter of the reasonable judgment of such authorities, in the absence of specific grounds on which pupils may be expelled or suspended as established by the legislature.

The authority of school personnel to suspend or expel pupils is not confined to punishing pupils for acts committed at school, but may be exercised in proper cases in respect to offenses committed off school property and outside of school hours, where the misconduct reflects adversely on the management and efficiency of the school, the good order and discipline of the pupils, or the respect and authority of a school employee. Such powers, however, must be exercised within matters of school jurisdiction as distinguished from the jurisdiction of the parents.

It has been judicially held that a child may be suspended or expelled for disrespect toward school authorities; for immorality; for drinking; for smoking; the use of cosmetics contrary to school regulations; irregular or tardy attendance at school; refusal to write a composition; refusal to follow proper orders; refusal to obey when told to read from a schoolbook; refusal to submit to the examination of the school physician on the grounds of conscientious objections; refusal to give the name of a pupil who has been guilty of a breach of rules when he knows the name of the pupil; making a speech in a school meeting criticizing the board of education; being drunk on Christmas Day; publishing in a newspaper a satirical poem reflecting on school policy; failure to maintain a required scholastic standing, although there is substantial authority to the contrary; failure to pay for school property wilfully or maliciously destroyed; and for general failure to obey the school rules or orders reasonably issued by any teacher or administrator.

It has been held that it is the duty of every teacher to maintain good order and discipline and to require of all pupils a faithful performance of their duties. To enable a teacher to discharge his duties properly, the school authorities must have the power to enforce prompt obedience to his reasonable commands. Hence, a pupil may be suspended or expelled for any breach of reasonable discipline while at school, or for any misbehavior injurious to the good government, discipline, or morals of the other pupils, whether specifically covered by adopted rules or regulations or not.

It has been held that the right of suspension or expulsion exists, regardless of the pupils' conduct, where acts by their parents interfere with school discipline, or where the parents refuse to subject themselves or permit their children to subject themselves to school rules and regulations.

As heretofore noted, the power of suspension or expulsion is not limited to cases involving infraction of rules theretofore adopted, but extends to cases where the school authorities are satisfied that the interests of the school require the expulsion of a child on account of his gross misbehavior. While the discretion vested in the school authorities in such connection is very broad, the authorities will not be allowed by the courts to act arbitrarily.

It has been held that a child cannot be suspended or expelled merely because of marriage, unless the married person's conduct is detrimental to the good order and discipline of the school; or the pupil is difficult to teach; or he refuses by direction of his parents to follow a particular branch of study; or he is involved in the loss of school property because of mere negligence.

In connection with the expulsion of a child from a public school, some statutes require that a hearing be held as a prerequisite to an expulsion. The authorities are not in agreement as to what kind of a hearing is contemplated under such procedure. In at least one case a formal hearing of the kind required in judicial proceedings has been required. Unless the statute specifically requires a formal hearing, the better rule appears to be that the hearing need not be clothed with all the attributes of a formal judicial hearing, but that the minimum requirements such as a fair hearing and the right to legal counsel should be observed.

Liability for Suspension or Expulsion. As a general rule, school authorities acting without malice or intention to wrong a pupil are not liable for errors of judgment in expelling a pupil. The basis of a claim for wrongful expulsion is bad faith or malice; hence, there can be no recovery of damages where the suspension or expulsion is the result of an error of judgment on the part of the school authorities, where they act in good faith, without malice, and in the line of what they honestly believe to be their duty.

Wrongful Exclusion Remedies. Where the school authorities act maliciously, in bad faith, or arbitrarily in suspending or expelling a child, an injury is committed which the law will redress by mandatory injunction, an action in mandamus, or a suit in damages. The general rules of practice and procedure would prevail in such cases. Where the action is one for damages, ordinarily, a parent cannot maintain such action for the wrongful suspension or expulsion of his child, but such action must be brought in the name of the child by the parent or guardian, for the child's benefit. If a parent has incurred tuition expenses for his child's attendance at another school directly resulting from the wrongful expulsion or suspension, an action to recover may be brought in his own name.

Where an action is brought for a wrongful suspension or expulsion, the defendants are the school authorities who authorized or directed that such suspension or expulsion be made. The presumption as to the good faith and reasonable conduct of the defendants is in their favor. Such presumption is that the school authorities act in good faith in exercising the authority which the law has vested in them, and the burden of proof is on the person who questions their conduct to establish that they were not actuated by proper motives. It has been held that in an action for the wrongful suspension or expulsion of a child, his guilt or innocence is not to be considered in such case, unless it appears that the child has been treated maliciously or arbitrarily. In a proper action, damages are recoverable by the pupil for depriving him of the benefit of attending school, as well as damages for injury to his feelings and to his standing in the community.

4.6. Married or Pregnant Pupils

Although the public and school officials during the past several years have expressed considerable concern about the matter of student marriages, there has been a scarcity of judicial decisions in such area. In the present century, less than a dozen court cases have been reported on this topic, the majority having occurred since 1957.

The trend seems to be for the courts to hold that marriage alone is not sufficient grounds to deny a person the right to attend school. On the other hand, the few reported cases on the subject seem to uphold the validity of board rules prohibiting a married student from participating in extracurricular student activities or athletics. In each case, however, the court pointed out that, under the facts before it, the rule was valid, and that other specifications in the rule were not being considered. It might be observed that while a child has the right to attend school, subject to statutory restrictions, participation in athletics or extracurricular student activities appears to be a privilege rather than a vested right. In the latter category, however, a board must act reasonably and not arbitrarily in the adoption of rules, and would be well advised to have a solid educational background on which to base its regulations, rather than the personal beliefs or prejudices of the board members.

The few cases in this country on the subject hold that pupils who marry are not subject to the compulsory attendance law, although the Supreme Court of Ohio has commented that a close examination of the Ohio statute fails to disclose that marital duties constitute a reason to legally justify the absence of a child of compulsory school age from school.

On the matter of the exclusion of pregnant pupils from school, whether such pupil is married or single, there is even less judicial determination. In an Ohio Common Pleas Court Case, Ohio ex rel. Idle v. Chamberlain, 175 NE (2d) 539 (1961), the board of education adopted a resolution providing for the withdrawal from school of any student upon knowledge of pregnancy and for the school officials to require a doctor's examination in cases of question. This case, which had to do with a married pupil, was decided in favor of the board of education. The court commented that the evidence showed that the pupil's further school attendance was denied in the interest of her physical well-being and not as a punitive measure. The court also stated that the board could calculate that the pupil's continued present might adversely affect the morale of the student body, cause disruption in the operation of the school's daily activities, and, to some extent, interfere with the discipline and government of the pupils. The court concluded that the board of education had not abused its discretion. It should be observed that the foregoing board rule would permit the pupil to return to school after the birth of her child. If the female pupil were unmarried and became pregnant, there would appear to be no legal doubt of the right of the school authorities to exclude her from school. Whether or not such exclusion could be permanent or for a limited time only would probably depend upon the pertinent statutory law, if any, of each state. There do not appear to be any specific, reported court decisions in this particular connection.

(For a comprehensive listing and analysis of cases on the subject of married pupils, reference is made to the following recent publication: *Law and Pupil Control,* by Anne Flowers and Edward C. Bolmeier, in the American School Law Series, published by The W. H. Anderson Company, Cincinnati, Ohio.)

4.7. Promotion and Retention

As a general legal proposition, a school board may prescribe rules governing the retention, promotion, and graduation of pupils, subject to specific statutory provisions. The determination by the local school authorities as to whether a pupil is entitled to graduate or be promoted or detained is a matter of local discretion for the most part. In some states, however, state statutes prescribe the minimum curriculum that must be met to entitle a child to graduate. The failure of a child to meet the school curriculum requirements or to receive passing grades in certain subjects is a matter of discretion of the school personnel. Such discretion is in the exercise of a quasi-judicial jurisdiction. Having been made in good faith, the acts of the school authorities are ordinarily conclusive, and will not usually be reversed by the courts.

Where a pupil completes the prescribed course of study and meets the standards fixed by the local board for graduation, generally, he is entitled to a diploma or the privilege of participating in a public graduation ceremony. The refusal of the pupil to wear a cap and gown at the graduation exercises will not deny him the right to a diploma if he is otherwise entitled to it.

4.8. Student Activities Funds

Laws and court decisions relative to such funds are very scarce. Generally, it is recognized that school districts, through their governing boards, are authorized to exercise a guiding control over them. In some states statutory laws have been passed relative to the handling of student activities funds. For the most part, however, it would seem that specific laws have not been passed to provide for the management of student activities in extracurricular or athletic activities, or the purposes for which the revenue derived from such activities may be lawfully expended. A gradually developing legislative awareness of the importance of such activities and the use of the revenue derived therefrom seems to be indicated. The courts for many years have upheld the authority of school principals to exercise control over the activities of students which occur in the school and which affect discipline and the proper efficiency of the school system. The authority of the school district to regulate, through its personnel, the proper handling of student activities and the use of the funds derived from such activities seems unquestioned. As a matter of fact, a court in Pennsylvania has held that revenue derived from athletics and student extracurricular activities is to be paid into the accounts of the school district treasurer, subject to official audit, the same as tax funds.

V

Teachers, Principals, and Superintendents

5.1. Generally

Public school teachers are ordinarily considered to be public employees, and not public officers. Their employment is customarily subject to the authority of a board of education in matters pertaining to their selection, control, and dismissal, subject for the most part to statutory regulations and reasonable rules and regulations which each board makes, promulgates, and enforces.

A person has no constitutional or vested right to be employed as a public school teacher. He has no right to serve except under such conditions and on such terms as may be prescribed by the state. The legislature must be free to act with respect to legislation relative to school teachers as it deems wise.

While a *teacher* is ordinarily defined as one whose occupation is to instruct, state statutes may define such term to include persons not regularly engaged as classroom instructors. Thus a *teacher* under law may be one who holds a teacher's certificate or whose employment requires such certificate, such as a superintendent, a principal, supervisor, or librarian. Ordinarily, the relationship between a teacher and managing board of a school district is created by contract which is subject to the ordinary rules of contract law, except that in public contracts of employment each statutory provision having to do with such employment is by implication made a part of such contract.

5.2. Qualifications

Subject to such limitations as may be imposed by a state constitution, the power to fix the qualifications of teachers may be exercised by the state legislature, delegated to a board, or conferred on boards of education, within the authority vested in such boards by statutory provisions.

In order for a person to be eligible for employment as a public school teacher, he must possess such qualifications as may be prescribed by state law, and by the employing board of education, such as possessing a legal certificate or license, experience, moral character, age, or general ability. Generally, in the absence of statutory regulations to the contrary, the employing board may prescribe specific qualifications for the employment of teachers. Thus, evidence of physical fitness may be required, or freedom from affiliation with certain organizations or groups may be specified. School boards have the right to screen their employees as to their fitness and loyalty, and in so doing, may consider not only a person's conduct, but also the persons or groups with whom he is now or has been associated. A school board may require its staff to take a loyalty oath, or non-Communist oath, unless prohibited by statutory or constitutional restrictions.

5.3. Certification

Each legislature may provide for a system of certification or licensing of persons to teach in the public schools. The administration of such a system may be delegated to a board or agency. Such certificates are not contracts protected by the due process clause of the Fourteenth Amendment, but confer rather a personal privilege, which may be revoked pursuant to statutory provisions.

Generally, it is a prerequisite to lawful employment as a teacher, or for recovery of wages under his contract, or for its breach that such person have a lawful certificate or license as a teacher.

There is considerable confusion as to the precise time that a teacher shall have a certificate to be lawfully employed or entitled to be paid. In some jurisdictions it has been held that the test of employment is controlling, that the teacher must have a valid certificate at the time that the contract is executed, and that obtaining a certificate during the life of the contract may not validate such contract. On the other hand, it has been held that a contract executed with that teacher who does not have a certificate at the time is not void from the beginning, provided the certificate is granted before the actual teaching begins. Under such circumstances it has been held that the entire transaction is valid. The intention here is not to guard against the making of a contract by an incompetent teacher, but the teaching of school by an incompetent person.

If the certificate of a teacher expires while he is teaching, his employment legally ends, unless the old certificate is renewed. There is authority to the contrary, however, to the effect that if a teacher has a proper certificate when he begins his employment for a definite term, and the certificate expires during the term, the contract remains in effect unless terminated in the way provided by law. The repeal of a statute, however, under which a certificate is obtained, will not affect the validity of a contract based on such certificate.

Subject to such restrictions as may be established by law, persons or boards authorized to issue teacher certificates are ordinarily vested with the right to exercise reasonable discretion in their issuance. When after proper examination or compliance with all statutory or other conditions it is determined that the applicant qualifies, the issuing authorities cannot refuse to issue a license, and if such is refused, such persons may be required to issue the certificate by an action in mandamus. If the issuing authorities act in good faith, they are not personally liable in damages for an error of judgment or fact in withholding a certificate, although they may be liable in withholding a certificate from a person entitled to one, if done maliciously.

The right of an applicant to appeal to a higher board or officer because of a refusal to issue him a certificate depends primarily on statutory regulations. Ordinarily, the decision on such appeal may be reviewed by the courts if the authorities have acted arbitrarily or in violation of the applicant's legal rights.

In reference to the revocation of a teacher's certificate, such is ordinarily regulated by statute. The grounds to revoke a certificate are generally set forth by statute, and usually include incompetency, immorality, general neglect, conduct unbecoming to a teacher, or commission of a crime. The license holder, by accepting a certificate, assents to the statutory grounds. If the authorities in the revocation of a certificate act in good faith they are not personally liable in damages even though their judgment or decisions were erroneous, but they may be liable if the facts disclose that they acted maliciously in revoking the certificate.

5.4. Selection and Employment

Only such boards or persons as may be specifically authorized by law to select and employ teachers, superintendents, and principals are permitted to do so. Ordinarily, by statutory authority, the power to select and employ teachers, superintendents, or principals is vested in school boards, including the power to enter into contract and fix the term of their employment and compensation. The discretion in a board in such connection is very broad. When a school board acts in good faith in such matters, and not contrary to law, the courts will not ordinarily interfere. The school board has the legal right to decide whom to employ and whom not to employ. The board has the absolute right to decide whether to employ or re-employ an applicant for any reason whatsoever, or for no reason at all, although in some jurisdiction it is held that a board cannot discriminate on the sole ground of the applicant's religious belief.

When the statutes confer exclusive authority on a school board to employ, such power cannot be delegated. The power of a board to select and employ teachers cannot be delegated to its superintendent of schools, even though the law requires the board to select teachers from recommendations or nominations made by such superintendents.

In order for the employment of a teacher to be valid, a board of education is bound by the statutes, and if the law is not observed, a teacher's contract may not be enforceable. Some courts hold that the statutes must be strictly adhered to in order for the employment of a teacher to be valid; while other courts hold there must be substantial compliance with the statutory requirements. It is fundamental that the matter of appointment of school employees is subject to constitutional provisions, within the exclusive power and control of the legislature, and that when the legislature has prescribed a specific mode of procedure for the employment of school personnel, such must be strictly followed, unless it is intended that such procedure be directory only. Generally, an appointment of a teacher becomes complete when, and only when, the last act required of the appointing body is performed, or when the contract of employment is executed by the parties.

The duty to hire teachers requires more than the mere appointment of licensed teachers, without regard to morals and competence, but ordinarily the employing body is the judge of an applicant's qualifications. In the absence of statutory provisions to the contrary, the appointing body may take sex, marital status, affiliation with an organization, so long as unlawful discrimination is not exercised.

5.5. Recommendation of Superintendent of Schools

Where a state law expressly provides that teachers or principals may be employed by a board of education only on the recommendation of the superintendent, a board of education has no power to employ a teacher or principal without such recommendation, and an appointment made without such recommendation is void, even though the board may have adopted a rule giving it exclusive power over the employment of teachers or principals. Even though the superintendent may attempt to ratify the employment of a teacher by giving his approval or recommendation subsequent to board action, such does not meet the requirements of law. Recommendations by the superintendent of schools gives the nominee a prima facie right of approval by the board of education, but ordinarily the board has the discretion to decide whether to employ the applicant. In some jurisdictions the board has no choice but to appoint the nominee of the superintendents, but ordinarily the superintendent's recommendation imposes no legal obligation on the board of education. The duty imposed by law on a superintendent to make a recommendation is a duty owed to the board of education. It is not a duty owed to an applicant seeking a position.

It should be observed that in many states the procedures to be followed, and the right and liabilities of the affected parties in relation to a superintendent's recommendation, are largely regulated by statute. Therefore, the law of each state should be particularly examined regarding problems relating to a particular state.

5.6. Term of Employment

Generally, the length of term of school employees is within the jurisdiction of the state legislature, and in many states statutes have been passed regulating such terms. Such statutes have been held valid and subject to such regulations. The appropriate school authorities may provide by contract the terms for which particular school employees are to serve. A law that provides that certain school employees may be employed for a specific term of years supersedes a board order limiting the term of a school employee to a shorter term. If during a particular term a statute is amended lengthening the term, a re-employment after the passage of the amended law is for the longer term.

Generally, under permissive state statutes school boards may grant leaves of absence, and they possess broad discretion with respect thereto. Thus, a board may grant a leave of absence for illness, and condition the granting of such or re-employment on a physical examination prescribed by the school authorities. Under certain statutes, a teacher may be placed on an unrequested leave of absence, provided in certain cases that he is given notice, and a hearing if he requests it.

5.7. Tenure

Generally, tenure statutes provide for a system of granting tenure rights to teachers, including the right to be employed for a continuing or indefinite period of time, subject to removal only for a designated cause in a manner prescribed by law. Such statutes have consistently been held valid. Passage of such laws has been justified on the theory that their purpose is to promote good order and the best interests and welfare of the state and school system by preventing the removal of capable teachers by political motives. It is generally held that tenure statutes should be liberally construed, although there is some authority to the effect that they should be strictly construed on the ground that they are in derogation of the common law. Retroactive effect will not be given to such statutes unless expressly provided by the terms.

There is some confusion as to the legal effect of the repeal or amendment of a tenure statute. The question turns on whether or not the teachers occupy a contractual status that cannot be disturbed. In some jurisdictions the tenure statutes have been interpreted merely to regulate the actions of school officials in the dismissal of teachers, or to declare a public policy to secure teachers against the whims of changing officeholders. Under the laws, the preferential right of employment created by the tenure statutes has been held to be a right, contractual in its nature, concerning which a teacher cannot be deprived of constitutionality by a repeal of the law. This latter position has been taken by the United States Supreme Court in the case of Indiana ex rel Anderson v Brand 303 U.S. 95,667,113 ALR 1482 under an Indiana statute. Even though a vested contractual right, however, has been acquired by a teacher under a tenure law, such a private right has been deemed to be subject to the police power of the state when properly exercised. Moreover, under tenure laws which provide for contracts of employment, such contracts being expressly made subject to the statutory provisions relating to schools—and the amendments thereto, such phrase is generally considered to be broad enough to include future amendments of the laws.

5.8. Rights Under Tenure Statutes

Whatever rights teachers have under such laws are largely regulated by the statutes of the various states. Under many statutes which provide permanent tenure for teachers, a period of probationary service is necessary before permanent status accrues. Such period of time ordinarily varies under the various tenure laws. Ordinarily, occasional absences during the probationary term will not affect the granting of permanent tenure. Generally, such probationary period must be served in the one school district. While some statutes provide that teachers shall automatically acquire permanent status at the end of a probationary period, in many states some action by the school board is necessary to actually grant such teachers permanent status. Under some statutes failure of the school authorities to follow the procedure set forth by law may result in a teacher acquiring permanent status by virtue of law.

Permanency of tenure does not result in the teacher holding an office, but it remains an employment. It carries with it no legal assurance against changes in salary. Generally, when the duty of fixing salaries is imposed on a school board, its power to reduce the salary of permanent teachers may be exercised, so long as it is done so reasonably, and not contrary to any statutory restrictions. The contract clause of the Federal Constitution does not prevent the reduction of salaries of teachers protected by such statutes.

Permanency of tenure does not freeze a teacher in one particular position or assignment. While a tenure teacher has the right to continued employment of the same rank or teaching area that he is qualified to hold under the law, the school authorities have the right to assign him to any teaching position for which he is qualified. A demotion, however, from a position of one rank or field to a position of another rank or teaching field, especially when accompanied by a substantial decrease in salary, in effect constitutes a removal from the original position. It should be noted that in some jurisdictions school authorities have complete discretionary authority to promote or demote teachers and to change their salaries. Nevertheless, as a general rule, no teacher has a vested right to be assigned to teach in any particular school building. Where a teaching certificate qualifies a teacher to teach more than one subject or in more than one grade, the particular subject or subjects and grades to which a teacher is assigned is a matter for the discretion of the authority having the power to assign.

Generally, the tenure rights of a teacher are lost by resignation. If a teacher resigns her permanent contract in one district and thereafter returns to teach in such district, she is not entitled to be classified as a permanent employee because of her prior service or contract. The acceptance of a position in another district may effect a relinquishment of tenure rights previously attained. Ordinarily, if a teacher in one district has acquired a permanent status and is thereafter transferred to an administrative post in such district, he does not forfeit his permanent status as a teacher, but on termination of his administrative position, he is entitled to be assigned to a position as a teacher under his permanent status.

Dismissal. While the remarks under this topic apply primarily to a permanent tenure teacher, in a jurisdiction where the statute provides the same kind of dismissal proceedings for permanent teachers and other teachers, these comments would also apply.

When a statute designates the causes for which a teacher may be dismissed, such grounds are exclusive to all other causes, and a board of education may not add to such causes one of their own creation. In many states, in addition to the enumerated statutes, the law also provides that teachers may be dismissed for "other good and just cause." Under such language it has been held that the school authorities have the power to determine reasonably the particular cause or basis on which they propose to dismiss a teacher, but they cannot act arbitrarily or unfairly, or create a cause which is irrelevant to the particular teacher or foreign to the school board's obligation of building up and maintaining an efficient school system. In interpreting such phrase, the courts hold that it may not only be a cause not resulting in or pertinent to the ground enumerated in the statute, but it includes any ground which bears a reasonable relation to the teacher's fitness. Indeed, some courts have held that *good and just cause* does not limit the cause set forth by the board to one of inefficiency or misconduct on the part of the teacher, but includes any ground that is asserted in good faith and is not arbitrary or unreasonable.

Thus, where faculty contracts are made with specific reference to or with full knowledge of a board rule or policy, adopted in good faith, that marriage will be a ground for terminating a woman teacher's employment, then the marriage of the teacher will be a good and just cause for terminating such contract. There is, however, some conflict on this point as some courts have held that marriage of a teacher as a good and just cause to dismiss is not a reasonable ground. There are not any recent cases available on this particular point, and because legal opinions often do change with the trend of the times, it is entirely possible that in this day and age a court might well consider the latter view more appropriate.

The particular incidents which may justify the dismissal of a teacher are largely tied in with the language of the statutes of the various states, and the court decisions construing such statutes, and for that reason to establish clear-cut principles of universal application is rather difficult. Generally, teachers are expected to bring to their work a reasonable amount of teaching competence, and if they do not do so, may be discharged for incompetency. The whole course of a teacher's conduct may be considered, in the evaluation of his competency, not only on the school premises while actually teaching pupils, but away from his classes. He is not expected to so conduct himself as to lose the respect of his associates or the community.

When teachers enter into contracts with boards of education, by implication they agree to abide by all reasonable rules and regulations adopted by the board of education, regardless of whether the rule was in effect at the time the contract was executed, or thereafter.

As to the power of the boards of education to dismiss a teacher for reasons of economy or because his services are no longer required, in the absence of express statutory authority, it would seem that the board would have no right to dismiss such teacher. Such is due to the fact that statutes regulating the dismissal of teachers are intended to regulate termination of the contract for causes personal to the teacher, and not dismissal for causes outside the control of the teacher, such as lack of a sufficient number of pupils or for reasons of economy. It should be pointed out, however, there is some authority to the effect that a board has the inherent right to terminate a teacher's contract where there has ceased to be any further need for the teacher's services through a program of economy instituted in good faith, or through a decrease in the number of pupils. This principle has been extended to include suspension or consolidation of schools or the abolition of an entire department in a school. However, such reasons must be based on good faith and cannot be used to circumvent the tenure law or to accomplish the dismissal for arbitrary reasons. In some jurisdictions, express statutory authority is given to school boards to suspend teachers' contracts because of reasons other than those set forth expressly as grounds to terminate a contract.

When a statute provides for the termination or suspension of a teacher's contract because of a decrease in the number of pupils, such is considered to refer generally to enrollment in a course, school, or school district. According to some authorities, where there is a decrease of students due to the installation of another department, such a decrease is one due to natural causes, and if a teacher is thereby rendered unnecessary for the operation of the school, his contract may be terminated.

Procedures and Remedies. The procedure relating to the dismissal of teachers is ordinarily regulated by the statutes in each state. Generally, there may be no material deviation from the procedure established by law. The primary purpose of a particular procedure for the dismissal of teachers established by law is to prevent arbitrary action by school boards, and to afford a fair consideration of the evidence. Even where the statutes provide that the board of education shall file the charges, and then act as a hearing board to hear the evidence, such is not deemed a denial of any legal right held by the teacher. Ordinarily, when a particular ground or cause is predicated against the teacher, the evidence introduced at such hearing must be confined to such ground.

In many jurisdictions, the statutes expressly grant the teacher the right of appeal to a court when his contract has been terminated by the board of education. His rights on appeal are largely regulated by the statutes of each state. In some states, the teacher has the right of a trial de novo before the court. In other jurisdictions, he does not have such right, but the authority of the court is to review the transcript and proceedings before the board of education to see that the teacher was granted a fair hearing, that all procedures prescribed by statute were properly observed, and whether the decision of the board of education was based on ample, sufficient, and credible evidence. In such jurisdictions, it is stated that the reviewing court cannot weight the evidence, or substitute its judgment for that of the board of education.

Under a tenure law which designated the causes for which a teacher may be dismissed and which provided that the decision of the board of education was final, it has been held that the action of the board in dismissing a teacher is not subject to review by the courts, unless the board acted outside of its authority, in bad faith, arbitrarily, fraudulently, or in gross abuse of discretion. Under a tenure statute, which provided it shall not be construed to deprive a person of his rights and remedies in a court of competent jurisdiction on a question of law and fact, it is the right of the dismissed teacher to have a trial court decide the truth of charges preferred without reference to the decision of the school board as to the merit of the charges. As heretofore noted, however, the right of direct appeal to a court, and the extent of the court's jurisdiction, is largely regulated by the statutes of each respective state.

The judicial remedies available in the wrongful discharge of a teacher would ordinarily be either an action in mandamus or an action for breach of contract, the latter remedy being available obviously only when the teacher was employed under a contract. There is substantial authority to the effect that a public employee who is wrongfully deprived of his right of employment may institute a mandamus action for restoration of employment, even though he is employed only under a contract arrangement and in spite of the argument that he has an available remedy in the form of an action for breach of contract. On the other hand, there is authority to the effect that mandamus will not lie for a teacher whose rights rest solely on a contract; but it is generally considered the appropriate method where the teacher's rights rest on tenure.

In an action for breach of contract by a teacher, the measure of damages is the salary or wage which was to be paid, minus any sum actually earned or which might have been earned by the plaintiff in the exercise of reasonable efforts in seeking other employment. There is authority to the effect that when the wrongful dismissal takes place during the school year which is covered by a contract, such constitutes a breach of contract for which the teacher may receive his salary for the balance of the year as damages for the wrongful breach.

5.9. Their Duties and Authority

Generally, teachers employed by boards of education are considered public employees, but not public officers. Their salaries are not ordinarily exempt from legal process. Although the duties of a school teacher are said to be purely secular, a teacher in a public school is under an implied duty to guard the morals of the children entrusted in his care. Teachers stand somewhat in place of the parents in training the minds and stamping the moral character of their pupils. They must endeavor to maintain good discipline over all pupils under their charge, and to guard the physical and mental welfare of such pupils, either in the classrooms or on field trips, or while on the playgrounds during the period in which such pupils are in the immediate care of such teacher. As discussed elsewhere, a teacher may be personally liable for injuries directly and proximately sustained by pupils under the care of such teacher for negligence or failure of duty.

In accepting employment as a teacher, a person agrees to perform his labor and duties under the control and direction of the board of education and its authorized administrative employees in conformity with board policy.

He is required to perform all duties that are included within the scope of his duties as a teacher, and may be required to assume reasonable additional or extracurricular duties, particularly if such duties are not foreign to his employment as a teacher or his responsibility to instruct, supervise, and discipline children.

Ordinarily, the hours of employment of each teacher, and the number of months on which his annual salary is based, are matters of the discretion of each employing board, subject to whatever regulations or restrictions may be imposed in regard to such matters by statute.

5.10. Discipline and Punishment of Pupils

It is generally considered that the discipline of pupils is a matter committed for the most part to teachers. The authority of a teacher in such respect, however, may be regulated by rules and regulations adopted by a board of education.

It was formerly held that the authority of a teacher over the pupil was on the same footing as that of a parent over his child. The modern view is that a teacher has such portion of the power of the parent committed to his charge as is necessary for the restraining and correction of the pupil. Such portion of the parents' power is impliedly delegated to the teacher.

Generally speaking, school officers and teachers have no concern with the individual conduct of the pupils wholly outside of the schoolrooms and grounds, while they are presumed to be under the control of the parents. When the pupil is sent to his home, the authority of the teacher ends and that of the parent begins; when the pupil enters the schoolrooms and grounds the authority of the teacher begins, and that of the parent ends.

This general rule, however, is modified under certain conditions. The misconduct of pupils on their way to and from school is within the scope of authority of teachers, and the pupils' conduct outside school hours and school property which directly relates to and affects the conduct of the school, its discipline, training, and efficiency, is within the control of the teachers.

After a child has returned to his home and his parents' control, parental authority is resumed so that all ordinary acts of misbehavior thereafter the parent alone has the power to punish. However, where an offense committed at home or away from school has a direct and immediate tendency to injure the school, and to bring the teacher's authority into contempt, the teacher has the right to punish the child for such acts when he returns to school. The authority of a board of education extends into the twilight zone between the home and school, and if a board adopts rules regulating the conduct of pupils while on their way to and from school, a teacher has the authority to enforce such rules, or in the absence of any board-adopted regulations, a teacher has the inherent right to punish and discipline a pupil.

The extent and method of punishment that may be inflicted is a matter for the wise judgment and discretion of a teacher. A teacher has the same right as a parent to inflict reasonable corporal punishment upon a pupil deserving it. As a general rule such punishment must be reasonable and confined within the bounds of moderation. It must not be cruel or excessive, and the teacher must not act wantonly or from malice or passion.

Each case must depend on its own circumstances. The instrument used must be proportioned to the gravity of the offense, the apparent motive and disposition of the offender, the influence of his example and conduct on others, and the age, size, sex, and physical strength of the pupil.

Where the punishment is moderate and is inflicted with a proper instrument, the teacher, as a rule, is not liable civilly in an action at law by either the child or the parent; but a teacher may be held liable for injuries resulting from any improper, immoderate, or excessive punishment. A teacher will not be held liable for injury caused in the administration of proper punishment by some hidden defect in the pupil's constitution, unless the teacher had knowledge of such defect or the punishment is otherwise excessive.

In a civil action against a teacher for damages caused by the improper punishment of a pupil, the burden of proof rests on the plaintiff to satisfy the jury that the teacher unlawfully beat and injured the child, and that damages resulted therefrom. Whether the punishment and the instrument used were proper are questions of fact for a jury to determine in a civil lawsuit.

Moderate and reasonable correction by a schoolmaster with a proper instrument is not a criminal offense. But if a teacher, in administering correction or punishment to pupils, uses his authority as a cover for malice, he is subject to the criminal laws; and the same holds true if the teacher is actuated by revenge, spite, or evil passion.

On the question of liability for excessive punishment administered under an error of judgment, the authorities are divided. Most adhere to the rule that mere immoderate and excessive punishment does not constitute a crime unless it is of such a nature as to produce or threaten lasting or permanent injury and is accompanied by express or implied malice.

A teacher stands in loco parentis, acts in a quasi-judicial capacity, and is not liable for an error in judgment in the matter of punishment of a pupil. In such punishment by a teacher of a pupil under his control there is a presumption of the correctness of his actions and that he acts in good faith.

Before a teacher can be convicted of assault and battery in the punishment of a pupil, the state must show beyond a reasonable doubt that the punishment was so severe, so excessive, and so cruel as to "shock the sensibilities of the average individual," and that the punishment was administered with either express or implied malice.

In the trial of a teacher charged with assault and battery of a pupil under his control, where there is no evidence which would indicate that the defendant was actuated by any malice, express or implied, or of any serious physical injury or punishment in excess of that which the law authorized one in loco parentis to inflict, and where there is ample evidence to indicate good faith and proper motive on part of the defendant, the trial court should direct the verdict for the defendant at the conclusion of the state's evidence.

5.11. Pupil Injuries

Generally, most teachers are continually involved in situations in which claims of personal liability may be brought against them because of injuries to pupils. This is due to the teacher's day by day contact with pupils and his obligation to supervise them. Conceivably, if a teacher is found negligent, and his negligence is the proximate cause of the pupil's injury, unless the teacher has a good defense in law, he may be held liable to pay damages for the pupil's injury.

Some injuries may be due to pure accident in which no claim of negligence is asserted against the teacher. Therefore, if a pupil is injured due entirely to accidental means, and the teacher was not negligent and is without fault, the teacher is not liable. If an injury is not caused by negligence, as legally defined, it is the result of an accident. If no negligence is associated with the injury, the accident may be said to have been unavoidable, and no liability can be asserted against the teacher.

Generally the rules of law which apply in reference to private individuals whose negligence harms others apply to teachers whose negligent conduct may result in injuries to the pupils. Because of the relationship that teachers have with their pupils, they are under the legal duty to exercise prudent or reasonable care not to injure them, and to prevent injuries to them. The claim that makes the teacher personally liable is found when the following factors are present: (1) there is present a breach of this duty; (2) there exists a reasonably close causal connection between the conduct of the teacher and the resulting injury; (3) the pupil is without fault that contributed to his own injury; and (4) the pupil suffers an injury or damage.

Ordinarily, a court in measuring the question of negligence considers the nature of the conduct of the teacher, the legal or proximate cause of the injury, and the foreseeability as to the possibility of injury to the pupil.

Negligence may be an act of commission or an act of omission. In each case negligence is determined by the particular facts involved. It is any conduct which does not meet the standard established by law for the protection of persons against harm. The standard of conduct is weighed or measured against what a reasonable person of ordinary prudence would have done or not have done under the same or similar circumstances.

There is a conflict of authority as to whether the standard would be that of a prudent teacher or a prudent parent. While a few courts have held that the standard of care required of a public school employee is that which a person of ordinary prudence charged with his duties would exercise under the same circumstances, other courts have held that a teacher or school employee may be charged only with reasonable care such as a parent of ordinary prudence would exercise under like circumstances.

Certain general observations are pertinent in the matter of negligence on the part of the teacher. There may be negligence per se or inherent in certain acts. It may involve a certain amount of unreasonable risk, even though done with reasonable care. In certain cases there may be negligence because of a teacher's lack of warning to the student, or the lack of skill or preparation on the part of the pupil, although the particular act itself would not constitute negligent conduct if reasonable care, ability, preparation, or warning had been exercised.

The special relation that exists between a teacher and a pupil creates a particular duty of care on the part of the teacher that may not be present in respect to one ordinary individual and another. It could be negligence on the part of a teacher to permit a child to use an instrument which conceivably could be dangerous to such child or to another person. It could be negligent for a teacher to permit a child to place himself in a situation where he could injure himself, or be the cause of injury to another. In any case, negligence is a question of fact to be decided by the jury from all the evidence presented in the particular case against such teacher.

Certain additional legal principles are also pertinent to the issue of negligence and liability on the part of a teacher. The degree of care expected of a teacher will also be measured in the light of the danger involved and the age or maturity of a child. Greater care will be expected of a teacher who supervises pupils who are exposed to dangerous machinery, chemicals, equipment, or similar situations, than of a teacher of English, history, or in teaching areas where hazards are not so immediate. In the former situation, the courts expect more constant and immediate supervision over the activities of the pupils, a greater degree of care to be exercised by the teacher in reference to foreseeing the possibility of an injury, and also evidence that the pupils had been adequately warned about or prepared for the hazards that they might be subject to, or adequately instructed in the proper use of the equipment, supplies, or machinery.

In respect to a teacher's liability, one factor often used to determine whether a person's conduct was negligent or proper is the matter of foreseeability. In a case where a reasonably prudent person should have seen the possible, harmful results of his action or inaction, or the possible harmful consequences of a child's action, such person, if he disregards the likely consequences, is responsible for his negligent conduct. Failure on the part of the teacher to take reasonable precautionary measures could be considered negligence.

Another factor necessary to establish liability on the part of the teacher is that his conduct must be established to be the proximate cause of a child's injury. It is that cause which in the natural and continuous sequence of events, without the interference of an independent, superseding cause or incident, resulted in the injury. To break the chain, such superseding cause must be a new and independent incident or factor which intervened to cause the injury to the pupil.

Absence from the Classroom. Generally, the temporary absence of a teacher from the classroom is not considered to be a negligent lack of proper supervision. If a child is guilty of misbehavior while the teacher is absent from the classroom and injures another child, the teacher is not liable. It cannot be said as a matter of law, in all cases, that the absence of the teacher is the proximate cause of the injury. The age, maturity, and intelligence of the pupils also bear on the question of negligent supervision on the part of the teacher. It shall be noted, however, that in a schoolroom where the class is engaged in projects involving the use of potentially dangerous machinery or equipment, a higher degree of supervision is expected over such room, and the teacher's absence from the room may be weighed in determining whether there was a lack of adequate supervision.

Playgrounds. Quite often, pupil injuries on playgrounds are the results of accidents in which negligence on the part of the teacher is not involved. Nor will a teacher be ordinarily held liable for an injury where supervision is proper and reasonable. While such supervision is to be suitable in relation to the apparatus on the grounds, the number and age of the pupils, and the size of the grounds, the courts appreciate the fact that a teacher cannot keep all pupils under continuous watch at all times, nor can a teacher be held to foresee or anticipate that the children by their own action might injure themselves under all circumstances.

Negligent supervision on the part of a teacher, which proximately causes an injury to a pupil, creates liability against the teacher. If a teacher knowingly permits a child to leave a supervised group, and he injures himself on an existing dangerous condition, the teacher may be held liable. While a teacher is not responsible to keep playground equipment in good repair, if a teacher permits a child to use a piece of equipment which he knows is defective and dangerous, conceivably the teacher could be held liable, especially if he did not warn the child of the hazards involved.

Shops and Laboratories. In this area of student participation, the hazards and dangers are more immediate and common than in ordinary elementary or secondary classrooms. Accordingly, the legal responsibility of the teacher to be diligent and watchful is a duty that goes with this area of teaching. Adequate supervision and instruction are essential. In many jurisdictions the shop or laboratory teacher has been held to be charged with the responsibility of exercising a high degree of care.

Constant and immediate supervision over the activities of all the pupils is expected on the part of the teacher. He is expected to adequately point out to the pupils the hazards of the equipment or material that they may use. He is expected to fully instruct the pupils as to the do's and don't's, to instruct them on good safety measures, to warn them of possible dangers, and to adequately instruct the pupils as to the proper methods of using a dangerous chemical or piece of machinery. Particularly in the laboratory, the teacher should also see that potentially dangerous chemicals should not be placed so that students have easy access to them. When he leaves the shop or laboratory, the prudent teacher should see that things are left in good order.

Physical Education and Driver Education. The physical education teacher is charged to exercise reasonable care over the pupils so as to prevent injuries, to assign students to such activities as are within their abilities, and to properly and adequately supervise pupil activities. There is a variety of cases that hold the physical education teacher or coach legally responsible for permitting children to engage in an athletic activity that is beyond their skill, ability, or physical fitness, or to participate in such an activity without proper preparation, training, or instruction. As in the case of playground equipment, while the teacher is not legally responsible to keep board-owned equipment in good repair, if he permits pupils to use apparatus which he knows is unsafe, he may be personally liable for resulting injuries.

In reference to the driver education teacher, unless excused by statute, he is under the duty to exercise reasonable prudence, and if he is negligent in such respect, he may be personally liable for resulting injuries. Correct supervision over the activities of the participating pupils, proper instruction as to the handling of the vehicle, and warning of possible hazards, are expected of the driver education teacher.

Field Trips. There is a scarcity of reported court decisions as to teacher liability for injuries resulting to pupils on field trips. More frequently there are lawsuits against the owner of plants for injuries to pupils in immediate charge of a teacher. As a general rule, the owner of a plant is liable for negligence to an injured person whom he invites to visit the plant if he fails to exercise proper care to keep his premises in a reasonably safe condition. On the other hand, if the person is considered a licensee in his use of the premises, the duty owed to such licensee is to point out to him hidden dangers known to the owners of which the licensee is not apt to be aware. If a person visits a plant at the request or invitation of the owner for the owner's benefit, or for the benefit of both the owner and the visitor, he is ordinarily considered an invitee. If he visits the plant for his own benefit and merely with the permission of the owner, the visitor is ordinarily considered a licensee.

The teacher in charge of a group of pupils on a field trip is expected to use reasonable care to protect the safety of the pupils. The extent of the care expected depends largely on the age and maturity of the pupils and the inherent dangers of the place visited, or the field trip itself.

Ordinarily, permission of the parents or the school administration to take the pupils on the field trip does not relieve the teacher of possible liability for his negligence. While it is legally possible for a parent to execute a legal waiver, releasing the teacher from a civil claim for damages because of medical or other expenses a parent may personally incur in the treatment of an injured pupil, the parent cannot waive away the pupil's claim for damage against the teacher for his negligence, on which the pupil can sue in his own name upon reaching a legal age to bring suit, or which the parent may bring at any time in behalf of his injured child.

Legal Defenses for a Teacher. The courts are not apt to impose liability against a teacher under any of the following conditions for injuries sustained by pupils:

(1) If there is contributing negligence on the part of the injured pupil, which has a causal connection with his injury. In determining whether a child may be charged with contributory negligence, the courts have said that the degree of care required may differ between adults and minors. An instruction that children are required to exercise ordinary care to avoid the injuries of which they complain (such care, as applied to them, is that degree of care which children of the same age, education, and experience are accustomed to exercise under similar circumstances), was held not erroneous when applied to plaintiff, a seventeen-year-old boy driving a motor driven bicycle. A child eleven years old can only be charged with that degree of care which children of the same age, maturity, and experience of ordinary care and prudence are accustomed to exercise under the same or similar circumstances. A child of tender age, in the absence of evidence that he has discretion and understanding to appreciate a danger which confronts him, is not chargeable with negligence.

While, generally, if both the teacher and the pupil are at fault and the negligence of each has a causal connection with the injury, there can be no liability against the teacher, this is not always the case. Several states have adopted the rule of comparative negligence, which means that if the teacher's negligence or want of care is greater than that of the injured pupil, then the damages would be prorated.

(2) If the injury sustained by the child is caused by an unavoidable and nonforeseeable accident. In such connection, however, the liability of the teacher for accidental injuries may turn on whether the teacher in the exercise of prudent behavior should have anticipated the danger of an accident, not necessarily the specific accident itself, and if in the exercise of due care on his part the teacher should have warned the pupil of the danger, or taken proper care to prevent the accident.

(3) In the case where, even though the teacher is negligent, his negligence is not the proximate cause of the injury, but rather the real cause of the injury was due to an intervening act or event which caused the injury, often resulting from the conduct of a third part.

(4) If the injured pupil assumed the risk. The terms *contributory negligence* and *assumption of risk* are not synonymous. The former is based on carelessness and the latter on venturousness. Assumption of risk is a matter of knowledge of the danger and intelligent acquiescence to it. Before a person may be charged with assumption of risk as a matter of law, it must be shown that the person accepted a danger that he clearly understood, and that he had a foresight of the consequences and a readiness to accept them. In reference to the assumption of risk by a child, the facts must establish that the child was old enough or had sufficient maturity to understand the danger involved, that he was aware of the danger involved in a contemplated course of action on his part, and that he willingly accepted the consequences of what might happen. Where a seven-year-old child jumped into a fire caused by the igniting of small pools of fire by another child, for the purpose of extinguishing it, reasonable minds can conclude only that he did not accept a danger that he clearly understood and that he did not have foresight of the consequences of his act together with a readiness to accept them.

5.12. Principals and Superintendents

Extensive material could be presented about the day-by-day responsibilities of principals and superintendents. They occupy important positions in the operation of school systems.

As a matter of law, the essential duties of a school superintendent are largely prescribed by statute. In some states, the superintendent has continuing tenure in his position; in others he is employed for a definite term of office, subject to statutory provisions. Ordinarily, he is considered to be the executive officer of the board of education. As a matter of law, in addition to his statutory duties, it would seem that such authority as he might possess would be in the field of duties that the board of education could properly delegate to him.

Statutory duties imposed on a principal of school buildings are rather scarce. In many states, the employment rights of principals generally follow the provisions of law respecting the employment of teachers. Their legal duties are such as may be prescribed by law, properly delegated by the board of education, or assigned to them by the superintendent of schools.

Superintendents and principals are not legally responsible for the negligence of other board employees. They are not responsible as a matter of law in keeping the school premises in good repair and safe condition. Accordingly, they would not be legally liable for injuries arising from the unsafe conditions of school premises. They are liable only for their personal acts of negligence which directly cause injuries.

VI

Tort Liability

6.1. Generally

It is a well-established principle of the common law that school boards in the exercise of their governmental functions are not liable in tort for injuries arising from the negligent acts of the board or its employees. This principle of the common law stems from the doctrine of governmental immunity from tort. There has been a long line of court cases holding that a school district, being merely an agency of the state and under the common law, is not, in the absence of a statute imposing such liability, liable for torts committed by its members or its employees. Based on the common law theory, a school board in its corporate capacity cannot commit a wrong or a tort; if it does so, in such respect it does not represent the district. The general rule of non-liability relieves the board from a legal responsibility for injuries to pupils suffered in connection with their attendance, even though such injuries may arise from the dangerous condition or improper construction of buildings, unsuitable or dangerous equipment, dangerous conditions of the school buildings or grounds, unsafe transportation of pupils, and the negligent acts of officers, agents, servants, or employees. Such doctrine of non-liability has, likewise, been extended to protect the board against tort actions for injuries claimed by persons other than school pupils.

The common law doctrine of governmental immunity, often phrased as "The king can do no wrong," appears to stem in the United States to two basic cases, the original case being decided in 1788 in England, and the other case in Massachusetts in 1812. This was pointed out by the Supreme Court of Minnesota in a rather recent case, Spanel v. Mounds View School District, 118 N.W. (2d) 799, in which opinion the court states in part as follows:

"All of the paths leading to the origin of governmental tort immunity

70

converge on Russell v. The Men of Devon, 100 Eng. Rep. 359, 2 T.R. 667 (1788). This product of the English common law was left on our doorstep to become the putative ancestor of a long line of American cases beginning with Mower v. Leicester 9 Mass. 247 (1812). Russell sued all of the male inhabitants of the County of Devon for damages occurring to his wagon by reason of a bridge being out of repair. It was apparently undisputed that the county had a duty to maintain such structures. The court held that the action would not lie because: (1) to permit it would lead to 'an infinity of actions,' (2) there was no precedent for attempting such a suit, (3) only the legislature should impose liability of this kind, (4) even if defendants are to be considered a corporation or quasi-corporation there is no fund out of which to satisfy the claim, (5) neither law nor reason supports the action, (6) there is a strong presumption that what has never been done cannot be done, and (7) although there is a legal principle which permits a remedy for every injury resulting from the neglect of another, a more applicable principle is 'that it is better that an individual should sustain an injury than that the public should suffer an inconvenience.' The court concluded that the suit should not be permitted 'because the action must be brought against the public.' There is no mention of the 'king can do no wrong,' but on the contrary it is suggested that plaintiff sue the county itself rather than its individual inhabitants. Every reason assigned by the court is born of expediency. The wrong to plaintiff is submerged in the convenience of the public. No moral, ethical, or rational reason for the decision is advanced by the court except the practical problem of assessing damages against individual defendants. The court's invitation to the legislature has a familiar ring. It was finally accepted as to claims against the Crown in 1947, although Russell had long since been overruled.

"In 1812, when Mower's horse was killed by stepping in a hole on the Leicester bridge, counsel argued that 'Men of Devon' did not apply since the town of Leicester was incorporated and had a treasury out of which to satisfy a judgment. The Massachusetts court nevertheless held that the town had no notice of the defect and that quasi-corporations are not liable for such neglect under the common law. On the authority of 'Men of Devon' recovery was decided. It was on this shaky foundation that the law of governmental tort immunity was erected in Minnesota and elsewhere."

The doctrine of the tort immunity of the school board would appear to rest essentially on the principle that a board of education is a state agency in that it performs a governmental function as a creature of the legislature and like the state itself is not liable in its corporate capacity unless made so specifically by statute. It has not been unusual, in addition, for the courts to point out that school districts manage funds which are trust funds and are not intended to be raised from tax sources to pay damages for injuries. Other courts have pointed out that the relationship of master and servant does not exist so as to make the board of education liable for the negligence of its employees. Some courts, also, have based their decisions on the fact that school board members in the performance of their duties exercise a public function and agency for the public welfare for which they receive no profit or corporate benefit.

In the past several years, the principle of governmental immunity has been abrogated in a few of the states either by statutory regulation or by judicial decree. Obviously, a court may abrogate a common law principle, although many courts have taken the position that if the doctrine of governmental immunity based on common law is to be changed, such should be done only by legislative mandate and not by judicial decree. Within the past few years, however, the Supreme Courts of Wisconsin, Arizona, Minnesota, and Illinois have abrogated the common law principle of governmental immunity, and in the states of Washington, New York, and California, laws have been passed which in legal effect abrogate the common law rule and make school boards liable for injuries sustained because of the negligence of school employees. It should be pointed out, however, that at the present time the principle of tort immunity of school boards remains in effect in a vast majority of the states, and because the common law principle is so well established and has existed for so many years it would seem that the process of changing the law, if such be done, would be very slow.

Many school districts, pursuant to legislative mandate, have been authorized to protect or insure school employees against negligent acts in the course of their employment. However, in most states where such statutes have been enacted, it has been judicially held that such statutes do not act to abrogate the common rule law of immunity.

6.2. Governmental—Proprietary Functions

In a few cases in this country, the courts have upheld the principle of tort liability of a school board when it is engaged in the performance of a proprietary function. The vast majority of courts, which adhere to the immunity doctrine, however, hold that such protects a board of education in all cases irrespective of whether the injury occurred as a result of a so-called proprietary or a so-called governmental function. Such courts hold that in the eyes of the law the board of education cannot be guilty of any wrong or commit an act of negligence; and not being liable in such capacity, it does not incur any legal responsibility because of the negligent acts of its employees. Some courts take the position that since a board of education is established to conduct schools, it acts completely within a governmental function, and as such, cannot lawfully engage in a proprietary function. Even those courts which may make a distinction between responsibility because of a governmental or proprietary function take the position that a particular activity of the school board does not lose its governmental definition because the activity may yield some profit or produce revenue.

6.3. Trespass or Nuisance

As a general rule of law, a board of education assumes no tort liability for trespass or the maintenance of a nuisance. This is based on the theory that a school board is not legally liable for any kind of tort, because it cannot represent the district in such respect and attempt to bind the district. In some jurisdictions, however, the immunity of the board does not extend to positive acts of misconduct in the nature of a trespass which invades the premises of another. In some jurisdictions, likewise, the school board has been held liable for damages to property caused by the maintenance of a nuisance on school property.

6.4. Personal Responsibility of Board Members

As a general rule, lawful liabilities existing against a school district should be maintained and enforced in an action against the board as a corporate body and not by actions against the individual members constituting such board. School members ordinarily are not personally responsible for actions within the scope of their authority, unless acting from corrupt motives. Board members cannot be made liable for any conscientious mistake or error in judgment.

The performance of many of the duties of the board members requires the exercise of judgment and discretion. When such occurs their acts are quasi-judicial. So long as the members of the board, in the exercise of such authority, act honestly and in good faith, within their jurisdiction, they will not be held liable for an injury growing out of an error of judgment, however great it may be. Such rule is based on sound public policy. An individual member of a board will not be held to answer in damages for the consequence of his acts, unless activated by malice, or intent to injure, or by a corrupt motive. Likewise, board members are not ordinarily personally liable for damages arising from their failure to perform a duty, or for negligent performance, where the specific duty is imposed on the board in its corporate capacity. Board members, however, may be personally liable for illegal expenditures made or approved by them.

6.5. Personal Tort Liability of School Employees

It appears to be generally accepted that the rule of immunity of school districts, school boards, or other agencies in charge of public schools ordinarily does not extend to their agents or employees, or other persons under contract with such public bodies, in the absence of a statute providing otherwise. Therefore, the rule has been applied or recognized that teachers in a public school, school bus drivers irrespective of whether they occupy the status of employees or independent contractors, and other school employees are personally liable for their own negligence.

If a school employee fails to exercise the duty of care expected of reasonably prudent persons in the same or similar situations, that person is said to be negligent; and if such negligence is the direct and proximate cause of injuries sustained by pupils to whom such employee owes a duty of care, such employee is personally responsible in damages. Under such rule, a teacher having charge of children in a classroom, a playground, on a field trip, or while engaging in athletic or other school activities may be personally responsible for injuries resulting from any negligence which directly and proximately causes such injuries, as discussed in detail elsewhere.

The same general principles of law would apply to cafeteria workers, custodial workers, principals, superintendents, bus drivers, and other school employees.

In the determination of the fundamental issue in reference to such personal liability, there are generally three main questions involved, namely: (1) Did the school employee owe a duty of care towards the plaintiff? (2) Was there a failure on the part of the employee to observe such duty? (3) Was such failure the direct and proximate cause of any resulting injury? If all three points each obtain an affirmative answer, in the eyes of the law, a case of personal liability is established.

The care expected of a bus driver, or a "shop" teacher, or a teacher of a class, where the hazards, and possibility of injuries are more immediate than in an ordinary classroom, is that of the highest degree. In the determination of whether or not a school employee is normally prudent, the courts tend to look closely at the following factors: (1) Did the employee exercise reasonable and adequate supervision for the safety and welfare of the pupils? (2) Did the employee, or should the employee, have reasonably foreseen the possibility of the child being injured? (3) Did the employee point out to the pupil the possible hazards that he might encounter in a particular activity or class, as well as inform him of the necessary safety rules and practices?

Court Cases
and Principles

I

Public School Structure

STATE ex rel. CLARK v. HAWORTH
122 Ind. 462, 23 N.E. 946 (1890)

Legal Principles

1. The control of schools and school affairs is vested in the law-making power of the state, upon the principle that schools are intrinsically matters of state control, and not of a local nature.

Opinion

. . . It is sufficient to say that the relator petitioned . . . to compel the appellee as school trustee to certify to the county superintendent the number of textbooks required . . . and the return of the appellee . . . is so framed as to present the question of the constitutionality of the act of March 2, 1889, and also the question of the duties of the school trustee under that act.

The act assailed does not impinge in the slightest degree upon the right of local self-government. The right of local self-government is an inherent, and not a derivative, one. Individualized, it is the right which a man possesses in virtue of his character as a free man. It is not bestowed by legislatures, nor derived from statutes. But the courts which have carried to its utmost extent the doctrine of local self-government have never so much as intimated that it exists as to a matter over which the Constitution has given the law-making power supreme control; nor have they gone beyond the line which separates matters of purely local concern from those of state control. Essentially and intrinsically, the schools in which are educated and trained the children who are to become the rulers of the commonwealth are matters of state, and not of local, jurisdiction.

In such matters the state is a unit, and the legislature the source of power. The authority over schools and school affairs is not necessarily a distributive one, to be exercised by local instrumentalities; but, on the contrary, it is a central power, residing in the legislature of the state. It is for the law-making power to determine whether the authority shall be exercised by a state board of education, or distributed to county, township, or city organizations throughout the state. With that determination the judiciary can no more rightfully interfere than can the legislature with a decree or judgment pronounced by a judicial tribunal. The decision is as conclusive and inviolable in the one case as in the other; and an interference with the legislative judgment would be a breach of the constitution which no principle would justify, nor any precedent excuse. . . .

Judge Cooley has examined the question with care, and discussed it with ability; and he declares that the legislature has plenary power over the subject of the public schools. He says, in the course of his discussion, that "to what degree the legislature shall provide for the education of the people at the cost of the state, or of its municipalities, is a question which, except as regulated by the Constitution, addresses itself to the legislative judgment exclusively." Again, he says, "The governing school boards derive all their authority from the statute, and can exercise no powers except those expressly granted, and those which result by necessary implication from the grant." . . .

If it be true that the power is a legislative one, then it is indisputably true that the courts cannot control the legislative discretion. This principle is elementary in Constitutional law, and it needs no support from precedents or decisions; but the principle has been so well expressed by Mr. Justice Bradley that we quote his language. Replying to an argument that the mode in which the power was exercised was improper, this great judge said: "The answer is: the legislative department, being the nation itself, speaking by its representatives, has a choice of methods, and is the master of its own discretion." . . . We have adopted and applied this rule, and, indeed, we could not depart from it without a disregard of principle that no decision or precedent would excuse.

As the power over schools is a legislative one, it is not exhausted by exercise. The legislature, having tried one plan, is not precluded from trying another. It has a choice of methods, and may change its plans as often as it deems necessary or expedient; and for mistakes or abuses it is answerable to the people, but not to the courts. It is clear, therefore, that even if it were true that the legislature had uniformly intrusted the management of school affairs to local organizations, it would not authorize the conclusion that it might not change the system. To deny the power to change is to affirm that progress is impossible, and that we must move forever "in the dim footsteps of antiquity." But the legislative power moves in a constant stream, and is not exhausted by its exercise in any number of instances, however great. It is not true, however, that the authority over schools was originally regarded as a local one. On the contrary, the earlier cases asserted that the legislature could not delegate the power to levy taxes for school purposes to local organizations, but must itself directly exercise the power; thus denying, in the strongest possible form, the theory of local control. This ruling was for many years regarded as the law of the state; but in the case of Robinson v. Schenck, 102 Ind. 307, 1 N. E. Rep. 698, it was held that the legislature might either exercise the power itself, or delegate it to local governmental in- strumentalities. It has, indeed, been the uniform course, since the organ- ization of the state, to regulate and control school affairs by legislation. All the public schools have been established under legislative enact- ments, and all rules and regulations have been made pursuant to statu- tory authority. Every school that has been established owes its existence to legislation, and every school officer owes his authority to the statute.

It is impossible to conceive of the existence of a uniform system of common schools without power lodged somewhere to make it uniform; and, even in the absence of express Constitutional provisions, that power must necessarily reside in the legislature. If it does reside there, then that body must have, as an incident of the principal power, the authority to prescribe the course of study and the system of instruction that shall be pursued and adopted, as well as the books which shall be used. This general doctrine is well entrenched by authority. . . . Having this au- thority, the legislature may not only prescribe regulations for using such books, but it may also declare how the books shall be obtained and dis- tributed. If it may do this, then it may provide that they shall be obtained through the medium of a contract awarded to the best or lowest bidder, since, if it be true, as it unquestionably is, that the power is legislative, it must also be true that the legislature has an unrestricted discretion and an unfettered choice of methods. It cannot be possible that the courts can interfere with this legislative power and adjudge that the legislature shall not adopt this method or that method; for, if the question is at all legislative, it is so in its whole length and breadth. Under our form of government, there is no such thing as a power partly judicial and partly legislative. . . .

If the power over the school system is legislative and exclusive, then the legislature has authority to impose upon all officers whose tenure is legislative such duties respecting school affairs as it deems proper. All such officers take their offices cum onere, and must do what the legisla- ture commands, or else resign.

It is a mistake to suppose that the statute under consideration imposes duties upon the school officers for the benefit of the book dealers. Not a word in it indicates such an intention.

MONAGHAN v. SCHOOL DISTRICT NO. 1
211 Ore. 360, 315 P. (2d) 797 (1957)

Legal Principles
1. Education is a governmental obligation of the state.
2. Public school teachers when engaged in their employment as such are employees.

Opinion
. . . our conclusion is that the word, "functions," embodies a definite meaning with no contradiction of the phrase "official duties"; that is, he who exercises the functions of another department of government may be either an official or an employee.

Is Mr. Monaghan, charged with official duties as a legislator, in his employment as a school teacher, exercising the functions of another department of government? We think he is and for the reasons which follow.

Education is a function or duty not regarded as a local matter. It is a governmental obligation of the state. Few of our administrative agencies are creatures of the organic law. But, as to schools, the Constitution mandates the legislature to provide by law "for the establishment of a uniform, and general system of Common schools." . . . It is a sovereign power and cannot be bartered away. Campbell v. Aldrich, 159 Ore. 208, 219, 79 P. 2d 257. The power ascribed to the legislature under the Constitution carries with it plenary power to establish the unit of the system, denominated a school district. . . .

A school district, as a legislatively created entity, enjoys closer proximation to the state than to the community it serves. It is a civil division of the state and has been referred to as a corporation having the most limited powers known to the law. It is a quasi-municipal corporation separate and distinct from pure municipal corporations such as cities and towns. . . .

When it so acts, it acts wholly as a governmental agency when performing duties imposed by statute. . . .

A public school teacher is an employee, employed in a public capacity. . . . 78 CJS 971, Schools and School Districts #154: 47 Am. Jur. 372, Schools #108. Teachers are employees hired by a state agency whose function it is to serve the state in the exercise of its sovereign power and duty as mandated by Art. VIII, par. 3 of the Oregon Constitution.

Recently, the Supreme Court of the United States has said: "Today, education is perhaps the most important function of state and local governments." Brown v. Board of Education of Topeka, 1954, 347 U.S. 483,

493, 74 S.Ct. 686, 691, 98 L.ed. 873, 880. It is a declaration to which we unhesitatingly subscribe. This judicially-emphasized importance of the place of education in our system of government casts upon us the duty to resolve doubts, if any, about the possibility of incursions of one department of government into the area occupied by education as an administrative function of the executive department in favor of a decisive separation of these powers, and with jealous vigilance bar its coercive influence or exercise, directly or indirectly, when that possibility becomes evident.

In the fulfillment of the obligation which our Constitution imposes (Art. VIII, par. 3, supra) the teacher is the most effective factor in its implementation.

A teacher's position in the scale of the relative importance of state employees serving a department of government is greater than most all others, particularly when compared to the stenographers and clerks. . . .

It is through the teacher, not the school district, that the state's standards of educational excellence are disseminated. When so engaged, they are exercising one of the functions of the executive department of our state government. . . .

As previously indicated, the respondent places some reliance upon Art. II, par. 10 of the Constitution, which inhibits any person from holding "more than one lucrative office at the same time." Inasmuch as Monaghan's position as a teacher is not an office, Art. II, par. 10 can have no applicability.

In emphasis of the importance and need of vigilance to avoid the trespass of one of the major departments of government upon the domains so wisely reserved to the other two, we conclude with the words of Madison, taken from 1 The Federalist, p. 340:

"It is equally evident that, in reference to each other, neither of them ought to possess, directly or indirectly, an overruling influence in the administration of their respective powers. It will not be denied that power is of an encroaching nature, and that it ought to be effectually restrained from passing the limits assigned to it."

PIERCE, et al. v. SOCIETY OF SISTERS
268 U. S. 510 (1925)

Legal Principles
1. The fundamental theory of liberty upon which all governments of this Union rest excludes any general power of the state to standardize its children by forcing them to accept instruction from public teachers only.

2. A state statute requiring parents to send their children to a public school, is an unreasonable interference with the liberty of parents and guardians to direct the upbringing of the children, and in that respect violates the Fourteenth Amendment.

Opinion

. . . The challenged Act requires every parent, guardian, or other person having control or charge or custody of a child between eight and sixteen years to send him "to a public school for the period of time a public school shall be held during the current year" in the district where the child resides; and failure so to do is declared a misdeameanor. The manifest purpose is to compel general attendance at public schools by normal children, between eight and sixteen, who have not completed the eighth grade. And without doubt enforcement of the statute would seriously impair, perhaps destroy, the profitable features of appellees' business and greatly diminish the value of their property. . . .

Under the doctrine of Meyer v. Nebraska, 262 U.S. 390, we think it entirely plain that the Act of 1922 unreasonably interferes with the liberty of parents and guardians to direct the upbringing and education of children under their control. As often heretofore pointed out, rights guaranteed by the Constitution may not be abridged by legislation which has no reasonable relation to some purpose within the competency of the state. The fundamental theory of liberty upon which all governments in this Union repose excludes any general power of the state to standardize its children by forcing them to accept instruction from public teachers only. The child is not the mere creature of the state; those who nurture him and direct his destiny have the right, coupled with the high duty, to recognize and prepare him for additional obligation.

Appellees are corporations and therefore, it is said, they cannot claim for themselves the liberty which the Fourteenth Amendment guarantees. Accepted in the proper sense, this is true. Northwestern Life Ins. Co. v. Riggs, 203 U.S. 243, 255; Western Turf Association v. Greenberg, 204 U.S. 359, 363. But they have business and property for which they claim protection. These are threatened with destruction through the unwarranted compulsion which appellants are exercising over present and prospective patrons of their schools. And this court has gone very far to protect against loss threatened by such actions. Truax v. Raich, 239 U.S. 33; Truax v. Corrigan, 257 U.S. 312; Terrace v. Thompson, 263 U.S. 197. . . .

Generally it is entirely true, as urged by counsel, that no person in any business has such an interest in possible customers as to enable him to restrain exercise of proper power of the state upon the ground that he will be deprived of patronage. But the injunctions here sought are not against the exercise of any proper power. Plaintiffs asked protection against arbitrary, unreasonable, and unlawful interference with their patrons and the consequent destruction of their business and property. Their interest is clear and immediate . . . within the rule approved in Truax v. Raich, Truax v. Corrigan and Terrace v. Thompson, and many other cases where injunctions have issued to protect business enterprises against interference with the freedom of patrons or customers. . . .

LEEPER v. STATE
103 Tenn. 500, 53 S.W. 962 (1899)

Legal Principles

1. The establishment and regulation of public schools are legislative functions. The legislative power, in this regard, is practically unlimited and is not exhausted by exercise.

2. The power of the legislature to regulate and control the public schools is based upon the police power and the right of the state to regulate institutions charged with a public use.

Opinion

. . . It is evident that the basic principle of it (the Act) is the power of the legislature to subserve the general welfare by prohibiting certain contracts and throwing around other restrictions tending to promote the general welfare and protect the citizen from oppression, fraud, and wrong. That the state may establish a uniform series of books to be taught in the schools, which it provides and controls, seems to be a proposition as evident as that it may provide a uniform system of schools, which we take it is not now an open question; and while the selection of textbooks may, in the earlier and cruder stages of the law, have been left to, and exercised by, local superintendents, directors, and teachers, it was not for want of authority in the state to prescribe a uniform system, but rather because the system had not reached that stage of development and progress that made it advisable, in the opinion of the legislature, to so provide. If we were allowed to look to the wisdom of such a provision, it would seem that a uniform series of school books, selected by men of large experience and extensive information, would be preferable to leaving such selection to superintendents, directors, and teachers, many without experience, some with limited education, and with limited opportunity of examining and comparing the different books.

But it is said that, if it be granted that a uniform series may be selected, still it is beyond the power of the legislature to confer upon one individual the right to publish and sell to the public school any particular book or books, and to prohibit teachers and patrons from using any other, thus forcing them to buy the books thus furnished or refusing them the benefits of the public school.

We think it clear that the state itself might, if it saw proper, publish the books to be used in its public schools, and might sell them to the children of the state or patrons of the schools; and, if it can do this, why may it not authorize another to do so, and prescribe the terms upon which it shall be done, in the interest of its citizens? . . . The authority of the state over schools is a legislative one, and it is difficult to see how a uniform system can be maintained which will confer equal benefits upon all sections of the state, unless it is done by legislative action. If the authority to regulate and control schools is legislative, then it must have an unrestricted right to prescribe methods, and the courts cannot interfere with it, unless some scheme is devised which is contrary to other provisions of the Constitution, so that the question recurs: Does the Act create such a monopoly as the Constitution inhibits?

It is said the schools do not belong to the state, but to the people, and while, in a certain sense, this is true, it is, at last, but a play upon words. The system is inaugurated, operated, shaped, supported, and controlled by the state through its legislature, but for the benefit of the people, and, as in all other matters of public concern, the people act through their immediate representatives, the legislature. . . .

It is said the Act denies local self-government. This, of course, is a general term, and no specific provision of the Constitution is referred to, upon this feature of the case, as being violated. It is said, in broad terms, that the people have an inherent fundamental and vested right to administer their own local affairs, as the people of each county and district shall deem right and proper. We cannot enter into a consideration of such general doctrine, but will attempt to discuss it so far as it touches upon the common-school system, and the manner of its execution. This system is supported in part by state funds, and in part by county taxes. But the latter, at last, are but state funds, provided by the state through the power delegated to the counties.

It is insisted that heretofore there has been more or less of local control and government of the public schools, but this local government was authorized by, and was the creature of, the statute, and the legislature is not precluded from framing other statutes if it deem it wise to do so, modifying former plans. . . . We are of the opinion that the legislature, under the constitutional provision, may as well establish a uniform system of schools and a uniform administration of them, as it may establish a uniform system of criminal laws and of courts to execute them. The object of the criminal laws is, by punishment, to deter others from the commission of crimes, and thus preserve the peace, morals, good order, and well-being of society, and the object of the public school system is to prevent crime, by educating the people, and thus, by providing and securing a higher state of intelligence and morals, conserve the peace, good order, and well-being of society. . . .

COLER & CO. v. SCHOOL TOWNSHIP
3 N.D. 249, 55 N.W. 587 (1893)

Legal Principles

1. If a school district is a de facto corporation, debts and liabilities assumed by such district under appropriate authorizing statutes become legally binding on such district.

Opinion

. . . At the threshold of this case, we are met with the proposition that there is no liability because there was no such corporation as School District No. 22 in existence when these instruments were executed and delivered.

It is asserted that the proceedings instituted to effect the organization of such a municipality were fatally defective. (The opinion then sets forth apparent defects that prevented the legal organization of the school district.) A municipal corporation may have life, although there are no officers in office. No claim is made that the officers who in fact signed the bonds and coupons were not at least de facto officers of the district, provided there was a legal organization thereof. Nor could it be successfully contended that such officers were not at least de facto officers, there having been an attempt to comply with the law requiring the furnishing and filing of the description before officers should be elected, and the officers being in actual possession of their respective offices and exercising the function thereof, and there being no other persons pretending to lay claim to such offices. Nor would we reach a different conclusion were we of opinion that the organization of the district was so defective that the proceedings would be set aside on certiorari, or the right of the district to act as such would be denied by judgment in quo warranto. At the time these bonds were issued the district was acting as a de facto district under at least color of organization. It had elected its district officers; had held its district meetings; had voted to borrow money to build a schoolhouse; and it appears to be undisputed that the proceeds of these bonds were used for that purpose, and the inhabitants received the benefit thereof. A schoolhouse has been built, and school has been taught therein. To allow the defense that the proceedings in the organization were defective to defeat the debt represented by these bonds would, under these circumstances, be to sanction repudiation of an honest obligation. We are firm in the opinion that the legality of the organization of a municipal corporation cannot be thus collaterally attacked. Citizens of the district who are opposed to the formation of such a corporation are not without remedy. Certiorari will reach the action of the county super-

LINCKE v. BOARD OF EDUCATION
245 Ill. App. 459 (1927)

Legal Principles

1. School districts are governmental agencies of the state existing for the sole purpose of maintaining an efficient system of free schools and have only such powers as are conferred by the state expressly or by necessary implication.

2. A board of education is an involuntary corporation, created by general law of the state to execute governmental duties, without private, corporate interests or benefits conferred upon it, and is simply an agency of the state that is not liable for neglect of duty except when made so by statute.

Opinion

. . . Plaintiff in error, instituted this suit in the circuit court of Rock Island against Moline Board of Education, defendant in error, to recover damages which she alleges were occasioned by falling upon an outdoor landing in the steps of the sidewalk on the high school grounds, leading from the street to the school building. The declaration alleges that by reason of the defective construction of the said landing ice accumulated thereon.

The question involved in this case is whether a school board is liable in damages under such circumstances as are alleged in the declaration. It is urged that defendant in error is a municipal corporation and by statute is capable of suing and being sued; that it was acting in a proprietary capacity and is therefore liable.

There is definite distinction between the liability of voluntary municipal corporations, such as cities created for their own benefit, and involuntary quasi corporations established by law as civil divisions of the state. At common law, actions for a dereliction of duty were maintainable against the former, but the latter, existing only as an agency of the state, were not liable. Such is the rule in Illinois. . . . The ground of distinction is that public, involuntary, quasi corporations are mere political divisions of the state created by general laws to aid in the general administration of the government and are not so liable, while those that are liable have privileges conferred upon them at their request, constituting a consideration for the duties imposed upon them. . . .

In regard to public, involuntary, quasi corporations, the rule is that there is no implied liability imposed upon them. These, such as counties, townships, school districts, road districts and other similar quasi corporations exist under general laws of the state, with territory apportioned into local subdivisions for the purposes of civil and governmental administration. In such organizations the duties, and their correlative powers, are assumed in invitum and there is no responsibility to respond in damages in a civil action for neglect in the performance of duties, unless a right of action is given by statute. . . .

A board of education is a corporation or quasi corporation created nolens volens, by the general law of the state to aid in the administration of the state government, and charged, as such, with duties purely governmental in character. It owns no property, has no private corporate interests, and derives no special benefits from its corporate acts. It is simply an agency of the state having existence for the sole purpose of performing certain duties, deemed necessary to the maintenance of an "efficient system of free schools" within the particular locality of its jurisdiction. The state acts in its sovereign capacity, does not submit its action to the judgments of courts, and is not liable for the torts or negligence of its agents; and a corporation created by the state as a mere agency for the more efficient exercise of governmental functions is likewise exempted from the obligation to respond in damages as master for negligent acts of its servants to the same extent as is the state itself, unless such liability is expressly provided by the statute creating such agency.

Plaintiff in error urges that defendant in error was exercising an authorized proprietary function under section 115 of the School Law. . . . It is elementary that the powers and duties of municipal corporations, such as cities, are of two kinds: first, public or governmental, and second, private or proprietary. They are not liable for negligence when exercising governmental functions. When performing proprietary functions they are chargeable with the same duties and obligations as private corporations and ordinary individuals. School districts derive their existence and all their powers from the legislature and have no inherent powers. . . . They have only such powers as are conferred expressly or by necessary implication. . . . School districts are charged with duties purely governmental in character and are agencies of the state, existing for the sole purpose of performing duties in connection with the maintenance of an efficient system of free schools . . . and differ from cities and other municipal corporations.

It is urged by plaintiff in error that the provisions of section 115 of the School Law delegate a proprietary function to school directors and boards of education and that the declaration therefore states a cause of action within its terms. That section provides for granting the use of assembly halls and classrooms when not otherwise needed, including light, heat, and attendants for public lectures, concerts, and other educational and social interests under such provisions and control as they may see fit to impose, and to conduct or provide for the conducting of recreational, social, and civic activities in the school buildings under their control; but it does not expressly nor by necessary implication authorize a grant for hire, reward, revenue, or profit as charged in the declaration. Any different construction would be utterly at variance with the single purpose for which school districts are created and maintained, as expressed in the constitution and the statutes and as limited by repeated decisions of the courts of this state. The use of school property for such purposes is not out of harmony with the object for which schools are conducted, but stimulates and fosters the interest of the pupils and patrons and promotes the efficiency of public schools. . . .

The fact that there is a provision in the statute that a school board may sue and be sued does not change the rule of their non-liability in tort actions of this kind. . . . Nor does the fact that boards of education are charged with the duty of making repairs and improvements to school-houses affect such rule. . . .

THORLAND, et al. v. SCHOOL DISTRICT
246 Minn. 96, 74 N.W. (2d) 410 (1956)

Legal Principles
1. School districts are subject to the control of the legislature, and their boundaries or territorial jurisdictions may be enlarged, diminished, or abolished in such manner and through such instrumentalities as the legislature may prescribe.
2. On appeal from an order of an agency to which has been entrusted the legislative function of formation or alteration of school districts, the inquiry of the court on the merits must be limited to a determination of whether the action of such agency was arbitrary, fraudulent, or oppressive, or an unreasonable disregard of the interests of the territory affected.

Opinion
. . . How far a court may go in setting aside an order of consolidation or an order of the county board, what quantum of proof is required, and what are the respective functions and scope of review of the trial court and this court are not so clearly defined by statute or by our decisions.

In the determination of these questions, certain fundamental rules of law must always be kept in mind. A school district, if technically not a municipal corporation, at least is a public corporation. School districts are subject to the control of the legislature, and their boundaries or territorial jurisdictions may be enlarged, diminished, or abolished in such manner and through such instrumentalities as the legislature may prescribe, except as limited by the constitution. . . .

Inasmuch as the action of such agency is legislative, the contention that to permit the court to determine whether such action is for the best interests of the territory affected permits the courts to invade the legislative field and thereby run afoul of the constitution is, as we said in Schweigert v. Abbott, 122 Minn. 383, 387, 142 N.W. 723, 724, not without merit. We there considered this question and disposed of it as follows:

". . . Whether public interests require and justify the organization of municipal or quasi-municipal corporations, including school districts, is a matter purely for the legislature, and cannot be conferred upon the courts. . . . If such authority cannot be directly conferred upon the courts, as held in the case cited, it would seem that an indirect method of conferring such jurisdiction would be equally invalid. . . . The court will, however, in determining whether the best interests of the territory affected justify a particular consolidation, limit its inquiry to the question whether the proceedings were arbitrary, resulting in unnecessary injustice to those who complain."

The discretion vested in the county board or other agency to which such legislative action is given must be fairly exercised in good faith for the best interests of the people in the districts affected. As long as it is so exercised, the courts will not interfere but, when it is exercised in a fraudulent, arbitrary, or unreasonable manner so as to constitute an abuse of discretion, then it generally is held that the courts may and will interfere on behalf of the district or the voters injured thereby.

The scope of review of the district court on appeal has been stated so frequently that it would seem unnecessary to repeat it again, but the frequency with which this question arises and is presented here indicates that it is not understood fully as yet by litigants and courts alike. Probably a restatement of the fundamental law will serve to clarify the matter to some extent. . . .

. . . The matter of establishing, enlarging the boundaries of, or of dissolving municipal corporations is purely legislative.

While the legislature cannot confer upon the courts legislative power, it can and does give to the court power to review the action of the administrative agency upon which it has conferred the legislative power to the extent that the courts will decide whether there has been an abuse of discretion vested in such agency. The power of review does not encompass the legislative function of determination but, rather, the power to prevent the administrative agency from exceeding its power by an arbitrary abuse of discretion. Thus, instead of an original right to determine, the court's function is to provide a check upon the arbitrary abuse of power vested in the agency entrusted by the legislature with the power of determination. In other words, the court's function, rather than being one of original determination, is to prevent the improper determination by the administrative agency.

BARTH v. SCHOOL DISTRICT

393 Pa. 557, 143 A. (2d) 909 (1958)

Legal Principles

1. A school district has no inherent powers of government.

2. A school district has only the powers that are granted by statute, specifically or by necessary implication.

Opinion

. . . A school district is a creature or agency of the legislature and has only the powers that are granted by statute, specifically or by necessary implication. . . .

In Slippery Rock Area Joint School System v. Franklin Township School District, 389 Pa. 435, . . . 133 A. 2d 848 . . . the Court said: " 'First it should be remembered that our entire school system is but an agency of the state legislature—maintained by them to carry out a constitutional duty. . . . The school system, or the school district, then, are but agencies of the state legislature to administer this constitutional duty. Wilson v. Philadelphia School District, 328 Pa. 225, 230. Within that school system, a school district is an agency of the state, created by law for the purpose of promoting education, deriving all of its powers from the statute, and discharging only such duties as are imposed upon it by statute. . . .' "

The Public School Code minutely details in approximately 270 pages, the powers, functions, and duties of a school district. It also provides in Article VI, par 610: "The use or payment of any public school funds of any school district, in any manner or for any purpose not provided in this act, shall be illegal." A study, nay a reading, of the Public School Code demonstrates that the legislature unquestionably intended and provided that the school district could possess and exercise only those powers and functions detailed in the Code, and that public school funds could be used only in the manner and for the purposes which are expressly or by necessary implication provided for in this detailed act.

Never heretofore have schools or school districts possessed or exercised, under the theory or name of education, the wide basic powers, functions, and duties of municipal government which are now claimed by the board of education, namely the prevention, suppression, correction, elimination, and punishment of juvenile delinquency—euphemistic language to describe vandalism, misdemeanors, and crimes committed by young persons—, gang control, and the improvement of living conditions. . . .

II

Administrative Government and Officers

BOWEN, et al. v. MEYER, et al.
255 S.W. (2d) (1953) 490

Legal Principles
1. A board of education has the discretion to establish transportation routes, and to determine a reasonable walking distance.
2. A court will not disturb the discretion of a board of education, unless it acts unreasonably and abuses its discretion.

Opinion
The Jefferson County Board of Education appeals from a judgment which requires the board to furnish transportation to the . . . school, for the pupils who reside in certain neighborhoods at a distance of from one mile to two and one-quarter miles from the school.

. . . We think it is clear that the distance alone, which at the most is two and one-quarter miles, is not unreasonable. . . . However, our decisions have recognized that hazards and conditions of the roads that must be traveled are factors to be taken into consideration in determining whether a particular distance is a reasonable walking distance. . . .

In the case before us, the school is located on Westport Road, about 1250 feet north of Hubbard Lane, which crosses Westport Road at right angles. Massie Avenue lies some 1250 feet west of, and parallel with, Westport Road, and Massie Avenue has its northern terminus at its intersection with Hubbard Lane. Massie Avenue has a traffic count of one car every minute in the morning, and one car every two minutes in the afternoon. The traffic count on Westport Road is one car every 10 seconds in the morning, and one car every 20 seconds in the afternoon. The morning traffic count on Hubbard Lane is one car every 15 seconds.

One group of school children would travel Massie Avenue on their way to and from school.

The second group of children would travel Westport Road. At the southern end of the road they would be required to cross some railroad tracks on which two trains are scheduled in the morning, and two in the afternoon, at hours when the children might be passing. Westport Road has a pavement 22 feet in width, with three-foot shoulders covered with short grass and weeds. The distance the children would be required to walk along Westport Road is less than half a mile. It is stipulated that school safety patrol boys are stationed at the intersection of Massie Avenue and Hubbard Lane, and that a county traffic patrolman is stationed at the intersection of Westport Road and Hubbard Lane, to assist pupils in crossing.

Another factor which we think may be given some consideration is the availability of common carrier bus transportation for the children, from their home neighborhoods to the intersection of Westport Road and Hubbard Lane, 1000 feet south of the school. The fare is five cents without transfer, and six and one-half cents with transfer. School safety patrol boys ride these buses to assist the younger children.

The board of education necessarily must be allowed some discretion in determining what is a reasonable walking distance in any particular situation, and the courts should not interfere unless the board has acted in an arbitrary and unreasonable manner in refusing to furnish transportation. Board of Education of Clay County v. Bowling, 312 Ky. 749, 229 S.W. (2d) 769.

We think the circumstances here are similar to those in the Clay County case, supra, and the hazards presented are not of such magnitude as to make it mandatory upon the board to furnish transportation. Westport Road, itself, presents no unusual dangers, and we do not consider the railroad tracks as being sufficient, alone, to require bus transportation to be supplied. Massie Avenue is narrow, it is true, but the traffic upon it is not heavy.

In a suburban area, such as this, children are exposed to the hazards of traffic in any of their outdoor activities. They will be upon the streets in play, in visiting their friends, and in going to the stores. They early in life must be trained to take care of themselves in traffic. Public bus transportation is a common convenience to them.

The situation of the suburban child is much different from that of the country boy, who ordinarily is not upon the highways on foot except in going to and from school; who is not conditioned to the hazards of constant automobile traffic; and who has no means of reaching school other than on foot or by school bus. In the Shelbyville case, Schmidt v. Payne 304 Ky. 58, 199 S. W. (2d) 990, the children would have been compelled to walk along a crooked, winding, heavily traveled county road, crossing a narrow bridge, a railroad, and a main federal highway. The hazards in the case now before us are not comparable to those in the Shelbyville case. . . .

RYAN v. HUMPHRIES
50 Okla. 343, 150 P. 1106 (1915)

Legal Principles

1. Where a school board has the original power to enter into a contract, such as the employment of teachers, such board may legally ratify a contract of employment made by the board in an irregular or unauthorized manner, and a ratification of such contract is equivalent to a full compliance with the authority originally given, and when done so renders the contract valid from its inception.

Opinion

. . . It appears that relator was employed by and entered into a written contract with the school board of said district. . . .

. . . The contention of the respondent upon the first proposition, that the contract of employment was made without his knowledge or consent, by the other two members of the board, and at a time when a meeting of the board had not been legally called and was not in session, would ordinarily present a complicated and serious question. We are of opinion that the evidence clearly shows that the contract was made by Abbott and Gamble, as director and clerk of the district, in the absence and without the consent or knowledge of the respondent.

This action of the board brings us to the question of its effect, in the way of ratification of the original contract entered into by Abbott and Gamble as director and clerk. In this connection it may not be out of place to say that the question of the power of municipal or quasi-municipal corporations to ratify unauthorized contracts is one of the generally recognized controversies of the court and bar. The authorities are absolutely irreconcilable; and after careful study of the proposition the writer hereof acknowledges himself at sea, in the midst of the storm of high rolling waves of uncertainty; but we gather from the weight of the authorities that, where the corporation had the power to enter into the contract under consideration, and the manner of making it being the only question involved, such contract may, as a rule, be ratified by an acceptance of the benefits of the contract by corporations, and by a subsequent recognition and substantial performance of the acts and conditions required by law in the execution of the legal contract, or by acquiescence in the conditions and benefits obtained by virtue of the contract.

This seems to be, in substance, the doctrine laid down in Hill v. City of Indianapolis (C.C.), 92 Fed. 467; Daires County v. Dickinson, 117 U.S. 657, 6 Sup. Ct. 897, 29 L. Ed. 1026; Town of Bloomfield v. Charter Oak Bank, 121 U.S. 121, 7 Sup. Ct. 865, 30 L. Ed. 923; and a long list of other authorities. . . .

As stated before herein, this seems to be the rule followed and approved by the weight of authorities on the subject; and upon the facts in the instant case, as necessarily found by the trial court, sustained by these authorities, we hold that the contract of employment of the relator was fully ratified by the board, so far as it relates to the services involved herein, and such ratification is equivalent to authority originally existing, and renders the contract valid from its date. . . .

STATE v. SCHOOL DISTRICT
141 S.W. (2d) 438 (Tex.) (1940)

Legal Principles
1. The discretion of a board of education cannot be restricted by prior policies or commitments.

Opinion
. . . About September 26, 1939, the court . . . made an order granting permission to the County Attorney, in the name of the state . . . to file an information in the nature of quo warranto. . . . The relief prayed . . . was to have a former consolidation . . . decreed to be void. An alternative purpose was that a certain pre-election agreement be held binding, and the Trent Independent School District be directed to "maintain the elementary schools at the Goodman schoolhouse according to their pre-election agreement and that said elementary schools be continuously maintained at the Goodman schoolhouse and school plant and that the trustees of the Trent Independent School District be directed by the order of this court to properly equip and maintain said school plant and the elementary school at the Goodman schoolhouse according to their pre-election agreement. . . .

The alleged pre-election agreement was not a contract to which the trustees of the Trent Independent School District and said individuals were respecting the parties. Persons acting upon such agreement were, as a matter of law, we think, charged with notice that the powers of the trustees were conferred by law for public purposes and the exercise thereof, involving, as it does, a matter of future policy, properly subject to change to meet changing conditions, and could not be restricted by an agreement of the nature of the one here involved.

The decisions relied upon by appellants are, we think, not at all applicable. In one of them (Black v. Strength, 112 Tex. 188, 246 S.W. 79, 80) is this significant statement: "The court was not binding itself to a certain course of action in the future." The agreement here in question, if effective as contended, did bind the board of trustees to a certain course of action in the future, namely, the perpetual maintenance of a school.

SCHOOL DISTRICT v. ANDREWS
333 S.W. (2d) 886 (Tex.) (1960)

Legal Principles
1. Courts will uphold actions of school authorities in promulgating rules to insure proper conduct and decorum of students designed for the good of the school as a whole where such rules are not shown to be a clear abuse of power and discretion or a violation of law.

2. Board of education did not abuse its discretion in promulgating regulation that high school children driving automobiles to school shall park same in designated lot and not move same until close of school unless by special permission.

Opinion
. . . Article 2780, Vernon's Ann. Tex. Civ. St. having to do with the authority of Independent School District Trustees provides in part, as follows: "Said trustees shall adopt such rules, regulations, and by-laws as they may deem proper; . . .

. . . The courts of Texas have consistently upheld the actions of school authorities in promulgating rules to insure proper conduct and decorum of the students designed for the good of the schools as a whole where such rules have not shown a clear abuse of power and discretion or a violation of law. So let us look at the facts.

The uncontroverted testimony given in this case by the President of the McLean Board of Trustees shows that before the rule in question was passed 50 to 60 automobiles driven to school by the children would be driven away at the noon hour. The record shows the high school, its grounds and parking areas, and the grade school and playgrounds were all located in the same immediate vicinity, the grade school and playground thereof being just north of the high school and its grounds; that small children would be there at the time the cars were leaving; that before passing the regulation "it got to be quite a traffic problem, a hazard, and our sole thought in passing this rule was for the protection of 350 or 360 children that we have in school. We didn't pick out any one person, we weren't trying to make a hardship case on anybody. Our only thought was for the benefit of our children in the McLean schools. That is the reason we passed the rule. Anybody I think that could be there at the time these 50 or 60 cars were trying to leave that parking lot and go to lunch could see the problem we had."

A former trustee of the school . . . testified his little girl . . . who rode her bicycle to and from school, was forced off the street into the gutter and injured by school children driving cars three abreast down the street. . . . He further testified he had seen as many as three cars of school boys and girls parked on a country road half a mile west of town at the noon hour. . . .

The high school principal testified he talked to Marsha on several occasions and warned her that she would have to be suspended if she did not comply with the rule in question. The testimony shows the following conversation between them: ". . . there is no reason in the world why you shouldn't drive it in the parking lot." She said, "I don't think my daddy wants me to do that."

The Superintendent of Schools testified:

"The traffic of the students leaving the school after having a joy ride around the school, up the streets and throughout the city of McLean, and also riding on the highways; that has been their big problem, and we are faced with it every year. It wasn't something we just thought up overnight. It was a problem that has been discussed every year, to my knowledge, since I have been in McLean." . . . "We have had cars run together, and the time when I was high school principal we had a little boy run over in front of the elementary school."

He further testified in effect that the problem had become more acute each year by reason of the economy of the area, making it possible for more students to have cars to drive to school, and that since the rule was invoked conditions had been a hundred per cent better.

The authority of the school officials has been further elaborated on in 47 American Jurisprudence, Section 173, "Schools," as follows:

> The authority of school officials assuredly extends into the twilight zone between the school and the home. The misconduct of pupils on the way to school, or on going home from school, is properly within the scope of the power of school officers. Hence, a school board may properly make and enforce a rule that scholars shall go directly to their homes after school hours, the liberty of neither the children nor their parents being at all unlawfully restrained by such a rule and its reasonable enforcement. . . .

When the rules announced above are applied to the facts of our case, we are forced to the conclusion that the learned trial judge was in error in holding that the Board of Trustees of the McLean Independent School District exceeded its authority in promulgating the rule in question. The regulation was not for the purpose of exercising authority over the use of public streets and highways at all (as suggested by the appellees' reply point) but for the purpose of controlling the conduct of the students.

JONES v. CODY

132 Mich. 13, 92 N.W. 495 (1902)

Legal Principles

1. School authorities may enforce reasonable rules governing the conduct of pupils away from the school grounds and on their way to the school and return.

Opinion

. . . No fault is to be found with the manner in which the defendant enforced the rule (requiring pupils to go directly to their homes at the close of school). . . .

. . . The rule and the method of enforcing it are reasonable, unless it be the law that those in control of our public schools have no jurisdiction over pupils outside the schoolhouse yard. It is not only the legal right, but the moral duty, of the school authorities, to require children to go directly from school to their homes. All parents who have a proper regard for the welfare of their children desire it. The state makes it compulsory for parents to send their children to school, and punishes them for failure to do so. The least that the state can in reason do is to throw every safeguard possible around the children who in obedience to the law are attending school. The dangers to which children are exposed upon the streets of cities are matters of common knowledge. Humanity and the welfare of the country demand that a most watchful safeguard should, so far as possible, accompany children when required or allowed to be on the streets. Parents have a right to understand that their children will be promptly sent home after school, and to believe that something untoward has happened when they do not return in time. In no other way can parents and teachers act in harmony to protect children from bad influences, bad companionship, and bad morals. No trader or merchant has the constitutional right to have children remain in his place of business, in order that they may spend money there, while they are on their way to and from school. The liberty of neither the children nor parent nor trader is at all unlawfully restrained by this rule and its reasonable enforcement. The rule does not interfere with the right of the parent to send his child upon an errand, to a store or other reputable place, or to the home of a relative or friend to visit. Neither does it restrict the authority of parents over their children. This action on the part of the school board of the city of Detroit and its teachers is fully sustained by the authorities. Larder v. Seamen, 32 Vt. 120; Deskins v. Gose, 85 Mo. 485; Sherman v. Inhabitants of Charleston 8 Cush 160; Mechem, Pub. Off. #730. Judgment is affirmed.

MARTIN v. CRAIG

42 N.D. 213, 173 N.W. 787 (1919)

Legal Principles

1. In order to prevent the spread of a communicable disease, pupils who are affected with such disease or who are suspected of being affected, may be excluded from school.

Opinion

This is an appeal from the order of the district court of La Moore County, quashing an alternative writ of mandamus.

. . . The plaintiff and appellant is the legal custodian of two children of school age and he petitioned for a peremptory writ compelling the defendants to admit them to school. The defendants justify the refusal on the ground that one of the children had been found by a reputable physician to be affected with trachoma, and the other to present a case where trachoma is suspected. . . .

The disease is communicable and of a very serious nature, frequently resulting in blindness and always in impairment of the normal functions of the tissues immediately affected. To prevent the spread of the disease and to secure proper treatment for those affected, the county board of health promulgated an order forbidding admission to school of children who, upon examination, were found to be or suspected of being afflicted, unless they were at the time under treatment for the disease.

In the instant case, the petitioner produced two doctors who presented what is generally considered to be first-class professional credentials qualifying them to give expert testimony. They had had ample opportunity to examine the patients and to diagnose the cases. In fact, the children had been patients of one of the doctors. These doctors testify that the children are not afflicted with trachoma but with folliculosis. One of them also testifies that it is injurious to the eye to treat it for trachoma when trachoma is not present, but a careful reading of his testimony discloses that the injury results from a species of treatment that is likely to be resorted to only when the disease is clearly present and when the necessity for radical treatment is indicated. We find nothing in the testimony or in the record that would justify us in presuming that any reputable physician would resort to treatment which must necessarily result in some degree of impairment, until the case indicates that such treatment is necessary.

The order of exclusion in the instant case cannot be said to be unreasonable. It only excludes those whose cases are positive and suspected, who are not at time under treatment. The seriousness of the disease and its communicable character afford ample foundation for such an order;

and, even conceding that it may be doubted in the instant case whether the children in question are affected, the doubt is one that must be resolved in favor of the authorities charged with the serious responsibility of preventing the spread of the disease. This is a case where mandamus does not issue as a matter of right, but where it will only issue in the exercise of a judicial discretion, and this discretion should not be exercised in a way that might result in needlessly exposing healthful children to a disease as serious as trachoma. See 26 Cyc. 143.

MATHEWS v. BOARD OF EDUCATION
127 Mich. 530, 86 N.W. 1036 (1901)

Legal Principles

1. In the absence of statutory authority, a board of education requirement that children be vaccinated as a prerequisite to attendance is invalid, where there is no imminent danger of the existence of disease against which the vaccination is sought.

Opinion

. . . We have already shown that it is made by law the duty of the child to attend school, and of the parent to send him; and, as long as the broad rule adopted by the board exists, the child must be vaccinated, or it and its parents must be lawbreakers. If the rule was that during the prevalence of the smallpox in Kalamazoo the child could not attend school unless vaccinated, a very different result would be reached. These epidemics never last very long, and the parent and child might well say, if they desired, that they would absent themselves from school during the epidemic. As the police power imposes restrictions and burdens upon the natural and private rights of individuals, it necessarily depends upon the law for its support, and, although of comprehensive and far-reaching character, it is subject to constitutional restrictions; and, in general, it is the province of the lawmaking power to determine in what cases or upon what conditions this power may be exercised. As applied to the present case, the relator had a right, secured by statutory enactment, to have his children continue to attend the city schools in which they were respectively enrolled as pupils; and they, too, had a right to so attend such schools. Whether it be called a "right" or "privilege" cannot be important, for in either view it was secured to the relator, and to his children as well, by the positive provisions of law, and was to be enjoyed upon such terms and under such conditions and restrictions as the lawmaking power, within constitutional limits, might impose. There is no statute in this state authorizing compulsory vaccination, nor any statute which requires vaccination as one of the conditions of the right or privilege of attending the public schools. . . . It is not a question as to what the legislature might do, under the police power, about requiring vaccination as a prerequisite to attending school.

BIDDLE v. WILLARD
10 Ind. 62 (1857)

Legal Principles

1. A prospective resignation, which is to take effect at a later date, may be withdrawn before it is accepted.

Opinion

. . . The case does not fall within the letter of the constitution or statutes relative to elections; it does not embrace the material fact of the expiration of the term of office. The elective term of the judicial office is, by the constitution, as we have seen, six years; for that period the successful candidate at an election is chosen; for that period he is disqualified to hold any political office; and for that period he has a right to hold the office of judge. That term of six years cannot expire except by its own limitation. It may be abandoned by the incumbent. It may be vacated of that incumbent by the act of God, and by law a new term may be made to then begin; but the term itself can only legally expire by the efflux of time. If, in the case of a prospective resignation, there is an expiration of any term, it is the term attempted to be created by the resignation itself. But such a term is not known to, or contemplated by, the constitution or statutes, and did not in law exist, in this case, if it can in any. This will appear when we consider what a resignation is.

To constitute a complete and operative resignation, there must be an intention to relinquish a portion of the term of the office, accompanied by the act of relinquishment. Webster and Richardson define the words "resign" and "resignation," substantially thus: "to resign, is to give back, to give up, in a formal manner, an office"; and resignation is the act of giving it up. Bouvier says, "resignation is the act of an officer by which he declines his office, and renounces the further right to use it. . . ."

Hence, a prospective resignation may, in point of law, amount but to a notice of intention to resign at a future day, or a proposition to so resign; and for the reason that it is not accompanied by a giving up of the office—possession is still retained, and may not necessarily be surrendered till the expiration of the legal term of the office, because the officer may recall his resignation—may withdraw his proposition to resign. He certainly can do this at any time before it is accepted; and after it is accepted, he may make the withdrawal by the consent of the authority accepting, where no new rights have intervened. The record nowhere shows us, in this case, that the prospective resignation of Judge Stuart was ever accepted; and, therefore, it does not show that any special term, not known to the law, was created by it, if in any event there could have been, which might have been filled at the October election.

III—IV

Pupils: Admission, Attendance, and Discipline

MEYER v. STATE OF NEBRASKA
262 U.S. 390 (1923)

Legal Principles

1. A state statute which prevents the teaching of foreign languages in private and parochial schools is an arbitrary interference with the rights of parents to control the education of their children.

Opinion

Plaintiff in error was tried and convicted . . . under an information which charged that on May 25, 1920, while an instructor in Zion Parochial School, he unlawfully taught the subject of reading in the German language to Raymond Parpart, a child of ten years, who had not attained and successfully passed the eighth grade. The information is based upon "An act relating to the teaching of foreign languages in the State of Nebraska," approved April 9, 1919. . . .

The problem for our determination is whether the statute as construed and applied unreasonably infringes the liberty guaranteed to the plaintiff in error by the Fourteenth Amendment. "No State shall . . . deprive any person of life, liberty, or property, without due process of law."

While this Court has not attempted to define with exactness the liberty thus guaranteed, the term has received much consideration and some of the included things have been definitely stated. Without doubt, it denotes not merely freedom from bodily restraint but also the right of the individual to contract, to engage in any of the common occupations of life, to acquire useful knowledge, to marry, establish a home, and bring up children, to worship God according to the dictates of his own conscience, and generally to enjoy those privileges long recognized at common law as essential to the orderly pursuit of happiness by free men. . . . The established doctrine is that this liberty may not be interfered with, under the guise of protecting the public interest, by legislative action which is arbitrary or without reasonable relation to some purpose within the competency of the state to effect. Determination by the legislature of what constitutes proper exercise of police power is not final or conclusive but is subject to supervision by the courts. . . .

The American people have always regarded education and acquisition of knowledge as matters of supreme importance which should be diligently promoted. The Ordinance of 1787 declares, "Religion, morality, and knowledge being necessary to good government and the happiness of mankind, schools, and the means of education shall forever be encouraged." Corresponding to the right of control, it is the natural duty of the parent to give his children education suitable to their station in life; and nearly all the states, including Nebraska, enforce this obligation by compulsory laws.

Practically, education of the young is only possible in schools conducted by especially qualified persons who devote themselves thereto. The calling always has been regarded as useful and honorable, essential, indeed, to the public welfare. Mere knowledge of the German language cannot reasonably be regarded as harmful. Heretofore it has been commonly looked upon as helpful and desirable. Plaintiff in error taught this language in school as part of his occupation. His right thus to teach and the right of parents to engage him so to instruct their children, we think, are within the liberty of the amendment.

The challenged statute forbids the teaching in school of any subject except in English; also the teaching of any other language until the pupil has attained and successfully passed the eighth grade, which is not usually accomplished before the age of twelve. The Supreme Court of the state has held that "the so-called ancient or dead languages" are not "within the spirit or the purpose of the act." . . . Latin, Greek, Hebrew are not proscribed; but German, French, Spanish, Italian and every other alien speech are within the ban. Evidently the legislature has attempted materially to interfere with the calling of modern language teachers, with the opportunities of pupils to acquire knowledge, and with the power of parents to control the education of their own.

It is said the purpose of the legislation was to promote civic development by inhibiting training and education of the immature in foreign tongues and ideals before they could learn English and acquire American ideals; and "that the English language should be and become the mother tongue of all children reared in this state." It is also affirmed that the foreign-born population is very large, that certain communities commonly use foreign words, follow foreign leaders, move in a foreign atmosphere, and that the children are thereby hindered from becoming citizens of the most useful type and the public safety is imperiled.

That the state may do much, go very far, indeed, in order to improve the quality of its citizens, physically, mentally, and morally, is clear; but the individual has certain fundamental rights which must be respected. The protection of the Constitution extends to all, to those who speak other languages as well as to those born with English on the tongue. Perhaps it would be highly advantageous if all had ready understanding of our ordinary speech, but this cannot be coerced by methods which conflict with the Constitution—a desirable end cannot be promoted by prohibited means.

For the welfare of his Ideal Commonwealth, Plato suggested a law which should provide: ". . . the proper officers will take the offspring of the good parents to the pen or fold, and there they will deposit them with certain nurses who dwell in a separate quarter; but the offspring of the inferior, or of the better when they chance to be deformed, will be put away in some mysterious, unknown place, as they should be." In order to submerge the individual and develop ideal citizens, Sparta assembled the males at seven into barracks and intrusted their subsequent education and training to official guardians. Although such measures have been deliberately approved by men of great genius, their ideas touching the relation between individual and state were wholly different from those upon which our institutions rest; and it hardly will be affirmed that any legislature could impose such restrictions upon the people of a state without doing violence to both letter and spirit of the Constitution.

The desire of the legislature to foster a homogeneous people with American ideals prepared readily to understand current discussions of civic matters is easy to appreciate. Unfortunate experiences during the late war and aversion toward every characteristic of truculent adversaries were certainly enough to quicken that aspiration. But the means adopted, we think, exceed the limitations upon the power of the state and conflict with rights assured to plaintiff in error. The interference is plain enough and no adequate reason therefor in time of peace and domestic tranquility has been shown.

The power of the state to compel attendance at some school and to make reasonable regulations for all schools, including a requirement that they shall give instructions in English, is not questioned. Nor has challenge been made of the state's power to prescribe a curriculum for institutions which it supports. Those matters are not within the present controversy. . . . No emergency has arisen which renders knowledge by a child of some language other than English so clearly harmful as to justify its inhibition with the consequent infringement of rights long freely enjoyed. We are constrained to conclude that the statute as applied is arbitrary and without reasonable relation to any end within the competency of the state.

As the statute undertakes to interfere only with teaching which involves a modern language, leaving complete freedom as to other matters, there seems no adequate foundation for the suggestion that the purpose was to protect the child's health by limiting his mental activities. It is well known that proficiency in a foreign language seldom comes to one not instructed at an early age, and experience shows that this is not injurious to the health, morals, or understanding of the ordinary child.

The judgment of the court below must be reversed and the cause remanded for further proceedings not inconsistent with this opinion.

BOARD OF EDUCATION v. MAAS

56 N.J.S. 245, 152 A. (2d) 394 (1959)

Legal Principles

1. A board of education policy requiring vaccination as prerequisite for school attendance was within the ambit of delegated legislative power.

2. The board of education is not required to recognize as exceptions to its policy exemptions predicated on the particular religious beliefs of the children or their parents.

Opinion

Defendant's main argument is that plaintiff board acted contrary to the statute . . . and restricted religious freedom guaranteed by the Federal and State Constitutions. . . .

The core question on this appeal is defendant's contention that the compulsory vaccination and immunization regulation adopted by the board deprived her of due process and religious freedom, within the contemplation of the United States Constitution, Amendments I or XIV, and the New Jersey Constitution (1947), Art. I, pars. 3 and 5.

A requirement that a child must be vaccinated and immunized before it can attend the local public schools violates neither due process nor (as defendant tangentially suggests) the equal protection clause of the Constitution. The rationale of this rule is rooted in traditional concepts recognizing the authority of a local board, acting under a legislative grant of power, to promote the community health, safety, and welfare. The fact that there may be differences of opinion as to the necessity or efficacy of vaccination or immunization does not deprive the state of the power to enact legislation requiring compulsory vaccination or immunization, or the local board from acting pursuant to such a power. . . .

. . . Defendant also argues that compulsory vaccination and immunization is not called for in Mountain Lakes because there has been no case of smallpox or diphtheria for almost a decade. The absence of an existing emergency does not warrant a denial to the regulative agency of the exercise of preventive means. A local board of education need not await an epidemic, or even a single sickness or death, before it decides upon action to protect the public. To hold otherwise would be to destroy prevention as a means of combatting the spread of disease. . . .

Nor did the local regulation abridge religious freedom within the meaning of the Federal and State Constitutions. In considering the compulsory vaccination of school children under R.S. 18:14–52, N.J.S.A. adopted by the local board of education in the Sadlack case, the court rejected the precise religious issue here raised by defendant, when it said: "So, too, with respect to the guaranty of religious liberty, the constitutional guaranty of religious freedom was not intended to prohibit legislation with respect to the general public welfare."

STREICH v. BOARD OF EDUCATION
34 S.D. 169, 147 N.W. 779 (1914)

Legal Principles
1. A board of education regulation which required pupils entering the schools to have a physical examination is valid.
2. Such regulation involves no question of religious liberty.

Opinion
. . . The sole question presented is the right of respondents to require of the children seeking admission into the schools under their charge, and as a condition to their admission, the furnishing of a certain report. . . .

Need a child suffer any indignity or a violation of any sacred right by submitting to such physical examination as would be necessary in order that a physician might fill out the report called for? Appellant did not prove, nor do we find anything in the report requiring, that there need be any exposure of the person of the child or any manipulation of its body such as would shock the sensibilities of the most refined person. Here again, we must not overlook the person who makes the examination; the conventionalities of our time recognize the absolute propriety of submitting one's body to the examination of a physician, whenever such examination is made for the purpose of gaining information concerning one's physical condition. The established customs—the conventionalities of the time—are matters to be considered in determining the reasonableness of a particular action; therefore a thing may be reasonable, though it conflicts with the individual views of the few, if it conforms to that of the many. . . .

COMMONWEALTH v. RENFREW, et al.

332 Mass. 492, 126 N.E. (2d) 109 (1955)

Legal Principles

1. Where a parent is charged with violation of the compulsory attendance law, he may not assert as a defense the fact that the requirements are contrary to his religious beliefs.

Opinion

The defendants, husband and wife, were charged jointly in two complaints, each complaint alleging a different time in neglecting to cause their minor children to attend school. . . . Both complaints were tried together and each defendant was found guilty on each complaint.

. . . None of the various other enumerated admitted facts constituted any defense to these complaints. Home education of their child by the defendants without the prior approval of the superintendent or the committee did not show a compliance with the statute and bar the prosecution of the complaints. State v. Hoyt, 84 N.H. 38. Rice v. Commonwealth, 188 Va. 224. The right to religious freedom is not absolute. For instance, the refusal of the one in control of a minor of school age to have him vaccinated or to procure a physician's certificate that he is an unfit subject for vaccination on account of the defendant's religious belief, thus preventing the child from attending school, is no defense to a violation of the compulsory school attendance law. Commonwealth v. Green, 268 Mass. 585. Commonwealth v. Childs, 299 Mass. 367. State v. Drew, 89 N.H. 54. Sadlack v. Board of Education, 137 N.J. L. 85. See Prince v. Massachusetts, 321 U.S. 158. The defendants and their child were Buddhists. One of the grievances of the defendants was that the mental health of the child was being affected because he was not being educated according to his capacity to learn. . . . Another grievance of the defendants is that some things that he was taught were causing conflict with the principles of Buddhism although they conceded that these principles were in no way in conflict with the law. There is no specification whatever as to what were "some of the things" just mentioned. They may well have been the secular subjects ordinarily taught in the public schools. The defendants state that their child has been taught the Twenty-Third Psalm and the Lord's Prayer. The mere reading of the Bible and the recital of the Lord's Prayer in the public schools do not justify the failure of the defendants to have him attend school. For more than a century our statute has provided that a portion of the Bible shall be read in the public schools without written note or comment and that no pupil shall be required to take any personal part in the reading if his parent or guardian informs the teacher in writing that he has conscientious scruples against the pupil participating in such reading. See now G.L. (Ter. Ed.) c. 71, #31. The purpose and validity of such a statute were explained and upheld, as was a regulation of a school committee that the schools should be opened each morning with a reading from the Bible and the offering of prayer, in Spiller v. Inhabitants of Woburn, 12 Allen 127. We think the case cited is in accord with the weight of authority. . . .

V

Teachers, Principals, and Superintendents

STATE ex rel. ANDERSON v. BRAND
303 U.S. 95 (1938)

Legal Principles

1. Issuance of a contract to a teacher pursuant to state law constitutes a contract which cannot be impaired by a subsequent law, unless in the proper exercise of police powers.

Opinion

The petitioner sought a writ of mandate to compel the respondent to continue her in employment. . . . Her complaint alleged that as a duly licensed teacher she entered into a contract . . . to teach in the township schools and, pursuant to successive contracts, taught continuously to and including the school year 1932–1933; that her contract for the school years 1931–1932 and 1932–1933 contained this clause: "It is further agreed by the contracting parties that all of the provisions of the Teachers' Tenure Law, approved March 8, 1927, shall be in full force and effect in this contract"; and that by force of that act she had a contract, indefinite in duration, which could be cancelled by the respondent only in the manner and for the causes specified in the act. . . . The complaint alleged the termination of her employment would be a breach of her contract with the school corporation. The respondent demurred on the grounds that the Teachers' Tenure Law had been repealed in respect to teachers in township schools.

The court below holds that in Indiana teachers' contracts are made but for one year; . . . that the law grants a privilege to one who has taught five years and signed a new contract to continue in employment under given conditions; that the statute is directed merely to the exercise of their powers by the school authorities and the policy therein expressed may be altered at the will of the legislature; that in enacting laws for the government of public schools the legislature exercises a function of sovereignty and the power to control public policy in respect of their management and operation cannot be contracted away by one legislature so as to create a permanent public policy unchangeable by succeeding legislatures. In the alternative the court declares that if the relationship be considered as controlled by the rules of private contract the provision for re-employment from year to year is unenforceable for want of mutuality.

As in most cases brought to this court under the contract clause of the Constitution, the question is as to the existence and nature of the contract and not as to the construction of the law which is supposed to impair it. The principal function of a legislative body is not to make contracts but to make laws which declare the policy of the state and are subject to repeal when a subsequent legislature shall determine to alter that policy. Nevertheless, it is established that a legislative enactment may contain provisions which, when accepted as the basis of action by individuals, become contracts between them and the state or its subdivisions within the protection of Art. I, Section 10. If the people's representatives deem it in the public interest they may adopt a policy of contracting in respect of public business for a term longer than the life of the current session of the legislature. This the petitioner claims has been done with respect to permanent teachers. The Supreme Court has decided, however, that it is the state's policy not to bind school corporations by contract for more than one year.

. . . By this Act (the Indiana Teachers' Tenure Act) it was provided that a teacher who has served under contract for five or more successive years, and thereafter enters into a contract for further service with the school corporation, shall become a permanent teacher and the contract, upon the expiration of its stated term, shall be deemed to continue in effect for an indefinite period, shall be known as an indefinite contract, and shall remain in force unless succeeded by a new contract or cancelled as provided in the Act. The corporation may cancel the contract, after notice and hearing, for incompetency, insubordination, neglect of duty, immorality, justifiable decrease in the number of teaching positions, or other good or just cause, but not for political or personal reasons. The teacher may not cancel the contract during the school term nor for a period of 30 days previous to the beginning of any term (unless by mutual agreement) and may cancel only upon five days' notice.

The respondent urges that every contract is subject to the police power and that in repealing the Teachers' Tenure Act the legislature validly exercised that reserved power of the state. . . . Thus in the declaration of the state's policy, ample reservations in aid of the efficient administration of the school system were made. The express prohibitions are that the contract shall not be cancelled for political or personal reasons. We do not think the asserted change of policy evidenced by the repeal of the statute is that school boards may be at liberty to cancel a teacher's contract for political or personal reasons. We do not understand the respondent so to contend. The most that can be said for his position is that, by the repeal, township school corporations were again put upon the basis of annual contracts, renewable at the pleasure of the board. It is significant that the Act of 1933 left the system of permanent teachers and indefinite contracts untouched as respects school corporations in cities and towns of the state. It is not contended, nor can it be thought, that the legislature of 1933 determined that it was against public policy for school districts in cities and towns to terminate the employment of teachers of five or more years' experience for political or personal reasons and to permit cancellation, for the same reasons, in townships.

Our decisions recognize that every contract is made subject to the implied condition that its fulfillment may be frustrated by a proper exercise of the police power but we have repeatedly said that, in order to have this effect, the exercise of the power must be for an end which is in fact public and the means adopted must be reasonably adapted to that end, and the Supreme Court of Indiana has taken the same view in respect of legislation impairing the obligation of the contract of a state instrumentality. The causes of cancellation provided in the Act of 1927 and the retention of the system of indefinite contracts in all municipalities except townships by the Act of 1933 are persuasive that the repeal of the earlier Act by the latter was not an exercise of the police power for the attainment of ends to which its exercise may properly be directed.

TRIPP v. MARTIN
210 Ga. 284, 79 S.E. (2d) 521 (1954)

Legal Principles

1. A contract of employment of a teacher, not made in compliance with the statute, is invalid.

2. Where the law requires the superintendent to recommend the employment of teachers, a board has no right to employ teachers without such recommendation.

Opinion

The pleadings in this case present but one question for determination in this court. How are the teachers in the public schools of the county to be selected and employed?

The plaintiffs contend that the power to select and employ teachers in the public schools is vested solely in the county board of education. . . .

Under the foregoing provisions of the Constitution, and in the absence of some constitutional limitation or prohibition, the general rule, long of force in this state, "that the general assembly of this state is absolutely unrestricted in its power of legislation so long as it does not undertake to enact measures prohibited by the State or Federal Constitution." . . . The language of this section, "shall be elected by the boards of education on the recommendation of the respective superintendents," is mandatory and not directive. . . .

Construing Article 8, Section 5, paragraph 1 of the Constitution of 1945, Code Ann. Section 2–6801, with reference to schools being confined to the control and management of the county board of education, in conjunction with Section 4 of the Minimum Foundation Program Act, Ga.L. 1949, p. 1406 et seq., as they must be construed (since the General Assembly is conclusively presumed to know the provisions of the Constitution), it would be the duty of the county school superintendent to recommend to the board of education all teachers having the necessary qualifications, ability, and character. The board of education must select and employ those teachers needed from the number recommended by the county school superintendent.

The expediency of legislation is a matter for determination by the General Assembly (Beall v. Beall 8 Ga. 210; Winter v. Jones, 10 Ga. 190, 54 Am. D. 379), and not by this court; nor will this court inquire into the motives of the General Assembly in the enactment of legislation. . . . Clements v. Powell, 155 Ga. 278 (116 S.E. 624).

The General Assembly having exercised a legislative power that is not in conflict with the Constitution, the trial court erred in making the mandamus absolute, so as to require the county school superintendent to execute contracts on behalf of the board of education with certain teachers whose employment was not recommended by the county school superintendent.

STATE v. WEBB
230 Wis. 390, 284 N.W. 6 (1939)

Legal Principles

1. The marriage of a teacher is not a valid ground to terminate her contract.

Opinion

. . . It is conceded that the marriage of a woman teacher in and of itself does not necessarily operate to make her less efficient or in any manner violate the requirement of good behavior. But the board contends that notwithstanding the provisions of Sec. 39.40, which provides that "such employment shall be permanent during efficiency and good behavior and until discharge for cause," it was proper for it in its discretion and sound judgment to adopt and maintain a policy against employing or continuing in employment married women teachers. . . .

We now come to the construction of the statute for the purpose of ascertaining what the legislature intended by the following language: "All employment of teachers as defined in subsection (1) of this section shall be on probation, and after continuous and successful probation for five years in the same school system or school, either before or after the taking effect of this section, such employment shall be permanent during efficiency and good behavior and until discharge for cause," and "no teacher who has become permanently employed, as herein provided, shall be refused employment, dismissed, removed, or discharged, except for cause. . . ."

The board contends that the language of the statute is broad enough to include a cause for discharge other than those relating to the efficiency and good behavior of a teacher and that the marriage of a woman teacher should be considered as a cause for discharge or reason for refusing further employment when the declared policy of the board is not to employ a married woman teacher. In our opinion, the contention is without merit. It is our opinion that the legislature intended that teachers who had acquired a permanent status should be continued in employment during efficiency and good behavior, and that the language "and until discharge for cause" was not intended to confer upon school boards the right to discharge teachers for reasons other than those connected or associated with efficiency or good behavior. . . .

JAMESON v. BOARD OF EDUCATION
74 W. Va. 389, 81 S.E. 1126 (1914)

Legal Principles
1. Where a statute sets forth the grounds for removal of a teacher, the statute must be strictly observed, and a teacher may not lawfully be dismissed on a ground not enumerated in the statute.

Opinion
. . . Plaintiff was Miss Hallie Jones. On July 20, 1911 she was married. . . . About August 11, 1911 she received a letter from the superintendent of schools, saying the board could not meet ahead of schedule, and when they did meet they . . . had declared her place vacant, and that they stood as a unit against the employment of a married woman. . . .

. . . Lastly, was plaintiff's marriage after her appointment good ground for revocation? While the fact of marriage was evidently the one, and the only one, on which defendant founded its action, it is apparently not relied upon, for it was not covered by briefs or oral arguments. The only grounds of removal prescribed by section 58, chapter 45, serial section 2099, Code 1913, are "incompetency, neglect of duty, intemperance, profanity, cruelty, or immorality." Marriage is not covered by any of these, and therefore does not constitute in and of itself ground of removal. This subject has been recently before the courts of New York, in the case of People v. Board of Education, 82 Misc. Rep. 684, 144 N.Y. Supp. 87, Supreme Court, New York County, November 15, 1913, and on appeal in the Supreme Court, Appellate Division, First Department, February 6, 1914, 160 App. Div. 557, 145 N.Y. Supp. 853. The court in the first case held, under the statute of New York, similar in its provisions to our own, that a female teacher in the public schools could not be removed because of her marriage. On appeal, the appellate division reversed the judgment, not upon the ground of marriage, but for other reasons, and among other things held, point 1 of the syllabus:

"That the absence of a married woman teacher that she might bear a child might be of such length as to give the board of education jurisdiction to remove her for neglect of duty, though she might not be removed on that ground merely because of absence for that purpose."

We have no question of absence or neglect of duty, or other ground of removal present in this case. As marriage is not a ground of removal under the statute of this state, the action of the board in removing plaintiff, or in revoking or attempting to revoke its action is unfounded.

Our conclusion is, therefore, to reverse the judgment below. . . .

TEACHERS' ASSN. v. BOARD OF EDUCATION
138 Conn. 269, 83 A. (2d) 482 (1951)

Legal Principles
1. Collective bargaining or professional negotiation is legally permissible between a board of education and an organization of its employees, if the strike threat is absent.

2. An organization of employees and a board of education may not negotiate a contract which involves the surrender of the board's legal discretion, is contrary to law, or is otherwise ultra vires.

Opinion
Few cases involving the rights of unions of government employees to strike to enforce their demands have reached the courts of last resort. That right has usually been tested by an application for an injunction forbidding the strike. The right of the governmental body to the relief has been uniformly upheld.

In the American system, sovereignty is inherent in the people. They can delegate it to a government which they create and operate by law. They can give to that government the power and authority to perform certain duties and furnish certain services. The government so created and empowered must employ people to carry on its task. These people are agents of the government. They exercise some part of the sovereignty entrusted to them. They occupy a status entirely different from those who carry on a private enterprise. They serve the public welfare and not a private purpose. To say that they (school employees) can strike is the equivalent of saying that they can deny the authority of government and contravene the public welfare. . . .

Questions (a) and (b) relate to the right of the plaintiff to organize itself as a labor union and to demand recognition and collective bargaining. The right to organize is sometimes accorded by statute or ordinance. . . . In Connecticut the statutes are silent on the subject. Union organization in industry is now the rule rather than the exception. In the absence of prohibitory statute or regulation, no good reason appears why public employees should not organize as a labor union. Springfield v. Clouse, 356 Mo. 1239, 1246, 206 S.W. 2d 539. It is the second part of the question (a) that causes difficulty. The question reads: "Is it permitted to the plaintiff under our laws to organize itself as a labor union for the purpose of demanding and receiving recognition and collective bargaining?" The question is phrased in a very peremptory form. The common method of enforcing recognition and collective bargaining is the strike. It appears that this method has already been used by the plaintiff and that the threat of its use again is one of the reasons for the present suit. As has been said, the strike is not a permissible method of enforcing the plaintiff's demands. The answer to questions (a) and (b) is a qualified "Yes." There is no objection to the organization of the plaintiff as a labor union, but if its organization is for the purpose of "demanding" recognition and collective bargaining the demands must be kept within legal bounds. . . .

Questions (c) and (d) in effect ask whether collective bargaining between the plaintiff and the defendant is permissible. The statutes and private acts give broad powers to the defendant with reference to educational matters and school management in Norwalk. If it chooses to negotiate with the plaintiff with regard to the employment, salaries, grievance procedure and working conditions of its members, there is no statute, public or private, which forbids such negotiations. It is a matter of common knowledge that this is the method pursued in most school systems large enough to support a teachers' association in some form. It would seem to make no difference theoretically whether the negotiations are with a committee of the whole association or with individuals or small related groups, so long as any agreement made with the committee is confined to members of the association. If the strike threat is absent and the defendant prefers to handle the matter through negotiation with the plaintiff, no reason exists why it should not do so. The claim of the defendant that this would be an illegal delegation of authority is without merit. The authority is and remains in the board. This statement is not to be construed as approval of the existing contracts attached to the complaint. Their validity is not in issue.

As in the case of questions (a) and (b), (c) and (d) are in too general a form to permit a categorical answer. The qualified "Yes" which we give to them should not be construed as authority to negotiate a contract which involves the surrender of the board's legal discretion, is contrary to law, or is otherwise ultra vires. For example, an agreement by the board to hire only union members would clearly be an illegal discrimination. . . . Any salary schedule must be subject to the purviews of the board of estimate and taxation.

RYAN v. HUMPHRIES
50 Okla. 343, 150 P. 1106 (1915)

Legal Principles

1. Where a school board has the original power to enter into a contract to employ teachers, such board may legally ratify a contract of employment made by the board in an unauthorized manner, and a ratification of such contract is equivalent to a full compliance with authority originally given, and when so done renders the contract valid from its inception.

Opinion

. . . We gather from the evidence that the claim was allowed by the board and warrant issued prior to the meeting above referred to, but the clerk failed to show the financial condition of the district on the warrant as required by law. . . .

. . . This action of the board brings us to the question of its effect, in the way of ratification of the original contract entered into by Abbott and Gamble as director and clerk. In this connection it may not be out of place to say that the question of the power of municipal or quasi-municipal corporations to ratify unauthorized contracts is one of the generally recognized controversies of the court and bar. The authorities are absolutely irreconcilable; and after careful study of the proposition the writer hereof acknowledges himself at sea, in the midst of the storm of high rolling waves of uncertainty; but we gather from the weight of the authorities that, where the corporation had the power to enter into the contract under consideration, and the manner of making it being the only question involved, such contract may, as a rule, be ratified by an acceptance of the benefits of the contract by corporations, and by a subsequent recognition and substantial performance of the acts and conditions required by law in the execution of the legal contract, or by acquiescence in the conditions and benefits obtained by virtue of the contract. This seems to be, in substance, the doctrine laid down in Hill v. City of Indianapolis (C.C.), 92 Fed. 467; Dairess County v. Dickinson, 117 U.S. 657, 6 Sup. Ct. 897, 29 L. Ed. 1026; Town of Bloomfield v. Charter Oak Bank, 121 U.S. 121, 7 Sup. Ct. 865, 30 L. Ed. 923; and a long list of other authorities.

BENSON v. SCHOOL DISTRICT, NO. 1
136 Mont. 77, 344 P. (2d) 117 (1959)

Legal Principles
1. A board of education lacks authority to require union membership on part of school teachers as a condition to receiving an increased salary.
2. A board of education has no power to discriminate between teachers employed by it as to amount of salary to be paid them on the basis of their membership in a labor union.
3. An agreement by a board of education to hire only union members would clearly be an illegal discrimination.

Opinion
. . . The complaint alleges that the plaintiffs are school teachers in School District No. 1 of Silver Bow County; that the defendants are the trustees of that school district; that on the 2d day of April, 1956, the defendant school district approved what is called a Master Agreement which among other things contained the following provisions that "The single salary principle of equal salary for equal training and experience shall prevail."

It established a salary schedule for the plaintiffs of $5100 per year for four of them and $4900 for the other four. The Master Agreement then contained these clauses:

"(a) All members now employed by the Board, who are not now members of the Union, must become members of the Union on or before the 4th day of September, 1956, and shall maintain their membership in the Union in good standing as defined by the constitution and by-laws of the Union during the term of their employment.

"(b) All teachers now employed by the Board, who are now members of the Union, shall maintain their membership in the Union in good standing as defined by the constitution and by-laws of the Union during the term of their employment.

"(c) All new teachers or former teachers employed by the Board shall become members of the Union within thirty (30) days after date of their employment and shall maintain their membership in good standing as defined in the constitution and by-laws of the Union during the term of their employment.

"The provisions of this Union Security Clause shall be adopted as a Board Rule and shall be a condition of all contracts issued to any teacher covered by this agreement.

"Any teacher who fails to sign a contract which includes the provisions of this Union Security Clause and who fails to comply with the provisions of this Union Security Clause shall be discharged on the written request of the Union, except that any such teacher who now has tenure under the laws of the State of Montana shall not be discharged but shall receive none of the benefits nor salary increases negotiated by the Union and shall be employed, without contract, from year to year on the same terms and conditions as such teacher was employed during the year 1955–1956." . . .

Hence we come to the question whether the Union Security Clause in the contract is void and illegal as contended by plaintiffs. We hold that it is.

It is not competent for the school trustees to require union membership as a condition to receiving the increased salary. So far as this case is concerned it is sufficient to say that the legislature has not given the school board authority to make the discrimination sought to be imposed here. We do not pass upon the point whether it would be competent for the legislature to place such authority in the school trustees. There is respectable authority holding that such action by the legislature would be unconstitutional. . . .

The court (Norwalk Teachers Assn. v. Board of Education, 138 Conn. 269) concluded by saying: "That right has usually been tested by an application for an injunction forbidding the strike. The right of the governmental body to this relief has been uniformly upheld." . . .

Other questions were considered by the court in that case. The court pointed out that some of the questions were too general to permit of a categorical answer, but the court did say that "an agreement by the board to hire only union members would clearly be an illegal discrimination." . . .

The case of People by Hoyne ex rel. Fursman v. City of Chicago, 199 Ill. App. 356, had a similar question before it. There the board of education adopted a rule forbidding the employment of teachers affiliated with the labor union. The court held that this was a discrimination between different classes of citizens conferring special privileges upon a class or group less than all. On consideration of the same question in 278 Ill. 318, 116 N.E. 158, L.R.A. 1917E, 1069, the Supreme Court of

Illinois reached a different conclusion and held that it was competent for the board of education of the City of Chicago to enforce the rule prohibiting the teachers from becoming members in a labor union. Whether we would agree with the court's opinion in that case, we need not here determine. The court upheld the rule there involved because the board of education recited in the rule that membership in a union was inimical to proper discipline, prejudicial to the efficiency of the teaching force, and detrimental to the welfare of the public school system. The board of education in that case was at least consistent. It refused to employ teachers who were members of a labor union. Here the defendant board does not refuse employment for not belonging to the union, but seeks to impose a penalty for not becoming members by seeking to withhold the increase in salary from those who do not belong to the union.

The same is true in the case of Seattle High School Chapter No. 200, of the American Federation of Teachers v. Sharples, 159 Wash. 424, 293 P. 994, 72 A.L.R. 1215, relied on by defendants. That case differs from this because in that case the very employment of the teachers was made dependent upon their belonging to a labor union. Here the defendant board is willing to employ the plaintiffs whether they belong to the Union or not but they undertake to deprive the plaintiffs of the increased salary unless they become members of the labor union. In other words, the plaintiff's employment, according to the board of trustees of the defendant school district, does not depend upon their affiliation with the union but only their right to the increased salary. Hence for this reason the Washington case is not controlling here.

For the purposes of this case it is sufficient to say that the school trustees have no authority or power to discriminate between the teachers employed by it as to the amount of salary paid to each because of their membership or lack of membership in a labor union. The school trustees have no authority to invade that field. As well might it be argued that the board of school trustees might provide that the increased salary shall not be allowed to those who do not affiliate with a certain lodge, service club, church or political party. . . .

STATE v. BOARD OF EDUCATION
19 Wash. 8, 52 P. 317 (1898)

Legal Principles

1. Where there is no appeal from a board of education on terminating a teacher's contract, a board member who has caused charges to be filed against a teacher because of personal hostility, and has announced a

determination to vote against him, whatever the evidence, may be restrained from participating in the hearing.

Opinion

It is conceded by the counsel for the respondents that this case overrules the former cases reported in the New York Supplement, but they insist the reasoning of the former cases is better, and that the decisions are more in consonance with the adjudicated cases. But we cannot agree on this proposition.

. . . The principle of impartiality, disinterestedness, and fairness on the part of the judge is as old as the history of courts; in fact, the administration of justice through the mediation of courts is based upon this principle. It is a fundamental idea, running through and pervading the whole system of judicature, and it is the popular acknowledgement of the inviolability of this principle which gives credit, or even toleration, to decrees of judicial tribunals. Actions of courts which disregard this safeguard to litigants would more appropriately be termed the administration of injustice, and their proceedings would be as shocking to our private sense of justice as they would be injurious to the public interest. The learned and observant Lord Bacon well said that the virtue of a judge is seen in making inequality equal, that he may plant his judgment as upon even ground. Caesar demanded that his wife should not only be virtuous, but beyond suspicion; and the state should not be any less exacting with its judicial officers, in whose keeping are placed not only the financial interests, but the honor, the liberty, and the lives of its citizens, and it should see to it that the scales in which the rights of the citizen are weighed should be nicely balanced, for, as was well said by Judge Bronson in People v. Suffolk Common Pleas, 18 Wend. 550, "next in importance to the duty of rendering a righteous judgment, is that of doing it in such a manner as will beget no suspicion of the fairness and integrity of the judge." . . . This presumption in certain cases may or may not be justified by the truth, but so solicitous is the law to maintain inviolate the principle that every litigant shall be secure in his right to a fair trial that he is accorded the benefit of the presumption. But what does a presumption amount to compared with the admitted fact that the judge will not accord the litigant a fair trial; that he will vote to remove him from his office, no matter what the evidence may be? To compel a litigant to submit to a judge who has already confessedly prejudged him, and who is candid enough to announce his decision in advance, and insist that he will adhere to it, no matter what the evidence may be, would be so farcical and manifestly wrong that it seems to us that the idea must necessarily be excluded by the very expression "administration of justice."

. . . While it is true that in some of the cases financial interest was claimed, yet, as a rule, the decisions are not based upon that ground, but upon the broad ground that the citizen is entitled to a judge who is absolutely impartial. . . .

SCHOOL CITY v. SIGLER
219 Ind. 9, 36 N.E. (2d) 760 (1941)

Legal Principles
1. The activities of a teacher which have a reasonable bearing on his ability, efficiency, and influence in the classroom are within the field of rules adopted by the school board.

2. A school board rule, general in terms and applying to all teachers, requiring a teacher to take a leave of absence to run for office is not an unreasonable rule.

3. To bind a teacher, it is not necessary that a rule be adopted prior to execution of a contract. A teacher is bound to observe all reasonable rules adopted by a board, prior to his employment, or adopted during the existence of his contract.

Opinion
. . . A statute requires school trustees to "take charge of the educational affairs of their respective townships, towns, and cities." Bruns' Stat. 1933, #28–2410, Baldwins 1934, #5967.

. . . They are required to furnish teachers and equipment "for the thorough organization and efficient management of the schools." The power to make reasonable rules and regulations to that end cannot be successfully challenged. . . . Activities of the teacher which have a reasonable bearing on his ability, efficiency, and influence in the classroom seem to us to be within the field of such regulation by the school board.

It will be conceded that he has the same privilege as any other citizen to become a candidate for public office. Such candidacy should not be and is not ground for cancellation of his contract as a permanent teacher. But anyone who has been a candidate recognizes that political activity is apt to interfere with one's usual avocation and this fact, independent of any possible involvement of the school system in political controversies, affords a sound reason for a temporary severance of the candidate's connection with the schools. This rule, general in terms and applying to all teachers, does not to us seem such an unreasonable exercise of the board's powers as to warrant judicial interference. The board, not the courts, is charged with the duty of managing the school system and so long as it acts with fairness its decisions on matters within its discretion are not subject to judicial review.

To bind the teacher it is not necessary that the rule be made prior to the execution of his contract. In express terms it contains his agreement to "observe all rules and regulations of the school authorities." Without such provision we think this agreement would be read into the contract. The tenure law does not purport to take from the school authorities the management of the schools. If only such rules could be enforced as were in existence when the contract was signed, the school system might be static for at least one year. New situations could not be met promptly; new problems would have to await solution until the close of the school year. We cannot find any such intent in the contract nor in the purpose behind the tenure law. "All rules and regulations" must, we think, include those adopted after as well as before the execution of the teacher's contract. Any other interpretation would unduly hamper the administration of the public school system by the authorities charged with its management. . . .

RUDY v. SCHOOL DISTRICT
30 Mo. App. 113 (1888)

Legal Principles

1. A board of education cannot violate a valid teacher's contract because of lack of funds to pay the teacher's compensation.

Opinion

. . . Now what is the defense to this action? The foregoing statement of the evidence and of the declaration of law refused by the court, show that it is that the directors have the power, without the consent of the teacher, to rescind the contract whenever they shall discover that enough money cannot be collected into the appropriate fund, under the levy made at the annual meeting of the qualified voters of the district, to meet the obligation incurred by the district under the contract. In support of this defense the defendant invokes the provision of section twelve, of article ten, of the constitution of the state. This, so far as material, reads as follows: "No . . . political corporation or subdivision of the state, shall be allowed to become indebted in any manner or for any purpose to an amount exceeding in any year the income and revenue provided for such year, without the assent of two-thirds of the voters thereof voting at an election to be held for that purpose." But the defense here set up fails to show that the revenue "provided for" the school year in question was not sufficient to pay all the teachers; it merely shows that there was a failure to pay into the school district treasury enough for that purpose. If this is a sound view, then the rights of the teacher, under his contract with the district, may be displaced by the negligence or fraud of the tax collector. If the collector negligently fails to collect the school taxes which are levied, or collects them and fails to turn them over, the directors for this reason may, even upon the brief notice of five days, cancel the contract with the teacher. We are of opinion that this is not the law. . . . Public Schools v. Patten, 62 Mo. 444; Householder v. City of Kansas, 83 Mo. 488. But, in order to make it appear that the contract with the teacher was ultra vires on the part of the directors, it must appear that not enough revenue was "provided" longer to continue the school, and not merely that not enough was collected and turned over to the treasurer of the school board.

But under any view of the case the defense fails, since it is shown by uncontradicted evidence that, after the closing of the school, one hundred and five dollars were collected and paid into the hands of the treasurer of the board, which might have been applied, as far as it went, in carrying out the contract between the defendant and the plaintiff. We allude to this circumstance more for the purpose of making it appear that the directors seem to have taken the view that they had the power to cancel the contract with the plaintiff in the exercise of a discretion, whenever they should be of opinion that sufficient revenue would not come in to continue the schools further.

CRABB v. SCHOOL DISTRICT, NO. 1

93 Mo. App. 254

Legal Principles

1. The law does not require a teacher to have a certificate at the time of making a contract to teach in the future, but such certificate must exist during the employment of teaching.

Opinion

. . . and that said contract is illegal and void, for the reason that at its date the plaintiff was not a legally qualified teacher . . . as she did not have a certificate of qualification. . . .

. . . At the time she entered into said contract she had a certificate to teach school, but it was defective. . . .

But it is the contention of the defendant, if the plaintiff did not have a proper certificate at the time the contract was entered into, it was for that reason invalid. This contention involves a construction of sections 8021, 8022, and 8023 of the Revised Statutes of 1889, in force at the date of the contract. Section 8021 is as follows: "No teacher shall be employed in any school supported by the public funds, or any part thereof, until he has received a certificate of qualification therefor, signed by the commissioner of the county where he or she intends to teach, except those

holding normal diplomas and certificates entitling them to teach under
section 8128 of the chapter on normal schools, and except those holding
certificates then in force from the state superintendent." Section 8022
prohibits any teacher from entering any school in the state to teach without such certificate, and as a penalty for so doing he forfeits all claim to
compensation, and subjects himself to a fine; and it further imposes a
fine upon any director who shall indorse or encourage any teacher in
such unlawful conduct. Section 8023 prescribes the qualifications of
teachers.

We do not think, taking sections 8021 and 8022, to be read together,
they mean that the teacher must have a certificate of qualification at the
time of making a contract to teach school in the future. The object of
the statute is that the qualification may exist during the term of the
employment. The language of the statute is that, "no teacher shall be
employed," and has reference to the employment and not to the contract
for employment. It means that he shall not be engaged in teaching without the required certificate, and the following section imposes a forfeiture
and punishment if he does so. . . .

It is further contended that as the school term began on the fourth day
of September, and plaintiff's certificate in evidence issued to her by the
State Superintendent of Schools was dated the fifth day of September,
she was not a qualified teacher at the beginning, and, therefore, she is
not in condition to enforce said contract. Time, it is true, is a material
essence of the contract in suit. But can it be said that the plaintiff's failure to have a proper certificate on the fourth day of September, when
defendant's school opened, taken in connection with the fact that she
received one on the next day dated the fifth of September, have the effect
of forfeiting her rights under the contract? There are instances when
time becomes of such material consequence, that a failure of a party to
comply with his contract in that respect at the time agreed upon, works
a forfeiture of his rights under such contract; but the courts are not
swift to enforce forfeitures, and only do so in extreme cases.

If the defendant had been forced to employ another teacher by reason
of plaintiff's failure to have a proper certificate on the fourth day of
September, the case would perhaps have been different. The defendant's
board knew that the plaintiff was to have a certificate to teach, for she
exhibited a telegram from the state superintendent that one had been
issued to her, which, however, when it came, was dated the fifth of September, one day after the school opened. If the defendant is to be permitted
to exact the literal terms of the contract, and demands the "pound of
flesh," the plaintiff's rights under her contract are forfeited. But ought it
to be permitted? It is good law that a party who commits the first breach
of his contract is not in a condition to enforce it against the other contracting party. Doyle v. Turpin, 57 Mo. App. 84. The defendant's records

introduced show that the defendant was the first to commit a breach of its contract. These records show that on the thirty-first day of August the defendant's board employed another teacher in place of the plaintiff and put it out of its power to comply with the contract. Under such circumstances it should not be permitted to deny plaintiff's right to recover because of her failure to have, for a single day, a teacher's certificate, for she substantially complied with her contract in that respect.

COLEMAN v. DISTRICT OF COLUMBIA
279 F. 990 (1922)

Legal Principles

1. The authority to employ teachers is ordinarily vested solely in a board of education.

2. Since the power of appointment requires an exercise of judgment, such power may not be delegated by the board of education.

Opinion

Grace Coleman filed her declaration . . . in which she averred that the District had breached a contract with her as a teacher . . . and she asked for damages. The District denied that it made the contract.

On September 14, 1920, Miss Coleman was advised by the assistant superintendent of schools that he had recommended her for a probationary appointment to a high school teachership, subject to a special examination by the health department of the District to determine physical fitness. On the next day, the board of education, acting on the recommendation, appointed the plaintiff to a probationary teachership in class 6–A, subject to the condition just mentioned. On the 17th of the same month the secretary of the board notified her of her appointment, and that she should appear and take the oath of office, but made no mention of the physical examination. Miss Coleman submitted herself to the examination. The school medical inspectors found that she was suffering from curvature of the spine, with resulting deformity of the chest, and other infirmities, and said that in their judgment she was capable of performing the duties of a probationary teacher, but not those of a permanent teacher. This report was laid before the health officer, who said that in his opinion Miss Coleman was not qualified to perform the duties of a teacher, because she would not be "able to stand the physical strain to which teachers are frequently subjected." He added that, if she was appointed, she would be entitled to share in the benefits of the Teacher's Retirement Act, which, he thought, in view of her physical condition, would be unfair to the District. In consequence the superintendent of schools, on September 21, same year, issued an order rescinding Miss

Coleman's appointment as a probationary teacher, and on October 6 following, the board of education ratified the superintendent's action. From a judgment against her, Miss Coleman brings the case here for review.

The board of education is not estopped by the secretary's letter to deny that she was appointed without condition. Before receiving the letter, she had been advised by the assistant superintendent of schools that her selection was upon the condition that she pass a satisfactory physical examination. This at least put her upon inquiry, when she received the secretary's letter, as to whether or not her appointment was subject to the condition named. That she understood the appointment was conditional is established by the fact that she submitted to the examination. Besides, no representative of the secretary could effectuate her appointment. He had no authority to employ teachers. That authority was vested solely in the board of education by section 2 of the Act of June 20, 1906. . . .

This power of appointment requires an exercise of judgment, and could not be delegated to the secretary or anybody else. The maxim "delegata potestas non potest delegari" applies. . . . Miss Coleman was charged with knowledge of this. "Parties dealing with a municipal corporation are bound to know the extent of the power lawfully confided to the officers with whom they are dealing in behalf of such corporation, and they must guide their conduct accordingly." Stone v. Bank of Commerce, 174 U.S. 412, 424, 19 Sup. Ct. 747, 752 (43 L.Ed. 1028). . . . Sometimes even the criminal law requires a person to know facts at his peril.

Nor may Miss Coleman invoke the doctrine that where an agent acts within the apparent scope of his authority, his principal is bound. The secretary had no authority, actual or apparent, to bind the board concerning the matter in hand, and could not have it under the statute. Of this Miss Coleman had at least constructive knowledge.

HODGE v. STEGALL
206 Okla. 161, 242 P. (2d) 720 (1952)

Legal Principles
1. When the state issues a teacher's certificate, such does not create a contract, and the certificate may be revoked for proper reasons.

Opinion
. . . L. R. Stegall, prior to March 23, 1951, held a lifetime teacher's certificate, and was engaged in teaching at the Burbank School in Osage County. On December 19th, 1950, twenty complainants from the Burbank School District appeared before the State Board of Education and filed

a formal written complaint with the Board, specifying twelve alleged violations of the Oklahoma Laws by Mr. Stegall. The complaint requested a hearing thereon and at the conclusion of such hearing that the certificate of the teacher be revoked. The State Board of Education set the hearing on the matter for 1:30 P.M., on Friday, January 26th, 1951. On December 29th, a letter containing an excerpt of the minutes of the State Board, showing the filing of the complaint and the setting of the same for hearing, was sent by the Secretary of the Board to Mr. Stegall. On January 11th, 1951, the State Superintendent, for the Board, advised Mr. Stegall further of the hearing and furnished to him an exact copy of the written complaint filed. This letter also advised that opportunity would be afforded the teacher for a full hearing at the time specified.

On January 21st, Mr. Stegall presented himself before the board with counsel and filed his protest against the hearing, on the grounds: (a) there was no statute or rules and regulations providing for the conduct of such a hearing, (b) the charges had no relation to the continuance of the certificate and did not authorize its revocation, (c) the charges were so indefinite and uncertain as to prevent a proper preparation of defense, (d) the charges purported to indict the teacher under the criminal laws of the state without trial in a proper tribunal, (e) the charges were unverified and unproven, (f) the entire proceeding was a travesty on justice and contrary to all established concepts of constitutional rights and due process of law. When the Board announced its intention to proceed with the hearing, counsel for Mr. Stegall demanded a shorthand record be taken of the proceedings. The Board advised counsel it had no provisions for such shorthand report of the proceedings, but offered to allow Mr. Stegall to make any record he might wish of the same. Considerable evidence was then taken, but no reporter's record of the same has been included in the record here. At the conclusion of this evidence the hearing was continued to March 2nd, 1951. Thereafter, on February 3rd, an amended complaint was filed with the State Board charging willful violations of the State laws, with reference to school matters. A copy of this was also made available to Mr. Stegall. On March 2nd, at the request of counsel for Mr. Stegall the matter was continued to March 23rd. At that time further continuance was sought by Mr. Stegall and his counsel on the same being refused they withdrew from the hearing. The State Board of Education then proceeded with the hearing and at the conclusion thereof revoked the certificate.

Under Article 1, Sec. 5, of the Constitution the legislature is charged with the responsibility of establishing and maintaining a system of public schools. By Article XIII, Sec. 5, of the Constitution, the supervision of instruction in the public schools is vested in the State Board of Education, with powers and duties to be prescribed by law. That the certificate to teach is a license and not an absolute right appears to be clearly established.

VI

Tort Liability

BUCK, et al. v. McLEAN, et al.
115 So. (2d) 764 (Fla.) 1959

Legal Principles
1. Boards of education are agencies of the state and as such are clothed with same degree of immunity from suit as is state.

2. Rule of immunity from liability for tort accorded boards of education is based equally upon doctrine of sovereignty and prohibitory provisions of the state constitution, and it matters not whether negligent act is committed while in performance of governmental or proprietary function.

3. Any change in rule of immunity of state and its agencies from suit must come by constitutional amendment, enactment of appropriate legislation, or both.

Opinion
. . . The crucial question presented for decision is whether a county school board may be held liable in tort for injuries sustained by a paying spectator as a result of negligence in the maintenance of an athletic stadium owned by the board. . . .

The immunity of the state from suit is absolute and unqualified and the constitutional provision securing it is not to be so construed as to place the state within reach of the court's process. County boards of public instruction are agencies of the state and as such are clothed with the same degree of immunity from suit as is the state. They are the creatures of the constitution, constituted as quasi corporations for the purpose of exercising under legislative authority such part of the governmental powers of the state as the law confides in them. In short, county school boards are part of the machinery of government operating at the local level as an agency of the state in the performance of public functions. The character of their functions, and the extent and duration of their powers, rests exclusively in the legislative discretion. Their powers may be enlarged, diminished, modified or revoked, and their acts set aside or confirmed, at the pleasure of the legislature.

As additional authority for the proposition that county school boards are not immune from liability for torts committed by their agents or employees while in the performance of a corporate or proprietary function, appellant refers us to the case of Hoffman decided in 1949 by a district court in Pennsylvania, and Sawaya decided in 1955 by the Supreme Court of Arizona. To these may be added the case of Molitor decided by the Supreme Court of Illinois on May 22, 1959, which extends the rule by withdrawing from county school districts immunity from tort liability for the negligent acts of their employees even when committed in the performance of governmental functions. We have carefully studied the cited decisions and in all frankness must agree that they are solid support for the position which appellants here take. They completely discredit and repudiate the ancient doctrine of sovereign immunity and reject as unsound the several reasons relied upon by our Supreme Court for the settled rule which immunizes county school boards against liability for torts committed by their agents or employees. We are compelled to the view, however, that such conflict in judicial opinion does not in any manner alter the established law of this jurisdiction.

We share the wonderment expressed by Mr. Justice Thomas in Suwannee County Hospital as to when the entry of government into businesses as well and as readily operatable by private enterprises will cease. Courts are not blind to the many instances within the personal knowledge of their members where departments and agencies of the state, as well as counties and local school boards, are engaged in activities which by any reasonable standard must be considered corporate and proprietary in nature. In so doing they are directly competing with private business in fields which could and in most instances are better served by the latter. It is a harsh doctrine indeed which leaves one without remedy for wrong suffered by him through the negligence of a state agent or employee committed while performing a proprietary function, but under similar circumstances imposes liability on everyone else engaged in the performance of similar functions.

Regardless of our personal views, we feel that a proper administration of justice invites respect for the admonition of Alexander Hamilton, who once wrote that courts "must declare the sense of the law; and if they should be disposed to exercise Will instead of Judgment, the consequences would equally be the substitution of their pleasure to that of the legislative body." If, therefore, a change in the long established rule of immunity prevailing in this state is to be made, it must come as it did in the states of New York, Washington and California either by constitutional amendment, or by enactment of appropriate legislation, or both. . . .

MOLITOR, et al. v. SCHOOL DISTRICT
18 Ill. (2d) 11, 163 N.E. (2d) (1959)

Legal Principles

1. The judicially created doctrine whereby the medieval rule of sovereign immunity from suit is extended to school districts, giving them immunity from tort liability, is abolished.

2. The doctrine of stare decisis is not an inflexible rule requiring the Supreme Court to blindly follow precedents and adhere to prior decisions, for where it appears that public policy and social needs require a departure from prior decisions, it is the court's duty as a court of last resort to overrule those decisions and establish a rule consonant with present-day concepts of right and justice.

Opinion

Plaintiff, Thomas Molitor, a minor, by Peter his father and next friend, brought this action . . . for personal injuries sustained . . . when the school bus in which he was riding left the road, allegedly as a result of the driver's negligence, hit a culvert, exploded, and burned.

The complaint alleged, in substance, the negligence of the school district, through its agent and servant, the driver of the school bus; that plaintiff was in the exercise of such ordinary care for his own safety as could be reasonably expected of a boy of his age, intelligence, mental capacity, and experience; that plaintiff sustained permanent and severe burns and injuries as a proximate result of defendant's negligence, and prayed for judgment in the amount of $56,000. Plaintiff further alleged that defendant is a voluntary unit school district organized and existing under sections 8–9 to 8–13 of the School Code. . . .

The complaint contained no allegation of the existence of insurance or other non-public funds out of which a judgment against defendant could be satisfied. Although plaintiff's abstract of the record shows that defendant school district did carry public liability insurance with limits of $20,000 for each person injured and $100,000 for each occurrence, plaintiff states that he purposely omitted such an allegation from his complaint.

Defendant's motion to dismiss the complaint on the ground that a school district is immune from liability for tort was sustained by the trial court, and a judgment was entered in favor of defendant. Plaintiff elected to stand on his complaint and sought a direct appeal to this court on the ground that the dismissal of his action would violate his constitutional rights. At that time we held that no fairly debatable constitutional question was presented so as to give this court jurisdiction on direct appeal, and accordingly the cause was transferred to the Appellate Court for the Second District. The Appellate Court affirmed the decision of the trial court and the case is now before us again on a certificate of importance.

In his brief, plaintiff recognizes the rule, established by this court in 1898, that a school district is immune from tort liability, and frankly asks this court either to abolish the rule in toto, or to find it inapplicable to a school district such as Kaneland which was organized through the voluntary acts of petition and election by the voters of the district, as contrasted with a school district created nolens volens by the state.

Historically we find that the doctrine of the sovereign immunity of the state, the theory that "the King can do no wrong," was first extended to a subdivision of the state in 1788 in Russell v. Men of Devon, 2 Term Rep. 671, 100 Eng. Rep. 359. . . .

It should be noted that the Russell case was later overruled by the English courts, and that in 1890 it was definitely established that in England a school board or school district is subject to suit in tort for personal injuries on the same basis as a private individual or corporation. Crisp v. Thomas, 63 L.T. N.S. (1890). Non-immunity has continued to be the law of England to the present day. See; Annotation, 160 A.L.R. 7, 84.

Coming down to the precise issue at hand, it is clear that if the above rules and precedents are strictly applied to the instant case, plaintiff's complaint, containing no allegation as to the existence of insurance, was properly dismissed. On the other hand, the complaint may be held to state a good cause of action on either one of two theories, (1) application of the doctrine of Moore v. Moyle, 405 Ill. 555, 92 N.E. 2d 81, or (2) abolition of the rule that a school district is immune from tort liability.

The original basis of the immunity rule has been called a "survival of the medieval idea that the sovereign can do no wrong," or that "the King can do no wrong" (38 Am. Jur. Mun. Corps sec. 573, p. 266). . . .

The other chief reason advanced in support of the immunity rule in the more recent cases is the protection of public funds and public property. This corresponds to the "no fund" or "trust fund" theory upon which charitable immunity is based. This rationale was relied on in Thomas v. Broadlands Community Consolidated School District, 348 Ill. App. 567, where the court stated that the reason for the rule is "that it is the public policy to protect public funds and public property, to prevent the diversion of tax moneys, in this case school funds, to the payment of damage claims. . . .

SPANEL, et al. v. SCHOOL DISTRICT
118 N.W. (2d) 795 (Minn.) (1962)

Legal Principles
1. Doctrine of sovereign tort immunity is archaic and is prospectively overruled as a defense with respect to tort claims against school districts, municipal corporations, and other subdivisions of government.

Opinion
Plaintiff sues on behalf of his 5-year-old son to recover damages from a school district and a teacher and principal employed by it for injuries resulting from the alleged negligence of defendants in permitting a defective slide to remain in the kindergarten classroom of an elementary school. . . .

The only issue before us is whether the doctrine of governmental tort immunity shall now be overruled by judicial decision.

We hold that the order for dismissal is affirmed, with the caveat, however, that subject to the limitations we now discuss, the defense of sovereign immunity will no longer be available to school districts, municipal corporations, and other subdivisions of government on whom immunity has been conferred by judicial decision with respect to torts which are committed after the adjournment of the next regular session of the Minnesota Legislature.

All of the paths leading to the origin of governmental tort immunity converge on Russell v. The Men of Devon, 100 Eng. Rep. 359, 2 T.R. 667 (1788). This product of the English common law was left on our doorstep to become the putative ancestor of a long line of American cases beginning with Mower v. Leicester, 9 Mass. 247 (1812). Russell sued all of the male inhabitants of the County of Devon for damages occurring to his wagon by reason of a bridge being out of repair. It was apparently undisputed that the county had a duty to maintain such structures. The court held that the action would not lie because: (1) To permit it would lead to "an infinity of actions" (100 Eng. Rep. 362, 2 T.R. 671), (2) there was no precedent for attempting such a suit, (3) only the legislature should impose liability of this kind, (4) even if defendants are to be considered a corporation or quasi corporation there is no fund out of which to satisfy the claim, (5) neither law nor reason supports the action, (6) there is a strong presumption that what has never been done cannot be done, and (7) although there is a legal principle which permits a remedy for every injury resulting from the neglect of another, a more applicable principle is "that it is better that an individual should sustain an injury than that the public should suffer an inconvenience." The court concluded that the suit should not be permitted "because the action must be brought against the public." There is no mention of the "king can do no wrong," but on the contrary it is suggested that plaintiff sue the county itself rather than its individual inhabitants. Every reason assigned by the court is born of expediency. The wrong to plaintiff is submerged in the convenience of the public. No moral, ethical, or rational reason for the decision is advanced by the court except the practical problem of assessing damages against individual defendants. The court's invitation to the legislature has a familiar ring. It was finally accepted as to claims against the Crown in 1947, although Russell had long since been over-ruled.

In 1812, when Mower's horse was killed by stepping in a hole on the Leicester bridge, counsel argued that "Men of Devon" did not apply since the town of Leicester was incorporated and had a treasury out of which to satisfy a judgment. The Massachusetts court nevertheless held that the town had no notice of the defect and that quasi corporations are not liable for such neglect under the common law. On the authority of "Men of Devon" recovery was denied. It was on this shaky foundation that the law of governmental tort immunity was erected in Minnesota and elsewhere. In 1871 we held that one who was injured by a defective bridge did have a cause of action against a municipal corporation for its negligence, citing "Men of Devon." A few years later we recognized the distinction between municipal corporations and quasi corporations with respect to liability to individuals for the negligence of municipal officers or agents. Without citing any authority we held that a plaintiff injured on a defective courthouse sidewalk could not recover damages against the county, basing our decision on what we said was a long-established doctrine which "the legislature alone should change."

The following year we reverted to "Men of Devon" in finding a town not liable for its negligent failure to repair a bridge, defendant citing also Mower v. Leicester. . . .

Some of the arguments advanced for retaining sovereign tort immunity are these: Stare decisis and stability in the law require it. There are no funds available to satisfy claims. The discretionary activities of adminis-trative officials would be seriously circumscribed by the specter of tort liability for mistakes in judgment. The functions of government are mandatory under our system, involving many dangerous and hazardous undertakings, exposing vast numbers of persons to potential harm. It is a practical impossibility to police all of the activities of school children. Many units of government do not have sufficient resources to absorb a substantial loss without the threat of bankruptcy.

Our consideration of the origins of tort immunity persuade us that its genesis was accidental and was characterized by expediency, and that its continuation has stemmed from inertia. The development of governmen-tal liability for proprietary functions was an acknowledgment that the original rule was unduly restrictive, and reflected an uneasiness in the corporate conscience. No student of the law has suggested any explanation for the arbitrary assumption of legal responsibility for negligence in the maintenance of municipal streets and sidewalks and contemporaneously a rigid adherence to immunity with respect to those maintained by towns and counties. It has been argued on behalf of defendants that if immunity is abolished public schools will be deluged with claims for injuries resulting from inadequate supervision, from frostbite while waiting for buses, from blows struck by other children, from forbidden and mischievous activities impulsively and foolishly inspired, and from a host of other causes. School children have a special status in the eyes of the law and in view of the compulsory attendance statutes deserve more than ordinary protection. Operating an educational system has been described as one of the nation's biggest businesses. The fact that subdivisions of government now enjoy no immunity in a number of areas of activity has not noticeably circumscribed their usefulness or rendered them insolvent, nor have our privately endowed schools and colleges been forced to close their doors . . . because the law has assessed them liability for the negligence of their employees. . . .

We recognize that by denying recovery in the case at bar the remainder of the decision becomes dictum. However, the court is unanimous in expressing its intention to overrule the doctrine of sovereign tort immunity as a defense with respect to tort claims against school districts, municipal corporations, and other subdivisions of government on whom immunity has been conferred by judicial decision arising after the next Minnesota Legislature adjourns, subject to any statutes which now or hereafter limit or regulate the prosecution of such claims. However, we do not suggest that discretionary as distinguished from ministerial activities, or judicial, quasi-judicial, legislative, or quasi-legislative functions may not continue to have the benefit of the rule. Nor is it our purpose to abolish sovereign immunity as to the state itself.

It may appear unfair to deprive the present claimant of his day in court. However, we are of the opinion it would work an even greater injustice to deny defendant and other units of government a defense on which they have had a right to rely. We believe that it is more equitable if they are permitted to plan in advance by securing liability insurance or by creating funds necessary for self-insurance.

LUNA, et al. v. SCHOOL DISTRICT
154 Cal. App. 803, 316 P. (2d) 773 (1957)

Legal Principles
1. The standard of care required of an employee of a school is that which a person of ordinary prudence, charged with his duties, would exercise under the same circumstances.

2. Where a child on a playground is injured while climbing a wall in violation of his teacher's orders, there can be no liability against the teacher for negligence.

Opinion

. . . There was no evidence that any accident had previously happened . . . or that respondent had notice of any dangerous character in the existing condition.

. . . The standard of care required of any officer or employee of such a school is that which a person of ordinary prudence, charged with his duties, would exercise under the same circumstances. Pirkle v. Oakdale Union Grammar School District 40 Cal. 2d 207 (253 P. 2d 1). There is no evidence here as to whether this accident occurred at a recess, whether school had closed for the day, or whether this boy had previously gone out to the main entrance. There is no evidence that the gate was used only as a service gate or that it was not used for the ingress or egress of kindergarten pupils. So far as appears from the record, school may have closed and there may have been no more than two other pupils there, aside from the boy who was hurt. The accident occurred while the boy was climbing the wall by the action of another boy who may have been merely on his way out of the gate. There is no evidence as to what the teacher was doing at the time or how long she had been in the room. There was no substantial evidence to show negligence on the part of the teacher, and negligence could not be inferred from the mere fact that the accident occurred on school ground while the teacher was not at the particular spot at that moment. There is no evidence that would justify the inference that this teacher should reasonably have expected not only that this boy would climb this wall but that his hand would slip at the very moment another boy was moving the gate. (Ford v. Riverside City School District, 121 Cal. App. 2d 554 (263 P. 2d 626.) This is the sort of accident that could happen at any door or gate, one which could well happen in spite of any possible supervision, and there was no substantial evidence that this injury was proximately caused by any negligence on the part of the respondent or its employees. Under the circumstances shown by the record the motion for a nonsuit was properly granted. . . .

United States
Supreme Court
Cases Review

THE DARTMOUTH COLLEGE CHARTER

Trustees of Dartmouth College v. Woodward

4 Wheat. 518 (U.S. 1819)

Majority opinion delivered by Chief Justice John Marshall

Dartmouth College was founded in the colony of New Hampshire in 1769. At this time the British granted to the college a charter which established authority for the school. After New Hampshire became a state, and due in part to political reasons, the legislature, in 1816, proceeded to reorganize the college for the purpose of bringing it under state control. The college trustees opposed the legislative act and a conflict arose.

The Supreme Court finally settled the problem when it held the charter of Dartmouth College to be an inviolable contract as defined in the Constitution of the United States. Chief Justice Marshall stated that: (1) the contract was protected by the Constitution, and (2) it had been impaired by the legislative act. Thus the decision of the state court of New Hampshire was reversed. The charter granted to Dartmouth College was in the nature of a contract, the terms of which could be changed only with the consent of those to whom it had been granted.

COLLECTION AND APPROPRIATION OF SCHOOL FUNDS

Springfield Township v. Quick

22 How. 56 (U.S. 1859)

Majority opinion delivered by Justice Catron

The "Land Ordinance" of 1785 dealing with the Northwest Territory reserved the 16th section of every township for the support of township schools. In 1826 Congress granted states the right to sell this land provided: (1) the township involved would consent, and (2) the money would be spent for school funds.

In 1855 the state of Indiana passed a law stating that township schools being supported by proceeds from their own lands should not receive additional money from the state until all other schools were receiving proportionately equal funds. Springfield Township protested this law and obtained an injunction against it. The state supreme court removed the injunction and the Supreme Court of the United States upheld this judgment.

Justice Catron delivered the opinion of the Court, saying that the state was not obligated to provide additional funds to a township receiving a bounty from Congress as long as that township's school had funds equal to, or higher than, other schools of the state. Thus the administration of consolidated funds by the state for the purpose of school support and equalization throughout the state was upheld.

INSTRUCTION BY CORRESPONDENCE AS INTERSTATE COMMERCE

International Text-Book Co. v. Pigg

217 U.S. 91, 30 Sup. Ct. 481 (1910)

Majority opinion delivered by Justice Harlan

International Text-Book Co. in Pennsylvania dealt in correspondence courses. In 1905, a Mr. Pigg from Kansas subscribed to a course in commercial law, but then failed to pay for it. A Kansas statute required any corporation doing business in the state for profit to file a detailed annual report showing the condition of that corporation. Failure to do this prohibited said corporation from doing further business in the state.

The company held that its business was by nature interstate and thus was not affected by the Kansas statute.

The Court ruled that even though this business was of an exceptional nature, it did involve commerce among the states. The Court also ruled that a valid contract had been made between Mr. Pigg and the company, the fulfillment of which involved interstate commerce. With Justice Harlan delivering the opinion of the Court, it was held that communication and business of this nature, and contracts related to it, was commerce among the states and could not be unnecessarily interfered with by the state.

FEDERAL TAXATION OF STATE EDUCATIONAL
INTERESTS-TARIFF ON IMPORTS

University of Illinois v. United States

289 U.S. 48, 53 Sup. Ct. 509 (1933)

Majority opinion delivered by Chief Justice Hughes

The state of Illinois felt that because one of its agencies used articles imported from a foreign country, the articles should not be subject to an import tax due to the sovereignty of that state. Scientific apparatus had been imported for use at the university and the state felt that it was entitled to import the articles free of duty.

The Court felt that under the Constitution, Congress' power to levy taxes has only one exception—that exports from a state may not be taxed. Even though our dual system of government may imply immunity of state agencies from federal taxation, this does not limit the power of Congress to control commerce with foreign nations. Thus the state is not rendered independent of federal power and the authority of Congress over foreign commerce and import duties. If this were not so, the idea of a single control over national matters, which was created by the Constitution, would be destroyed.

FEDERAL TAXATION OF STATE EDUCATIONAL INTERESTS-EXCISE ON GATE RECEIPTS

Allen v. Regents of University System of Georgia

304 U.S. 439, 58 Sup. Ct. 980 (1938)

Majority opinion delivered by Justice Roberts

Georgia University officials claimed that having to pay a federal excise tax on admission receipts was a burden on a part of the educational program. They felt that since the proceeds went to the support of the educational institution, and since this was a state agency, the agency should have tax immunity.

The Court held that deviations from the ordinary functions of state government were subject to a federal tax, citing the federal liquor tax as an example. The conduct of any business which is comparable to those usually conducted by private businessmen causes a state to forfeit any tax immunities and in turn be treated as a private concern. By entering a business which would normally be taxable, the state is exercising a governmental power which does not render it immune to federal taxation.

(On April 1, 1954, Public Law No. 324 was released. This law held that admission to regular athletic events would be excluded from federal taxes, providing the proceeds were used for the institution sponsoring the event. Post-season events, however, were still subject to the tax.)

TEACHER TENURE, STATUTORY

Phelps v. Board of Education

300 U.S. 319, 57 Sup. Ct. 483 (1937)

Majority opinion delivered by Justice Roberts

During the depression years many school boards found it necessary to reduce teachers' salaries. This case arose when a teacher from New Jersey claimed that the tenure status which he had achieved was contractual in nature and could not be impaired by the legislation, which sought to reduce his salary.

The Court ruled that public positions do not establish contractual obligations, but instead fall under statutory terms, which may be regulated by the legislature. The nature of the contract and certain qualifying phrases such as "during good behavior" establish the right and responsibility of the legislature to exercise such rules and regulations as are needed for the efficient operation of the public trust. As long as all teachers of like qualifications are treated the same, with no individual discriminations being made, the legislature may take any reasonable action to operate the schools.

TEACHER TENURE, CONTRACTUAL

Indiana ex rel. Anderson v. Brand

303 U.S. 95, 58 Sup. Ct. 443 (1938)

Majority opinion delivered by Justice Roberts

In 1927 the state of Indiana adopted the Teachers' Tenure Law. A teacher who served, under contract, for five or more consecutive years was recognized as a permanent teacher with an indefinite contract. Specific reasons were listed as causes for dismissal—incompetency, insubordination, etc.—but political and personal reasons were not among those listed. In 1933 the legislature amended this act to omit township school corporations. Brand was informed that she was not to be re-hired for 1933–4, but then was permitted to teach anyway, and was again threatened the following year in the same manner.

The Court held that the legislative enactment of 1927 creating the Teachers' Tenure Law contained provisions which, when accepted by both parties, involved a contract. Thus, the legislature could not, by a subsequent act, pass any law which would alter agreements formerly entered into by the parties involved. While the laws made by one legislature may be repealed or changed by a later one, certain provisions in said law may, when accepted by two parties, create a contract which may not be abridged.

TEACHER RETIREMENT, STATUTORY

Dodge v. Board of Education of Chicago

302 U.S. 74, 58 Sup. Ct. 98 (1937)

Majority opinion delivered by Justice Roberts

This case involves an Illinois plan known as the Miller Law, which dealt with retirement provisions for teachers. This plan was effected entirely through the use of public funds, since the teachers made no contributions of their own to the fund. This was an important point made by the Court in its decision to uphold the state's action.

In 1935 an amendment to the plan lowered the retirement age and also reduced the annuities. These reduced annuities affected not only teachers who subsequently retired, but also those who had previously retired. Those previously retired contended that this was a violation of a contract and therefore should be repealed.

The Court held that the legislative act setting up the retirement plan was statutory in nature, that it did not create private contractual or vested rights, but merely declared a policy to be pursued by the legislature. "If, upon a construction of the statute, it is found that the payments are gratuities, involving no agreement of the parties, the grant of them creates no vested right." Thus no contract had been formed.

(Had a joint-contributory retirement system been set up, the member, by direct participation in creating the fund, would have secured for himself a vested right which could not have been impaired by the legislature.)

SECTARIAN INSTRUCTION NEED NOT BE INCLUDED IN A COURSE OF STUDY (THE GIRARD COLLEGE CASE)

Vidal v. Girard's Executors

2 How. 127 (U.S. 1844)

Majority opinion delivered by Justice Story

Stephan Girard was an immigrant who became very wealthy after coming to America. In 1831 he died leaving an estate of some six million dollars. A part of his will left some real estate and two million dollars for the purpose of establishing a college for poor, male orphans. Some of his relatives, disappointed at not getting more than they received, seized upon a stipulation that no sect, person representing a sect, or course promulgating a sect be allowed in the college, as grounds for breaking the will since it was repugnant to the Christian religion. They also contended that the city of Philadelphia could not accept a legal bequest of real estate.

It was brought out during the trial that Girard had not forbidden the teaching of Christian principles by the college instructors. The Court then noted, in a unanimous opinion, that this charitable donation was not derogatory to Christianity nor was it opposed to any known policy of the state of Pennsylvania. There was no law questioned here. The Court merely refused to question a will which had created an endowment for a college and provided that no religion be taught or any cleric be permitted on the school property.

INDIANS' TRIBAL FUNDS FOR PAROCHIAL SCHOOLS

Quick Bear v. Leupp

210 U.S. 50, 28 Sup. Ct. 690 (1908)

Majority opinion delivered by Justice Fuller

Charles E. Leupp, Commissioner of Indian Affairs on the Rosebud Agency in South Dakota, made a contract with the Bureau of Catholic Indian Missions in Washington, D.C. for the purpose of educating a number of Indian pupils. Payment for this was to be made from the Sioux treaty fund, trust fund, or both. Some of the Indians protested any use of funds for sectarian education. They declared that the Commissioner's action, in behalf of the Indians, violated the policy of the government to make no appropriation for education in any sectarian school.

The Commissioner declared that appropriations of public moneys were not involved, but that money belonging to the Indians as a matter of right was being used. The Court upheld the action and view of the Commissioner. The United States had entered into treaties with the Indians, under which the Indians gave up certain lands and other rights when promised aid from the government. The trust funds and treaty funds belonged to the Indians as a result of such treaties. Thus they were not the same as a congressional appropriation. A portion of the Court's opinion stated that it is ". . . the moral right of the Indians to have this 'trust fund' applied to the education of the Indians in schools of their choice, . . ." This was the only money which the Indians could claim as theirs, and even though it wasn't delivered directly to them, they have the privilege of directing its expenditure for their benefit.

FREE TEXTBOOKS FOR PRIVATE SCHOOLS

Cochran v. Louisiana State Board of Education

281 U.S. 370, 50 Sup. Ct. 335 (1930)

Majority opinion delivered by Chief Justice Hughes

Louisiana, which has a heavy Catholic population, had a statute which provided free textbooks to all school children regardless of what school they attended. When the statute was questioned, the state court upheld the law, declaring that it was the children and not the schools which benefited from the law. All school children in the state were meant to be included within the meaning of the statute.

The Supreme Court of the United States sustained Louisiana's action of using public funds for this purpose and developed the "child benefit theory." In this case the books aided all children and since they were not religious in nature, could not be construed as useful to any particular religion or sect. Thus, there was no violation of any law dealing with the separation of education and religion. Had a book of specifically religious nature been provided by the state, the opinion would probably have been different. The interest of the legislature is that of education in general. It does not have the power, in this situation, to interfere with, or to segregate, any private school.

Some, however, still question this decision, wondering if, in fact, the schools in question actually did benefit from the provision of the textbooks.

FREE BUS TRANSPORTATION FOR PAROCHIAL SCHOOLS

Everson v. Board of Education

330 U.S. 1, Sup. 67 Ct. 504 (1947)

Majority opinion delivered by Justice Black

In the state of New Jersey a statute was passed making it possible for school authorities to reimburse parents of children attending parochial schools, in this case Catholic. Everson, a taxpayer in the school district in question, challenged the right of the school board to make payments of reimbursements to parents sending their children to Catholic schools. The language of the statute was also cited, since it expressly indicated the inclusion of parochial schools within its scope, but excluded any school operated in whole or in part for profit.

The state court upheld the statute and Everson appealed the Supreme Court. The Court, in affirming the previous decision, enlarged upon the "child benefit theory" by reasoning that the tax money used in this manner did not necessarily benefit the parochial school but did serve the state's purpose of providing education without regard to religion. In part, the majority opinion stated that the Constitution requires the state to be neutral in matters regarding religion, but not an adversary of religion. This specific legislation aids parents only in getting their children to and from school. It does not aid or promote religion or the parochial school itself.

However, the Court itself was sharply divided on the issue, since in this case one particular group benefited while others were seemingly excluded. A second point of controversy was that the majority of the Court assumed that the township involved was rightly concerned with a type of service which in actuality it should not have been concerned with— namely furnishing transportation, since in this case the buses were operated by the public transportation system.

COMPULSORY MILITARY TRAINING IN A STATE UNIVERSITY

Pearson v. Coale

290 U.S. 597, 54 Sup. Ct. 131 (1933)

Per curiam decision

This case deals with a requirement of the University of Maryland making it obligatory that male students enroll in the ROTC program. Coale was a member of the Methodist Episcopal Church, which had recently passed a resolution opposing this program and urging that Methodists be exempt from the program. Coale refused to participate and was suspended until he would comply with the requirement. The university was upheld by the state court. The appeal from here to the Supreme Court (federal) was dismissed because the facts of the case provided no reason to question the university's action.

However, a later case arising in California was more skillfully developed and the Court did reach a decision concerning a similar question.

UPHOLDING RIGHT OF UNIVERSITY TO REQUIRE MILITARY TRAINING OF STUDENTS

Hamilton v. Regents of the University of California

293 U.S. 245, 55 Sup. Ct. 197 (1934)

Majority opinion delivered by Justice Butler

The University of California had a requirement that all physically able male students must take military training. This regulation was an effect of the state's acceptance of the terms in the Morrill Act of 1862. In 1933, two young men, both sons of ordained Methodist ministers, enrolled, but refused to comply with the military requirement on the grounds of conscientious objection. The courts of California consistently upheld the requirement of the university and the case was taken to the Federal Supreme Court.

The Court upheld the previous court action, stating that neither the rights of religion nor the privileges and immunities of private citizens were impaired by the university requirement. Not doubting the sincerity of the students' assertions, the Court held that nothing unconstitutional had occurred and that the students did not have to attend the university in question.

The Court went further to make a distinction between the military training requirement and actual military service, saying that Congress had made provisions to exempt conscientious objectors and that fulfillment of the university requirement did not imply later military service. It was also pointed out that Congress, not the Constitution, exempted conscientious objectors, and that the spirit of the Constitution implied the obligation of all citizens to defend their country. Thus the university requirement was not in conflict with the Federal Constitution.

COMPULSORY FLAG SALUTING

Minersville School District v. Gobitis

310 U.S. 586, 60 Sup. Ct. 1011 (1940)

Majority opinion delivered by Justice Frankfurter

The question involved in this case was whether or not compulsory flag saluting violated the individual's freedom of religious belief. It arose when the school district passed a rule that students should participate in a ceremony designed to promote national loyalty and unity. Gobitis was a member of the Jehovah's Witness sect, which opposed any recognition of "graven images," which in this instance was the flag. They would declare their respect, but would not salute it. The state courts upheld the religious convictions of Gobitis and the school district appealed the Supreme Court. In reaching its decision, the Court actually circumvented the idea of religious freedom involved in the First Amendment and based its decision on the idea that a state had the right to set up and demand certain acts in maintaining national feeling and unity. In approaching the case from this angle, the Court reversed the decisions of the state courts and upheld the rule of the school district.

Recognizing that claims of liberty versus claims of authority both involve fundamental rights, the Court felt that in order to maintain a country in which the rights and privileges afforded by the Constitution would be upheld, it is sometimes necessary to subordinate individual liberty to the authority of the state. The holding of religious convictions does not relieve an individual from his political responsibilities. Three years later, however, the Court was to reverse its decision made here.

COMPULSORY FLAG SALUTE BY PUPILS INVALID

West Virginia State Board of Education v. Barnette

319 U.S. 624, 63 Sup. Ct. 1178 (1943)

Majority opinion delivered by Justice Jackson

This case is similar to the one just mentioned concerning compulsory flag saluting. The outcome was different, however, because it was approached from a different viewpoint. In the case of *Minersville School*

District v. Gobitis, the Court recognized but did not consider the idea of religious freedom, but instead based its decision upon rights belonging to the state. In the present case the Court faced the religious issue and decided that the state of West Virginia had unconstitutionally invaded "the sphere of intellect and spirit which it is the purpose of the First Amendment of our Constitution to reserve from all official control."

Some differences do exist in the two cases. Here the ruling was made by the state rather than the local board. Also, and probably more significant, is the fact that parents could be held accountable for refusal to comply, whereas in the earlier case the child was expelled but no further action was designated. The Court felt that an "affirmation of belief and an attitude of mind" could not be regulated or enforced against an individual or a group. Refusal to perform the act in question did not interfere with the rights and privileges of any other person.

The Court also pointed out that the Congress of the United States had dealt with similar questions concerning conscientious objectors and made such acts voluntary. Concerning national unity, the Court held that persuasion and example, but not force or coercion, were permissible. The use of compulsion to promote nationalism has proven throughout history to be futile.

Thus, according to the Court's decision, schools could include, and even require, patriotic exercises in their programs as long as those with true conscientious objections were excused from the exercises.

RELEASED TIME FOR ON-PREMISE RELIGIOUS INSTRUCTION

Illinois ex rel. McCollum v. Board of Education

333 U.S. 203, 68 Sup. Ct. 461 (1948)

Majority opinion delivered by Justice Black

In 1940 the school board of Champaign, Illinois, permitted religious instruction to be held in the schools for those children whose parents signed "request cards." Any religious group could participate. An organization representing Catholic, Jewish, and some Protestant faiths sponsored the program, which was held during school hours. Attendance was compulsory only for those designated by parents.

McCollum, an atheist, claimed that this program made her son conspicuous and left him open to ridicule. The state court affirmed the decision of a lower court which had dismissed her petition, so an appeal was accepted by the Federal Supreme Court.

The Court ruled that the use of tax-supported property and the use of time designated for secular education, plus the close cooperation of public school officials, violated the establishment of religion clause in the Constitution. The fact that school attendance was compulsory was also cited as being an aid to the religious group because it, in a sense, provided the group to be instructed.

It should be noted that the Court did not take away the right of a school to study ethics and the values of religion, but it did remove the spreading of specific religious principles or, as it might be phrased, the indoctrination of a group in religious principles.

RELEASED TIME FOR OFF-PREMISE RELIGIOUS INSTRUCTION

Zorach v. Clauson

343 U.S. 306, 72 Sup. Ct. 679 (1952)

Majority opinion delivered by Justice Douglas

This case is similar to the *McCollum* case from Illinois in that religious instruction of public school students takes place during regular school hours. There are two differences, however, which were significant to the Court. First, the religious instruction took place in private premises; and second, there was little real cooperation between school authorities and the religious groups.

Zorach (and Gluck), taxpayers and residents of New York City, challenged the right of a school board ruling which permitted a "released-time" program of religious instruction. This took place during public school hours, but away from the school building. The *McCollum* case was cited as setting a precedent for the charge that the ruling by the school board was unconstitutional, but the New York Court of Appeals distinguished it from the *McCollum* case and upheld the school board ruling.

The Supreme Court held that no one was forced to attend the religious instructions, that this was no different from the practice of excusing students for various holy day observances, and that the school system itself was not using coercion or in any way providing the religious instructors with an audience. All that was required was an excuse explaining where the student was, which is the procedure followed in case of any absence. Thus the ruling of the lower court was sustained.

TEACHERS' FREEDOM OF SPEECH AND
ANTI-SUBVERSIVE LEGISLATION

Adler v. Board of Education

342 U.S. 485, 72 Sup. Ct. 380 (1952)

Majority opinion delivered by Justice Minton

This case arose not because of any overt action, but because of a challenge on the part of a school teacher, against the ruling of a legislative act. In 1948, the state of New York passed the Feinberg law, which was designed to keep subversive influences out of the schools. This law consisted of three major parts. The board of regents was made responsible for enforcement of the law, for making a list of organizations held to be subversive and the membership of any organization, plus an annual report to the legislature concerning any action taken with respect to this law.

Adler, with others, obtained an injunction against the school board's enforcement of the law, but various other state courts reversed this decision, and then upheld the reversal. The Federal Supreme Court also sustained the reversal, holding that no constitutional violation had been made. In part the Court said that employees have no right to employment upon their terms, but must abide by the rules and decisions of their employer. As long as reasonable terms were laid down by the proper authorities, no usurpation of individual freedoms had been made. The fact that the school was an agency of the state did not mean that it was unable to require its employees to prove their conduct fit for public service. The Court did not agree that the guilt of a teacher should be confirmed only by overt acts, but held that membership in an organization advocating forceable overthrow of the government indicated support of its ideas. This, in turn, was reason enough to prohibit employment of such a person in the public schools. This was not a denial of individual freedom, since a person did not have to accept employment under these terms if they were repugnant to him.

TEACHERS' FREEDOM OF SPEECH AND LOYALTY OATHS

Wieman v. Updegraf

344 U.S. 183, 73 Sup. Ct. 215 (1952)

Majority opinion delivered by Justice Clark

The state of Oklahoma passed a statute which had a purpose similar to that of the Feinberg law in New York. In this case, the Court held that the law was invalid because of a conflict with the "due process" clause of the Fourteenth Amendment. This decision should not be taken as a reversal of the Court's earlier opinion in the *Adler* case however, since there was a difference involved in the specific laws. The Oklahoma law required subscription to a loyalty oath which had omitted the "knowingly" clause; that is, it overlooked the possibility that an innocent person may have belonged to a subversive group unknowingly, or he may have joined the group, then, at a later date when he became aware of the group's character, severed relationship with the group. The law was challenged on four points. It was said to be a bill of attainder, an *ex post facto* law, an impairment of contracts, and violation of the "due process" clause.

The Court held that a state could not bar employment solely on the basis of organizational membership and disregard a person's lack of knowledge concerning the organization to which he belonged. Teachers must have freedom of thought, inquiry, and action in order to interpret and impart knowledge and ideas of the differing facets of their society and the world. This is not meant as encouragement to join subversive groups but to protect a teacher who may become innocently involved while pursuing new ideas.

From the two previous cases, three inferences may be drawn. The Court may: (1) refuse to countenance guilt by association; (2) hold invalid those loyalty oaths which penalize teachers for innocent affiliation with organizations listed as subversive; and (3) uphold those loyalty oaths which penalize teachers knowingly affiliated with such organizations.

CENSORSHIP OF EDUCATIONAL MATERIALS
OFFENSIVE TO RELIGIOUS GROUPS

Burstyn v. Wilson

343 U.S. 495, 72 Sup. Ct. 777 (1952)

Majority opinion delivered by Justice Clark

This case involves the question of censorship and the right of a state to refuse a license to show motion pictures which are deemed obscene, immoral, etc. This question becomes involved with education because of the increasing use of motion pictures as instructional materials. In this case certain school officials were involved because they were serving as censors. Catholics had objected to the showing of an Italian production called *The Miracle,* claiming that it was sacrilegious.

The state courts of New York upheld the censors' ruling that the film should not be shown, but upon appeal, this decision was reversed by the Supreme Court. The Court was concerned mainly with the old principle of a free press. It recognized the fact that films, like other means of communication, could be harmful, but felt that films enjoyed the same freedoms as those of a newspaper. The Court looked with disfavor upon the New York statute involved because it provided for a prior restraint to be used, allowing censors complete control over the matter and leaving no responsibility with the film producer or the person responsible for showing the film.

Many different groups can claim that something is derogatory to them because of something which may have evolved from a film or a book, even though no such intent or purpose was meant. Only if maliciousness is directly intended can a censor be placed on that material.

CONTROL OVER SECRET SOCIETIES IN SCHOOLS

Waugh v. Mississippi University

237 U.S. 589, 35 Sup. Ct. 720 (1915)

Majority opinion delivered by Justice McKenna

J. P. Waugh, a citizen of Mississippi, had applied for admission to the state university law department. One requirement for admission was that he renounce his affiliation with Kappa Sigma, a Greek-letter fraternity, because of state legislation which required students transferring to Mississippi University to disavow allegiance to all fraternities. Mr. Waugh alleged that he was being deprived of property rights and happiness protected by the Fourteenth Amendment. A county court decided in favor of Mr. Waugh, but the state court reversed the decision. The Federal Supreme Court later upheld the reversal.

The state legislation was universal, prohibiting all societies. It was not retroactive, however, which meant that those belonging to such societies before the legislation was passed were permitted to retain membership. The Court said that the right to attend the university was a conditional right, not an absolute one, and the state had the privilege of imposing regulations providing for the discipline and welfare of the school. As the Court said, "It is not for us to entertain conjectures in opposition to the views of the state, and annul its regulations upon disputable considerations of their wisdom or necessity." The right of "life, liberty, and happiness" are, in some degree, by necessity, limited by law.

COMPULSORY VACCINATION OF SCHOOL CHILDREN

Zucht v. King

260 U.S. 174, 43 Sup. Ct. 24 (1922)

Majority opinion delivered by Justice Brandeis

The city of San Antonio, Texas, passed an ordinance requiring a certificate of vaccination as a condition of entering school. Zucht refused to comply, was barred from public school, and also caused to be excluded from a private school. An injunction against enforcement of the ordinance, a writ compelling admission, and damages, were sought but denied. The denial was upheld by the Federal Supreme Court.

In 1905, the case of *Jacobson v. Massachusetts* had dealt with the same question and was cited here. In agreement with this decision, the Court held that public officials had the right and responsibility to require vaccination as a means of protecting the public health. This right is contained in the police power of the state and is used as a means of protecting the general welfare of the people. Thus, even in the absence of an epidemic, provided there is legislation to this effect, the state may require enforcement of compulsory vaccination.

RIGHTS OF TEACHERS AND PARENTS IN THE MATTER OF FOREIGN LANGUAGE INSTRUCTION

Meyer v. Nebraska

262 U.S. 390, 43 Sup. Ct. 625 (1923)

Majority opinion delivered by Justice McReynolds

On April 9, 1919, the state of Nebraska passed an act relating to the use and instruction of foreign language in the schools. No person, in any type of school, could teach in a foreign language nor could a foreign language be taught as a course until a student reached the ninth grade.

Meyer, a teacher in a Lutheran parochial school, taught German reading to a ten-year-old boy and thus violated the state law regarding this. The courts of Nebraska upheld the law, but the Federal Supreme Court ruled it in violation of the liberty guaranteed in the Fourteenth Amendment. The legislation was arbitrary and without reasonable purpose. Had the use or knowledge of a foreign language intimated harm or danger to the citizens of Nebraska, then this would have been a valid exercise of police power. But mere use or knowledge was not thought to be harmful.

The courts of Nebraska had ruled that the ancient, or dead, languages —Latin, Greek, Hebrew—were not included in the spirit of the legislation. The Supreme Court took this as an unlawful interference with the modern-language teachers and therefore denied the liberty of parents to control their children's education and of teachers to follow their chosen occupation.

The Court emphasized its desire to allow the state to retain control over the curriculum, organization, and functions of its educational systems, but held that the state, as well as the federal government was restricted by certain fundamental liberties of the individual person.

RIGHT OF ATTENDANCE AT PRIVATE SCHOOLS
(THE OREGON CASE)

Pierce v. Society of the Sisters of the Holy Names of Jesus and Mary

(and Pierce v. Hill Military Academy)

268 U.S. 510, 45 Sup. Ct. 571 (1925)

Majority opinion delivered by Justice McReynolds

During the wave of nationalism and prosperity which followed World War I, many efforts to make the world safe for democracy went too far. Such was the case concerning a law passed in Oregon on November 7, 1922, to become effective in 1926. It stated, with minor exceptions, that children of school age must be sent to the public schools in their district. Two Oregon corporations mentioned above received an injunction from the U. S. District Court in Oregon and the Supreme Court upheld the injunction.

The question of religion played very little part in the reasons given by the Court in upholding the decision of the lower court. Again, as in the *Meyer* case, the Court stated that it would not interfere with the power of the state to reasonably regulate its schools. However, the Oregon statute unreasonably hampered the business and property of the appellees without due process of law, constituting a violation of the Fourteenth Amendment. The Court felt that as long as a private or parochial school develops competent and intelligent citizens, the needs of the state have been met, and in such a case the state may not require children to attend the public schools.

RIGHT OF ATTENDANCE AT FOREIGN LANGUAGE SCHOOLS

Farrington v. Tokushige

273 U.S. 284, 47 Sup. Ct. 406 (1927)

(and Stainback v. Mo Hock Ke Lok Po)

336 U.S. 368, 69 Sup. Ct. 606 (1949)

Majority opinion delivered by Justice McReynolds

Through a series of acts beginning in 1920, the territorial legislature of Hawaii sought to limit foreign language schools in the territory. According to the acts, only pupils who regularly attended a public school or an approved private school, or had completed the eighth grade, or were over fourteen years of age, could attend a foreign language school, which conducted lessons in the speaking, reading, and writing of Japanese for one hour every day in each grade. Japanese parents received an injunction against enforcement of the act on grounds that it illegally deprived them of liberty and property since nothing contrary to American principles was taught at the schools.

The Supreme Court upheld the injunction, ruling that the law went beyond reasonable regulation and interfered with the parents' right of educating their children. The Court also felt that this action would probably destroy the schools, thus taking away property for no just cause.

(Since the Fourteenth Amendment is a limitation on states, only the Fifth Amendment was cited here because Congress is responsible for the territories.)

After World War II, a similar question arose, this time concerning the instruction of Chinese. The statute involved barred any foreign language instruction before a child went through four years of school. The Court cited the *Meyer* case, which granted the right of parents to educate their children in a foreign language. It was also stated that the right to teach was God-given and not normally subject to state limitation, and that the right to teach was also a property right.

The *Stainback* case, however, was not accepted by the Supreme Court because of procedural grounds.

SCHOOL AUTHORITIES MAY TEMPORARILY SUSPEND FOR ECONOMIC REASONS THE NEGRO HIGH SCHOOL ALONE

Cumming v. County Board of Education

175 U.S. 528, 20 Sup. Ct. 197 (1899)

Majority opinion delivered by Justice Harlan

During a time of economic stress the school board of Richmond County, Georgia, suspended support of a Negro high school, while maintaining the white school and a Negro elementary school. An injunction was sought to stop support of the white high school if the Negro high school was not to be maintained. A local court granted the injunction, but the state supreme court reversed the action of the lower court, and this decision was upheld by the Federal Supreme Court.

The Court gave the impression through its decision that had the Negroes used a different approach in their action, they might have been successful. Had they demanded establishment of a school for Negroes rather than the abandonment of the school for whites, and had the authorities' refusal of the demands appeared arbitrary, a different decision might have arisen. This, however, seems to be a weak stand and points out the fact that the Court did not want to interfere with the state's right of controlling its educational systems.

SEGREGATED INSTRUCTION MAY BE IMPOSED ON A CHARTERED PRIVATE SCHOOL

Berea College v. Commonwealth of Kentucky

211 U.S. 45, 29 Sup. Ct. 33 (1908)

Majority opinion delivered by Justice Brewer

Berea College was chartered by the state of Kentucky as a coeducational, non-denominational school. It admitted both white and Negro students equally. In 1904 a state law was passed making it unlawful to operate integrated schools. Berea College was convicted under this law and the conviction was upheld by the Federal Supreme Court.

The question involved was whether or not the state had the right to make such a regulation and, if so, was such a regulation constitutional. The Court felt that no violation of the Federal Constitution had been made, that the state court of Kentucky had already ruled no violation of the state laws, and that the state had the right to regulate its own corporations. The Court agreed with the statement that Berea College had no natural right to teach, but existed solely at the pleasure of the state itself.

There was also a question of individual versus corporation raised and the interpretation was that a corporation was not entitled to the same rights that the individual could claim. Thus a statute which might violate the Constitution when applied to an individual may not be a violation when applied to a corporation created by the state.

A CHINESE CHILD MAY BE CLASSIFIED AS COLORED FOR SCHOOL SEGREGATION PURPOSES

Gong Lum v. Rice

275 U.S. 78, 48 Sup. Ct. 91 (1927)

Majority opinion delivered by Chief Justice Taft

This case involves not the legality of segregation in the public schools, which has been previously established, but the decision as to what constitutes "colored" as defined in relation to the segregation of the schools. Martha Lum was pure Chinese, born a U.S. citizen. She was denied admittance in the white public schools of Mississippi and instead was pointed to the availability of the colored public schools or the private schools.

The state held that she came under the classification of "colored" as opposed to "white" and was therefore not permitted to enter the white school. Since a colored public school was maintained in every county, she was not being deprived of the equal opportunity which was afforded her as a U.S. citizen.

The Supreme Court upheld this viewpoint. Again it pointed out the right and power of the state to maintain and regulate its own schools within limits of reasonability. The Court felt that there was no new question involved here; that this was able to be settled by the state legislature without federal intervention. Thus, the constitutionality of the "separate but equal" doctrine was still adhered to as being compatible with the Fourteenth Amendment.

EQUAL OPPORTUNITY FOR A LEGAL EDUCATION MUST BE PROVIDED WITHIN A STATE'S OWN BORDERS

Missouri ex rel. Gaines v. Canada

305 U.S. 337, 59 Sup. Ct. 232 (1938)

Majority opinion delivered by Chief Justice Hughes

Lloyd Gaines was a Negro citizen of Missouri who had graduated from Lincoln University and wished to enter law school, which was not offered there. He applied for admission at the University of Missouri, but was denied admission because of his race. He was offered tuition fees to attend an out-of-state school comparable to the University of Missouri, but instead sought a writ of mandamus to gain admission at Missouri. The court refused his petition.

The Supreme Court accepted this case in order to determine whether the constitutional provision of equal protection was satisfied or not. The Court felt that Missouri was evading its responsibilities by utilizing out-of-state institutions because each state is required to provide equal opportunity within its own borders. The duty of the state is to furnish training to its residents on the basis of an equality of right, and color is not a valid consideration in establishing a question of right. A state may fulfill constitutional requirements only within itself; ". . . the obligation of the state to give the protection of equal laws can be performed only where its laws operate, that is, within its own jurisdiction."

The Court denied the university's right to exclude Gaines and held the state responsible for failing to provide an equal opportunity for all. However, this decision did not make the practice of offering to pay out-of-state tuition to Negroes illegal, and, if this proved acceptable to both parties, it could still be done.

WHITE AND COLORED PUBLIC SCHOOL TEACHERS SIMILARLY SITUATED AND QUALIFIED MUST BE PAID EQUAL SALARIES

Alston v. School Board of the City of Norfolk

311 U.S. 693, 61 Sup. Ct. 75 (1940)

Majority opinion delivered by Judge Parker

This case was never really heard by the Supreme Court for the purpose of rendering a decision because the Court sustained a judgment given by the U.S. Circuit Court of Appeals and refused a petition to review the case.

A Negro school teacher in Norfolk claimed that he was being paid less although he was equally prepared and qualified. He claimed this was a violation of the "due process" and "equal protection" laws of the Constitution. At first the U.S. District Court dismissed the case on the grounds that a contract had been made and this limited action to the two parties involved. Upon appeal to the circuit court, however, a decision was rendered according to three questions. (1) Had the school board shown unconstitutional discrimination in fixing the salaries? (2) Were the individual's rights thereby infringed? (3) Had right of complaint been waived by the signing of a contract?

The Court ruled that unconstitutional discrimination had been shown, that the individual's rights were denied, and that the individual still had the right to seek correction of a wrong. All citizens are equal before the law and this action by the school board was a direct violation of the Fourteenth Amendment.

OPPORTUNITY FOR A LEGAL EDUCATION MUST BE PROVIDED ONE RACE AS SOON AS ANOTHER

Sipuel v. Oklahoma Board of Regents

332 U.S. 631, 68 Sup. Ct. 299 (1948)

(and Fisher v. Hurst)

333 U.S. 147, 68 Sup. Ct. 389 (1948)

A per curiam decision

In 1946 Oklahoma had only one state-supported law school. When Ada Sipuel was refused admittance because of her race, an appeal was taken to the courts. The state courts upheld the university's standing, so the case reached the Federal Supreme Court. Here the state court's decision was reversed. The Court referred to the *Gaines* case ten years earlier and declared the equal rights guaranteed by the Constitution were being violated. The state attempted to point out a difference between the two cases by saying that Sipuel had given no advance warning of her intent to enter school and thus there had been no time to prepare separate but equal facilities.

The Court stated that this had no bearing on the case. The university must be prepared to offer the same education to all people at the same time. An attempt to do this immediately resulted in a temporary "law school" in the state capitol building staffed by a faculty of three. Sipuel refused to attend because it was not accredited.

Again the Court was appealed, this time by Mrs. Fisher, who had earlier been Miss Sipuel. Here the Court refused to accept the case because of no new issues being raised, but it did stand firm on its first ruling against the state of Oklahoma.

FACILITIES AND SERVICES FOR A LEGAL EDUCATION MUST BE TRULY EQUAL

Sweatt v. Painter

339 U.S. 629, 70 Sup. Ct. 848 (1950)

Majority opinion delivered by Chief Justice Vinson

The circumstances of this case are similar to those of some earlier cases, but with the final decision rendered, the Supreme Court, although not reversing the ruling in *Plessy v. Ferguson,* came closer to the opinion that separate facilities must be truly, or in all respects, equal. Merely the idea or token establishment of equal facilities was no longer enough.

The Court refused to consider this case as one whose decision would have broad effects covering all other similar situations, but kept this issue narrow, that is, related to this case only. The University of Texas Law School had refused admission to the petitioner solely on the grounds of his race. At that time no law school for Negroes existed in Texas. The state realized that this was a denial of equal rights, but continued the case in order to allow time for substantially equal facilities to be supplied. The petitioner, however, refused to attend the newly created school and his appeal to the Supreme Court was accepted.

The Court could find no substantial equality between the two schools in question. The faculty, size of student body, extent of library, variety of courses, etc. were factors which must be considered as affecting the education offered by a school. It was also pointed out that a school which excluded eighty-five percent of the population of the state—people with whom the petitioner will deal with in the course of his work—could not be considered substantially equal. Thus, the state's judgment was reversed and petitioner was to be admitted to the University of Texas Law School.

AN ENROLLED GRADUATE STUDENT MUST NOT BE SEGREGATED WITHIN A STATE UNIVERSITY

McLaurin v. Oklahoma State Regents

339 U.S. 637, 70 Sup. Ct. 851 (1950)

Majority opinion delivered by Chief Justice Vinson

Another situation was presented here which was leading away from the *Plessy v. Ferguson* decision, although this decision was still not reversed. In Oklahoma, after the U.S. District Court had so directed, McLaurin was admitted to the University of Oklahoma Graduate School to study those courses not offered in Negro schools. However, even though petitioner had gained admittance, he was still segregated within the university by being appointed to specific areas in classrooms, library, and cafeteria. It was at this time that McLaurin appealed the Supreme Court to remove these restrictions. It was argued by the state that these restrictions were only nominal, that the appellant was not put at any disadvantage since he was using the same facilities as the other students were using.

The Court, however, felt that undue restrictions had been caused McLaurin. Even though he was using the same facilities, he had been set apart from the other students and this resulted in a handicap in his pursuance of a graduate education. His ability to study, enter into conversations, and to learn his profession had been impaired. Furthermore, the Court felt that there was a constitutional difference between restrictions imposed by law and those imposed by personal preference. McLaurin should at least have the opportunity to secure his acceptance by others on his own merits and therefore must receive the same treatment as the other students receive.

" 'SEPARATE BUT EQUAL' HAS NO PLACE" IN PUBLIC EDUCATION

Brown v. Board of Education of Topeka (Kansas)

347 U.S. 483, 74 Sup. Ct. 686 (1954)

Bolling v. Sharpe (District of Columbia)

347 U.S. 497, 74 Sup. Ct. 693 (1954)

Majority opinion delivered by Chief Justice Warren

These two cases brought to an end the "separate but equal" doctrine put forth in *Plessy v. Ferguson*. They represent the conclusion of a trend started in the cases cited earlier, i.e. *Missouri ex rel. Gaines v. Canada, Sipuel v. Oklahoma State Regents, Sweatt v. Painter,* and *McLaurin v. Oklahoma State Regents.* The results of these cases were similar to the

results of the present cases, but the previous cases were decided individually and the results pertained to that peculiar case. In the present cases
the results affected the entire country.

A total of five cases was involved in the two decisions rendered here.
Four dealt with the states and one with the District of Columbia. The
nature of these cases was such that a consolidated opinion could be given
and in each one the question of the "separate but equal" doctrine was
presented so directly that avoidance of this issue could no longer be
maintained. The five cases were, briefly:

1. Delaware
   Lebhart v. Belton—Negro parents asserted substantial inequalities in the
   separate schools. This assertion was a fact. Children were granted admittance by the court until equal facilities could be provided. This was then
   taken to the Federal Supreme Court by the school authorities involved.

2. Kansas
   Brown v. Board of Education of Topeka—Negro parents admitted equal
   facilities but charged that segregation was socially and psychologically
   damaging to their children. The state agreed with them but held that this
   was not pertinent to the question and refused their petition. The parents
   then appealed the Federal Supreme Court.

3. South Carolina
   Briggs vs. Elliott—Negro parents sought to have facilities made equal. The
   court upheld the constitutionality of the request, ordered the inequalities
   removed within six months. Parents then appealed Federal Supreme Court,
   which could not hear the case for six months, so it was returned to the
   state. The progress after six months was satisfactory to the state court, but
   the parents still questioned segregation itself and appealed the Supreme
   Court again.

4. Virginia
   Davis v. County School Board—About the same as the South Carolina case
   except that the facilities were to be made equal immediately.

5. District of Columbia
   Bolling v. Sharpe—Negro parents held that the intent of Congress under
   the Fifth Amendment was not meant to provide for segregated schools.
   School authorities, as in *Brown v. Board of Education of Topeka*, held
   that since no inequality of schools had been shown, there was no grounds
   for a case. The court agreed. Parents then appealed the Supreme Court on
   grounds that segregation was unconstitutional.

In the four cases cited earlier as leading up to the present cases, it was
not necessary to involve the *Plessy v. Ferguson* decision because in each
instance it was possible to grant relief to the Negroes without such involvement. Here, however, it is asserted that even though the separate
facilities are equal as far as tangible factors are concerned, the act of
segregation itself causes inequalities. The Court felt that the question of
intangible factors must be considered.

It was mentioned that at the time of *Plessy v. Ferguson* the historical setting was such that it could not be compared to the present situation. For example, in the South the movement for free public schools was not advanced to a great degree. Most of the schools were still privately organized. Thus, the decision involved at that time could not be too pertinent to the present day.

The Court phrased the question before it as such: "Does segregation of children in public schools solely on the basis of race, even though the physical facilities and other 'tangible' factors may be equal, deprive the children of the minority group of equal educational opportunities?" Their answer was: "We believe that it does."

The cases of *Sweatt v. Painter* and *McLaurin v. Oklahoma State Regents* were cited as ones involving the intangible factors of association with faculty and students, use of good libraries, etc. This, the Court held, generates a feeling of inferiority and since those discriminated against are to be leaders, they may pass on this feeling of inferiority to those who follow them.

On the basis of social, psychological, and other intangible factors then, separate educational facilities were held to be inherently unequal.

The case of *Bolling v. Sharpe* was considered separately because it involved the Fifth Amendment and the Congress of the United States rather than the Fourteenth Amendment and states. The decision for this case was identical to the previous one because, as the Court stated, "In view of our decision that the Constitution prohibits the states from maintaining racially segregated public schools, it would be unthinkable that the same Constitution would impose a lesser duty on the Federal Government."

ENGEL v. VITALE
370 U.S. 421 (June 25, 1962)

Majority opinion delivered by Justice Black (Actual opinion follows)

The respondent Board of Education of Union Free School District No. 9, New Hyde Park, New York, acting in its official capacity under state law, directed the School District's principal to cause the following prayer to be said aloud by each class in the presence of a teacher at the beginning of each school day:

"Almighty God, we acknowledge our dependence upon Thee, and we beg thy blessings upon us, our parents, our teachers and our country."

This daily procedure was adopted on the recommendation of the State Board of Regents, a governmental agency created by the State Constitution to which the New York Legislature has granted broad supervisory, executive, and legislative powers over the state's public school system. These state officials composed the prayer which they recommended and published as a part of their "Statement on Moral and Spiritual Training in the Schools," saying: "We believe that this statement will be subscribed to by all men and women of good will, and we call upon all of them to aid in giving life to our program."

Shortly after the practice of reciting the Regents' prayer was adopted by the school district, the parents of ten pupils brought this action in a New York State Court insisting that use of this official prayer in the public schools was contrary to the beliefs, religions, or religious practices of both themselves and their children. Among other things, these parents challenged the constitutionality of both the state law authorizing the school district to direct the use of prayer in public schools and the school district's regulation ordering the recitation of this particular prayer on the ground that these actions of official governmental agencies violate that part of the First Amendment of the Federal Constitution which commands that "Congress shall make no law respecting an establishment of religion"—a command which was "made applicable to the State of New York by the Fourteenth Amendment of the said Constitution." The New York Court of Appeals, over the dissents of Judges Dye and Fuld, sustained an order of the lower state courts which had upheld the power of New York to use the Regents' prayer as a part of the daily procedures of its public schools so long as the schools did not compel any pupil to join in the prayer over his or his parents' objection. We granted certiorari to review this important decision involving rights protected by the First and Fourteenth Amendments.

We think that by using its public school system to encourage recitation of the Regents' prayer, the State of New York has adopted a practice wholly inconsistent with the Establishment Clause. There can, of course, be no doubt that New York's program of daily classroom invocation of God's blessings as prescribed in the Regents' prayer is a religious activity. It is a solemn avowal of divine faith and supplication for the blessings of the Almighty. The nature of such a prayer has always been religious, none of the respondents has denied this, and the trial court expressly so found:

> "The religious nature of prayer was recognized by Jefferson and has been concurred in by theological writers, the United States Supreme Court and State courts and administrative officials, including New York's Commissioner of Education. A committee of the New York Legislature has agreed.

> "The Board of Regents as amicus curiae, the respondents and intervenors all concede the religious nature of prayer, but seek to distinguish this prayer because it is based on our spiritual heritage. . . ."

The petitioners contend among other things that the state laws requiring or permitting use of the Regents' prayer must be struck down as a violation of the Establishment Clause because that prayer was composed by governmental officials as a part of a governmental program to further religious beliefs. For this reason, petitioners argue, the state's use of the Regents' prayer in its public school system breaches the constitutional wall of separation between church and state. We agree with that contention since we think that the constitutional prohibition against laws respecting an establishment of religion must at least mean that in this country it is no part of the business of government to compose official prayers for any group of the American people to recite as a part of a religious program carried on by government.

It is a matter of history that this very practice of establishing governmentally composed prayers for religious services was one of the reasons which caused many of our early colonists to leave England and seek religious freedom in America. The Book of Common Prayer, which was created under governmental direction and which was approved by Acts of Parliament in 1548 and 1549, set out in minute detail the accepted form and content of prayer and other religious ceremonies to be used in the established, tax-supported Church of England. The controversies over the Book and what should be its content repeatedly threatened to disrupt the peace of that country as the accepted forms of prayer in the established church changed with the views of the particular ruler that happened to be in control at the time. Powerful groups representing some of the varying religious views of the people struggled among themselves to impress their particular views upon the government and obtain amendments of the Book more suitable to their respective notions of how religious services should be conducted in order that the official religious establishment would advance their particular religious beliefs. Other groups, lacking the necessary political power to influence the government on the matter, decided to leave England and its established church and seek freedom in America from England's governmentally ordained and supported religion.

It is an unfortunate fact of history that when some of the very groups which had most strenuously opposed the established Church of England found themselves sufficiently in control of colonial governments in this country to write their own prayers into law, they passed laws making their own religion the official religion of their respective colonies. Indeed, as late as the time of the Revolutionary War, there were established churches in at least eight of the thirteen former colonies and established religions in at least four of the other five. But the successful Revolution against English political domination was shortly followed by intense opposition to the practice of establishing religion by law. This opposition crystallized rapidly into an effective political force in Virginia where the minority religious groups such as Presbyterians, Lutherans, Quakers and Baptists had gained such strength that the adherents to the established Episcopal Church were actually a minority themselves. In 1785–1786, those opposed to the established church, led by James Madison and Thomas Jefferson, who, though themselves not members of any of these dissenting religious groups, opposed all religious establishments by law on grounds of principle, obtained the enactment of the famous "Virginia Bill for Religious Liberty" by which all religious groups were placed on an equal footing so far as the state was concerned. Similar though less far-reaching legislation was being considered and passed in other states.

By the time of the adoption of the Constitution, our history shows that there was a widespread awareness among many Americans of the dangers of a union of Church and State. These people knew, some of them from bitter personal experience, that one of the greatest dangers to the freedom of the individual to worship in his own way lay in the Government's placing its official stamp of approval upon one particular kind of prayer or one particular form of religious services. They knew the anguish, hardship and bitter strife that could come when zealous religious groups struggled with one another to obtain the Government's stamp of approval from each King, Queen, or Protector that came to temporary power. The Constitution was intended to avert a part of this danger by leaving the government of this country in the hands of the people rather than in the hands of any monarch. But this safeguard was not enough. Our Founders were no more willing to let the content of their prayers and their privilege of praying whenever they pleased be influenced by the ballot box than they were to let these vital matters of personal conscience depend upon the succession of monarchs. The First Amendment was added to the Constitution to stand as a guarantee that neither the power nor the prestige of the Federal Government would be used to control, support or influence the kinds of prayer the American people can say—that the people's religions must not be subjected to the pressures of government for change each time a new political administration is elected to office. Under that Amendment's prohibition aganist governmental establishment of religion, as reinforced by the provisions of the Fourteenth Amendment, government in this country, be it state or federal, is without power to prescribe by law any particular form of prayer which is to be used as an official prayer in carrying on any program of governmentally sponsored religious activity.

There can be no doubt that New York's state prayer program officially establishes the religious beliefs embodied in the Regents' prayer. The respondents' argument to the contrary, which is largely based upon the contention that the Regents' prayer is "non-denominational" and the fact that the program, as modified and approved by state courts, does not require all pupils to recite the prayer but permits those who wish to do so to remain silent or be excused from the room, ignores the essential nature of the program's constitutional defects. Neither the fact that the prayer may be denominationally neutral, nor the fact that its observance on the part of the students is voluntary can serve to free it from the limitations of the Establishment Clause, as it might from the Free Exercise Clause, of the First Amendment, both of which are operative against the States by virtue of the Fourteenth Amendment. Although these two clauses may in certain instances overlap, they forbid two quite different kinds of governmental encroachment upon religious freedom. The Establishment Clause, unlike the Free Exercise Clause, does not depend upon any showing of direct governmental compulsion and is violated by the enactment of laws which establish an official religion whether those laws operate directly to coerce nonobserving individuals or not. This is not to say, of course, that laws officially prescribing a particular form of religious worship do not involve coercion of such individuals. When the power, prestige and financial support of government is placed behind a particular religious belief, the indirect coercive pressure upon religious minorities to conform to the prevailing officially approved religion is plain. But the purposes underlying the Establishment Clause go much further than that. Its first and most immediate purpose rested on the belief that a union of government and religion tends to destroy government and to degrade religion. The history of governmentally established religion, both in England and in this country, showed that whenever government had allied itself with one particular form of religion, the inevitable result had been that it had incurred the hatred, disrespect and even contempt of those who held contrary beliefs. That same history showed that many people had lost their respect for any religion that had relied upon the support of government to spread its faith. The Establishment Clause thus stands as an expression of principle on the part of the Founders of our Constitution that religion is too personal, too sacred, too holy, to permit its "unhallowed perversion" by a civil magistrate. Another purpose of the Establishment Clause rested upon an awareness of the historical fact that governmentally established religions and religious persecutions go hand in hand. The Founders knew that only a few years after the Book of Common Prayer became the only accepted form of religious services in the established Church of England, an Act of Uniformity was passed to compel all Englishmen to attend those services and to make it a criminal offense to conduct or attend religious gatherings of any other kind—a law which was consistently flouted by dissenting religious groups in England and which contributed to widespread persecutions of people like John Bunyan who persisted in holding "unlawful [religious] meetings . . . to the great disturbance and distraction of the good subjects of this kingdom. . . ." And they knew that similar persecutions had received the sanction of law in several of the colonies in this country soon after the establishment of official religions in those colonies. It was in large part to get completely away from this sort of systematic religious persecution that the Founders brought into being our Nation, our Constitution, and our Bill of Rights with its prohibition against any governmental establishment of religion. The New York laws officially prescribing the Regents' prayer are inconsistent with both the purposes of the Establishment Clause and with the Establishment Clause itself.

It has been argued that to apply the Constitution in such a way as to prohibit state laws respecting an establishment of religious services in public schools is to indicate a hostility toward religion or toward prayer. Nothing, of course, could be more wrong. The history of man is inseparable from the history of religion. And perhaps it is not too much to say that since the beginning of that history many people have devoutly believed that "More things are wrought by prayer than this world dreams of." It was doubtless largely due to men who believed this that there grew up a sentiment that caused men to leave the cross-currents of officially established state religions and religious persecution in Europe and come to this country filled with the hope that they could find a place in which they could pray when they pleased to the God of their faith in the language they chose. And there were men of this same faith in the power of prayer who led the fight for adoption of our Constitution and also for our Bill of Rights with the very guarantees of religious freedom that forbid the sort of governmental activity which New York has attempted here. These men knew that the First Amendment, which tried to put an end to governmental control of religion and of prayer, was not written to destroy either. They knew rather that it was written to quiet well-justified fears which nearly all of them felt arising out of an awareness that governments of the past had shackled men's tongues to make them speak only the religious thoughts that government wanted them to speak and to pray only to the God that government wanted them to pray to. It is neither sacrilegious nor antireligious to say that each separate government in this country should stay out of the business of writing or sanctioning official prayers and leave that purely religious function to the people themselves and to those the people choose to look to for religious guidance.

It is true that New York's establishment of its Regents' prayer as an officially approved religious doctrine of that State does not amount to a total establishment of one particular religious sect to the exclusion of all others—that, indeed, the governmental endorsement of that prayer seems relatively insignificant when compared to the governmental encroachments upon religion which were commonplace 200 years ago. To those who may subscribe to the view that because the Regents' official prayer is so brief and general there can be no danger to religious freedom in its governmental establishment, however, it may be appropriate to say, in the words of James Madison, the author of the First Amendment:

> "It is proper to take alarm at the first experiment on our liberties. . . . Who does not see that the same authority which can establish Christianity, in exclusion of all other Religions, may establish with the same ease any particular sect of Christians, in exclusion of all other sects? That the same authority which can force a citizen to contribute three pence only of his property for the support of any one establishment, may force him to conform to any other establishment in all cases whatsoever?"

The judgment of the Court of Appeals of New York is reversed and the cause remanded for further proceedings not inconsistent with this opinion.

Reversed and remanded.

SCHOOL DIST. OF ABINGTON TP. PA. v. SCHEMPP; MURRAY v. CURLETT

83 Sup. Ct. Rep. 1560 (Decided June 17, 1963)

Majority opinion delivered by Justice Clark (Actual opinion follows)

Once again we are called upon to consider the scope of the provision of the First Amendment to the United States Constitution which declares that "Congress shall make no law respecting an establishment of religion, or prohibiting the free exercise thereof. . . ." These companion cases present the issues in the context of state action requiring that schools begin each day with readings from the Bible. While raising the basic questions under slightly different factual situations, the cases permit of joint treatment. In light of the history of the First Amendment and of our cases interpreting and applying its requirements, we hold that the practices at issue and the laws requiring them are unconstitutional under the establishment clause, as applied to the states through the Fourteenth Amendment.

The Facts in Each Case: No. 142. The Commonwealth of Pennsylvania by law, 24 Pa. Stat. Sec. 15–1516, as amended, Pub. Law. 1928 (Supp. 1960) Dec. 17, 1959, requires that "At least ten verses from the Holy Bible shall be read, without comment, at the opening of each public school on each school day. Any child shall be excused from such Bible reading, or attending such Bible reading, upon the written request of his parent or guardian." The Schempp family, husband and wife and two of their three children, brought suit to enjoin enforcement of the statute, contending that their rights under the Fourteenth Amendment to the Constitution of the United States are, have been, and will continue to be violated unless this statute be declared unconstitutional as violative of these provisions of the First Amendment. They sought to enjoin the appellant school district, wherein the Schempp children attend school, and its officers and the Superintendent of Public Instruction of the Commonwealth from continuing to conduct such readings and recitation of the Lord's Prayer in the public schools of the district pursuant to the statute. A three-judge statutory District Court for the Eastern District of Pennsylvania held that the statute is violative of the Establishment Clause of the First Amendment as applied to the states by the Due Process Clause of the Fourteenth Amendment and directed that appropriate injunctive relief issue. D.C., 201 F. Supp. 815. On appeal by the District, its officials and the Superintendent, under 28 U.S.C. par. 1253, we noted probable jurisdiction. 371 U.S. 807, 83 S.Ct. 25, 9 L.Ed. 2d 52.

The appellees, Edward Lewis Schempp, his wife Sidney, and their children, Roger and Donna, are of the Unitarian faith and are members of the Unitarian Church in Germantown, Philadelphia, Pennsylvania, where they, as well as another son, Ellory, regularly attend religious services. The latter was originally a party but having graduated from the school system pendente lite was voluntarily dismissed from the action. The other children attend the Abington Senior High School, which is a public school operated by appellant district.

On each school day at the Abington Senior High School between 8:15 and 8:30 A.M., while the pupils are attending their home rooms or advisory sections, opening exercises are conducted pursuant to the statute. The exercises are broadcast into each room in the school building through an intercommunications system and are conducted under the supervision of a teacher by students attending the school's radio and television workshop. Selected students from this course gather each morning in the school's workshop studio for the exercises, which include readings by one of the students of 10 verses of the Holy Bible, broadcast to each room in the building. This is followed by the recitation of the Lord's Prayer, likewise over the intercommunications system, but also by the students in the various classrooms, who are asked to stand and join in repeating the prayer in unison. The exercises are closed with the flag salute and such pertinent announcements as are of interest to the students. Participation in the opening exercises, as directed by the statute, is voluntary. The student reading the verses from the Bible may select the passages and read from any version he chooses, although the only copies furnished by the school are the King James version, copies of which were circulated to each teacher by the school district. During the period in which the exercises have been conducted the King James, the Douay and the Revised Standard versions of the Bible have been used, as well as the Jewish Holy Scriptures. There are no prefatory statements, no questions asked or solicited, no comments or explanations made, and no interpretations given at or during the exercises. The students and parents are advised that the student may absent himself from the classroom or, should he elect to remain, not participate in the exercises.

It appears from the record that in schools not having an intercommunications system the Bible reading and the recitation of the Lord's Prayer were conducted by the homeroom teacher, who chose the text of the verses and read them herself or had students read them in rotation or by volunteers. This was followed by a standing recitation of the Lord's Prayer, together with the Pledge of Allegiance to the flag by the class in unison and a closing announcement of routine school items of interest.

At the first trial Edward Schempp and the children testified as to specific religious doctrines purveyed by a literal reading of the Bible "which were contrary to the religious beliefs which they held and to their familial teaching." 177 F.Supp. 398, 400. The children testified that all of the doctrines to which they referred were read to them at various times as part of the exercises. Edward Schempp testified at the second trial that he had considered having Roger and Donna excused from attendance at the exercises but decided against it for several reasons, including his belief that the children's relationships with their teachers and classmates would be adversely affected.

Expert testimony was introduced by both appellants and appellees at the first trial, which testimony was summarized by the trial court as follows:

"Dr. Solomon Grayzel testified that there were marked differences between the Jewish Holy Scriptures and the Christian Holy Bible, the most obvious of which was the absence of the New Testament in the Jewish Holy Scriptures. Dr. Grayzel testified that portions of the New Testament were offensive to Jewish tradition and that, from the standpoint of Jewish faith, the concept of Jesus Christ as the Son of God was 'practically blasphemous.' He cited instances in the New Testament which, assertedly, were not only sectarian in nature but tended to bring the Jews into ridicule or scorn. Dr. Grayzel gave as his expert opinion that such material from the New Testament could be explained to Jewish children in such a way as to do no harm to them. But if portions of the New Testament were read without explanation, they could be, and in his specific experience with children Dr. Grayzel observed, had been, psychologically harmful to the child and had caused a divisive force within the social media of the school.

"Dr. Grayzel also testified that there was significant difference in attitude with regard to the respective Books of the Jewish and Christian Religions in that Judaism attaches no special significance to the reading of the Bible per se and that the Jewish Holy Scriptures are source materials to be studied. But Dr. Grayzel did state that many portions of the New, as well as of the Old, Testament contained passages of great literary and moral value.

"Dr. Luther A. Weigle, an expert witness for the defense, testified in some detail as to the reasons for and the methods employed in developing the King James and the Revised Standard Versions of the Bible. On direct examination, Dr. Weigle stated that the Bible was non-sectarian. He later stated that the phrase 'non-sectarian' meant to him non-sectarian within the Christian faiths. Dr. Weigle stated that his definition of the Holy Bible would include the Jewish Holy Scriptures, but also stated that the 'Holy Bible' would not be complete without the New Testament. He stated that the New Testament 'conveyed the message of Christians.' In his opinion, reading of the Holy Scriptures to the exclusion of the New Testament would be a sectarian practice. Dr. Weigle stated that the Bible was of great moral, historical, and literary value. This is conceded by all the parties and is also the view of the court." 177 F.Supp. 398, 401-402.

The trial court, in striking down the practices and the statute requiring them, made specific findings of fact that the children's attendance at Abington Senior High School is compulsory and that the practice of reading 10 verses from the Bible is also compelled by law. It also found that:

"The reading of the verses, even without comment, possesses a devotional and religious character and constitutes in effect a religious observance. The devotional and religious nature of the morning exercises is made all the more apparent by the fact that the Bible reading is followed immediately by a recital in unison by the pupils of the Lord's Prayer. The fact that some pupils, or theoretically all pupils, might be excused from attendance at the exercises does not mitigate the obligatory nature of the ceremony for . . . Section 1516 . . . unequivocally requires the exercises to be held every school day in every school in the Commonwealth. The exercises are held in the school buildings and perforce are conducted by and under the authority of the local school authorities and during school sessions. Since the statute requires the reading of the 'Holy Bible,' a Christian document, the practice . . . prefers the Christian religion. The record demonstrates that it was the intention of . . . the Commonwealth . . . to introduce a religious ceremony into the public schools of the Commonwealth." 201 F.Supp., at 819.

No. 119. In 1905 the Board of School Commissioners of Baltimore City adopted a rule pursuant to Art. 77, Par. 202 of the Annotated Code of

Maryland. The rule provided for the holding of opening exercises in the schools of the city consisting primarily of the "reading, without comment, of a chapter in the Holy Bible and/or the use of the Lord's Prayer." The petitioners, Mrs. Madalyn Murray and her son, William J. Murray, III, are both professed atheists. Following unsuccessful attempts to have the respondent school board rescind the rule this suit was filed for mandamus to compel its rescission and cancellation. It was alleged that William was a student in a public school of the city and Mrs. Murray, his mother, was a taxpayer therein; that it was the practice under the rule to have a reading on each school morning from the King James version of the Bible; that at petitioners' insistence the rule was amended to permit children to be excused from the exercise on request of the parent and that William had been excused pursuant thereto; that nevertheless the rule as amended was in violation of the petitioners' rights "to freedom of religion under the First and Fourteenth Amendments" and in violation of "the principle of separation between church and state, contained therein. . . ." The petition particularized the petitioners' atheistic beliefs and stated that the rule, as practiced, violated their rights

> "in that it threatens their religious liberty by placing a premium on belief as against non-belief and subjects their freedom of conscience to the rule of the majority; it pronounces belief in God as the source of all moral and spiritual values, equating these values with religious values, and thereby renders sinister, alien, and suspect the beliefs and ideals of . . . Petitioners, promoting doubt and question of their morality, good citizenship and good faith."

The respondents demurred and the trial court, recognizing that the demurrer admitted all facts well pleaded, sustained it without leave to amend. The Maryland Court of Appeals affirmed, the majority of four justices holding the exercise not in violation of the First and Fourteenth Amendments, with three justices dissenting. 228 Md. 239, 179 A. 2d 698. We granted certiorari. 371 U.S. 809, 83 S.Ct. 21, 9 L.Ed. 2d 52.

It is true that religion has been closely identified with our history and government. As we said in Engel v. Vitale, 370 U.S. 421, 434, 82 S.Ct. 1261, 1268, 8 L.Ed. 2d 601 (1962), "The history of man is inseparable from the history of religion. And . . . since the beginning of that history many people have devoutly believed that 'More things are wrought by prayer than this world dreams of.' " In Zorach v. Clauson, 343 U.S. 306, 313, 72 S.Ct. 679, 684, 96 L.Ed. 954 (1952), we gave specific recognition to the proposition that "we are a religious people whose institutions presuppose a Supreme Being." The fact that the Founding Fathers believed devotedly that there was a God and that the inalienable rights of man were rooted in Him is clearly evidenced in their writings, from the Mayflower Compact to the Constitution itself. This background is evidenced today in our public life through the continuance in our oaths of office from the Presidency to the Alderman of the final supplication, "So help me God." Likewise, each House of the Congress provides through its Chaplain an opening prayer, and the sessions of this Court are declared open by the crier in a short ceremony, the final phrase of which invokes the grace of God. Again, there are such manifestations in our military forces, where those of our citizens who are under the restrictions of military service wish to engage in voluntary worship. Indeed, only last year an official survey of the country indicated that 64% of our people have church membership, Bureau of Census, U.S. Department of Commerce, Statistical Abstract of the United States, 48 (83d ed. 1962), while less than 3% profess no religion whatever. Id., at p. 46. It can be truly said, therefore, that today, as in the beginning, our national life reflects a religious people who, in the words of Madison, are "earnestly praying, as . . . in duty bound, that the Supreme Lawgiver of the Universe . . . guide them into every measure which may be worthy of his . . . blessing. . . ." Memorial and Remonstrance Against Religious Assessments, quoted in Everson v. Board of Education, 330 U.S. 1, 71–72, 67 S.Ct. 504, 538–539, 91 L.Ed. 711 (1947) (Appendix to dissenting opinion of Rutledge, J.).

This is not to say, however, that religion has been so identified with our history and government that religious freedom is not likewise as strongly imbedded in our public and private life. Nothing but the most telling of personal experiences in religious persecution suffered by our forebears, see Everson v. Board of Education, supra, 330 U.S., at 8–11, 67 S.Ct., at 507–509, 91 L.Ed. 711, could have planted our belief in liberty of religious opinion any more deeply in our heritage. It is true that this liberty frequently was not realized by the colonists, but this is readily accountable to their close ties to the Mother Country. However, the views of Madison and Jefferson, preceded by Roger Williams, came to be incorporated not only in the Federal Constitution but likewise in those of most of our states. This freedom to worship was indispensable in a country whose people came from the four quarters of the earth and brought with them a diversity of religious opinion. Today, authorities list 83 separate religious bodies, each with memberships exceeding 50,000, existing among our people, as well as innumerable smaller groups. Bureau of Census, op. cit., supra, at 46–47.

Almost a hundred years ago in Minor v. Board of Education of Cincinnati, Judge Alphonzo Taft, father of the revered Chief Justice, in an unpublished opinion stated the ideal of our people as to religious freedom as one of

"absolute equality before the law of all religious opinions and sects. . . ."

*   *   *   *   *   *   *   *   *   *

"The government is neutral, and, while protecting all, it prefers none, and it disparages none."

Before examining this "neutral" position in which the Establishment and Free Exercise Clauses of the First Amendment place our government, it is well that we discuss the reach of the Amendment under the cases of this Court.

First, this Court has decisively settled that the First Amendment's mandate that "Congress shall make no law respecting an establishment of religion, or prohibiting the free exercise thereof" has been made wholly applicable to the states by the Fourteenth Amendment. Twenty-three years ago in Cantwell v. Connecticut, 310 U.S. 296, 303, 60 S.Ct. 900, 903, 84 L.Ed. 1213 (1940), this Court, through Mr. Justice Roberts, said:

> "The fundamental concept of liberty embodied in that Fourteenth Amendment embraces the liberties guaranteed by the First Amendment. The First Amendment declares that Congress shall make no law respecting an establishment of religion or prohibiting the free exercise thereof. The Fourteenth Amendment has rendered the legislatures of the states as incompetent as Congress to enact such laws. . . ."

In a series of cases since Cantwell the Court has repeatedly reaffirmed that doctrine, and we do so now. Murdock v. Commonwealth of Pennsylvania, 319 U.S. 105, 108, 63 S.Ct. 870, 872, 87 L.Ed. 1292 (1943); Everson v. Board of Education, supra; Illinois ex rel. McCollum v. Board of Education, 333 U.S. 203, 210–211, 68 S.Ct. 461, 464–465, 92 L.Ed. 648 (1948); Zorach v. Clauson, supra; McGowan v. Maryland, 366 U.S. 420, 81 S.Ct. 1101, 6 L.Ed. 2d 393 (1961); Torcaso v. Watkins, 367 U.S. 488, 81 S.Ct. 1680, 6 L.Ed. 2d 982 (1961); and Engel v. Vitale, supra.

Second, this Court has rejected unequivocally the contention that the establishment clause forbids only governmental preference of one religion over another. Almost 20 years ago in Everson, supra, 330 U.S., at 15, 67 S.Ct., at 511, 91 L.Ed. 711, the Court said that "neither a state nor the Federal government can set up a church. Neither can pass laws which aid one religion, aid all religions, or prefer one religion over another." And Mr. Justice Jackson, dissenting, agreed:

> "There is no answer to the proposition . . . that the effect of the religious freedom Amendment to our Constitution was to take every form of propagation of religion out of the realm of things which could directly or indirectly be made public business and thereby be supported in whole or in part at taxpayers' expense. . . . This freedom was first in the Bill of Rights because it was first in the forefathers' minds; it was set forth in absolute terms, and its strength is its rigidity."
> Id., 330 U.S., at 26, 67 S.Ct., at 516, 91 L.Ed. 711.

Further, Mr. Justice Rutledge, joined by Justices Frankfurter, Jackson, and Burton, declared:

"The First Amendment's purpose was not to strike merely at the official establishment of a single sect, creed, or religion, outlawing only a formal relation such as had prevailed in England and some of the colonies. Necessarily it was to uproot all such relationships. But the object was broader than separating church and state in this narrow sense. It was to create a complete and permanent separation of the spheres of religious activity and civil authority by comprehensively forbidding every form of public aid or support for religion." Id., 330 U.S., at 31–32, 67 S.Ct., at 519, 91 L.Ed. 711.

The same conclusion has been firmly maintained ever since that time, see Illinois ex rel. McCollum, supra, 333 U.S., at pp. 210–211, 68 S.Ct., at pp. 464–465, 92 L.Ed. 648; McGowan v. Maryland, supra, 366 U.S., at 442–443, 81 S.Ct., at 1113–1114, 6 L.Ed. 2d 393; Torcaso v. Watkins, supra, 367 U.S., at 492–493, 495, 81 S.Ct., at 1682–1683, 1684, 6 L.Ed. 2d 982; and we reaffirm it now.

While none of the parties to either of these cases has questioned these basic conclusions of the Court, both of which have been long established, recognized, and consistently reaffirmed, others continue to question their history, logic, and efficacy. Such contentions, in the light of the consistent interpretation in cases of this Court, seem entirely untenable and of value only as academic exercises.

The interrelationship of the Establishment and the Free Exercise Clauses was first touched upon by Mr. Justice Roberts for the Court in Cantwell v. Connecticut, supra, 310 U.S., at 303, 60 S.Ct., at 903, 84 L.Ed. 1213, where it was said that their "inhibition of legislation" had

"a double aspect. On the one hand, it forestalls compulsion by law of the acceptance of any creed or the practice of any form of worship. Freedom of conscience and freedom to adhere to such religious organization or form of worship as the individual may choose cannot be restricted by law. On the other hand, it safeguards the free exercise of the chosen form of religion. Thus the Amendment embraces two concepts,—freedom to believe and freedom to act. The first is absolute but, in the nature of things, the second cannot be."

A half dozen years later in Everson v. Board of Education, supra, 330 U.S., at 14–15, 67 S. Ct., at 511, 91 L.Ed. 711, this Court, through Mr. Justice Black, stated that the "scope of the First Amendment . . . was designed forever to suppress" the establishment of religion or the prohibition of the free exercise thereof. In short, the Court held that the Amendment "requires the state to be a neutral in its relations with groups of religious believers and non-believers; it does not require the state to be their adversary. State power is no more to be used so as to handicap religions, than it is to favor them." Id., 330 U.S., at 18, 67 S.Ct. at 513, 91 L.Ed. 711.

And Mr. Justice Jackson, in dissent, declared that public schools are organized

"on the premise that secular education can be isolated from all religious teaching so that the school can inculcate all needed temporal knowledge and also maintain a strict and lofty neutrality as to religion. The assumption is that after the individual has been instructed in worldly wisdom he will be better fitted to choose his religion." Id., 330 U.S., st 23–24, 67 S.Ct. at 515, 91 L.Ed. 711.

Moreover, all of the four dissenters, speaking through Mr. Justice Rutledge, agreed that

"Our constitutional policy . . . does not deny the value or the necessity for religious training, teaching, or observance. Rather it secures their free exercise. But to that end it does deny that the state can undertake or sustain them in any form or degree. For this reason the sphere of religious activity, as distinguished from the secular intellectual liberties, has been given the two-fold protection and, as the state cannot forbid, neither can it perform or aid in performing the religious function. The dual prohibition makes that function altogether private." Id., 330 U.S., at 52, 67 S.Ct., at 529, 91 L.Ed. 711.

Only one year later the Court was asked to reconsider and repudiate the doctrine of these cases in McCollum v. Board of Education. It was argued that "historically the First Amendment was intended to forbid only government preference of one religion over another. . . . In addition they ask that we distinguish or overrule our holding in the Everson case that the Fourteenth Amendment made the 'establishment of religion' clause of the First Amendment applicable as a prohibition against the States." 333 U.S., at 211, 68 S.Ct., at 465, 92 L.Ed. 648. The Court, with Mr. Justice Reed alone dissenting, was unable to "accept either of these contentions." Ibid. Mr. Justice Frankfurter, joined by Justices Jackson, Rutledge, and Burton, wrote a very comprehensive and scholarly concurrence in which he said that "separation is a requirement to abstain from fusing functions of Government and of religious sects, not merely to treat them all equally." Id., 333 U.S., at 227, 68 S.Ct., at 473, 92 L.Ed. 648. Continuing, he stated that: "the Constitution . . . prohibited the Government common to all from becoming embroiled, however innocently, in the destructive religious conflicts of which the history of even this country records some dark pages." Id., 333 U.S., at 228, 68 S.Ct., at 473, 92 L.Ed. 648.

In 1952 in Zorach v. Clauson, supra, Mr. Justice Douglas for the Court reiterated:

"There cannot be the slightest doubt that the First Amendment reflects the philosophy that Church and State should be separated. And so far as interference with the 'free exercise' of religion and an 'establishment' of religion are concerned, the separation must be complete and unequivocal. The First Amendment within the scope of its coverage permits no exception; the prohibition is absolute. The First Amendment, however, does not say that in every and all respects there shall be a separation of Church and State. Rather, it studiously defines the manner, the specific ways, in which there shall be no concert or union or dependency one on the other. That is the common sense of the matter." 343 U.S., at 312, 72 S.Ct., at 683, 96 L.Ed. 954.

And then in 1961 in McGowan v. Maryland and in Torcaso v. Watkins each of these cases was discussed and approved. Chief Justice Warren in McGowan, for a unanimous Court on this point, said:

"But, the First Amendment, in its final form, did not simply bar a congressional enactment establishing a church; it forbade all laws respecting an establishment of religion. Thus, this Court has given the Amendment a 'broad interpretation . . . in the light of its history and the evils it was designed forever to suppress. . . .'" 366 U.S., at 441–442, 81 S.Ct., at 1113, 6 L.Ed.2d 393.

And Mr. Justice Black for the Court in Torcaso, without dissent but with Justices Frankfurter and Harlan concurring in the result, used this language:

"We repeat and again reaffirm that neither a State nor the Federal Government can constitutionally force a person 'to profess a belief or disbelief in any religion.' Neither can constitutionally pass laws or impose requirements which aid all religions as against nonbelievers, and neither can aid those religions based on a belief in the existence of God as against those religions founded on different beliefs." 367 U.S., at 495, 81 S.Ct., at 1683, 6 L.Ed.2d 982.

Finally, in Engel v. Vitale, only last year, these principles were so universally recognized that the Court without the citation of a single case and over the sole dissent of Mr. Justice Stewart reaffirmed them. The Court found the 22-word prayer used in "New York's program of daily classroom invocation of God's blessings as prescribed in the Regents' prayer . . . to be a religious activity." 370 U.S., at 424, 82 S.Ct., at 1264, 8 L.Ed. 2d 601. It held that "it is no part of the business of government to compose official prayers for any group of the American people to recite as a part of a religious program carried on by the government." Id., 370 U.S., at 425, 82 S.Ct., at 1264, 8 L.Ed.2d 601. In discussing the reach of the Establishment and Free Exercise Clauses of the First Amendment the Court said:

> "Although these two clauses may in certain instances overlap, they forbid two quite different kinds of governmental encroachment upon religious freedom. The Establishment Clause, unlike the Free Exercise Clause, does not depend upon any showing of direct governmental compulsion and is violated by the enactment of laws which establish an official religion whether those laws operate directly to coerce non-observing individuals or not. This is not to say, of course, that laws officially prescribing a particular form of religious worship do not involve coercion of such individuals. When the power, prestige, and financial support of government is placed behind a particular religious belief, the indirect coercive pressure upon religious minorities to conform to the prevailing officially approved religion is plain." Id., 370 U.S. at 430–431, 82 S.Ct., at 1267, 8 L.Ed.2d 601.

And in further elaboration the Court found that the "first and most immediate purpose of the Establishment Clause rested on a belief that a union of government and religion tends to destroy government and to degrade religion." Id., 370 U.S. at 431, 82 S.Ct., at 1267, 8 L.Ed.2d 601. When government, the Court said, allies itself with one particular form of religion, the inevitable result is that it incurs "the hatred, disrespect, and even contempt of those who hold contrary beliefs." Ibid.

The wholesome "neutrality" of which this Court's cases speak thus stems from a recognition of the teachings of history that powerful sects or groups might bring about a fusion of governmental and religious functions or a concert or dependency of one upon the other to the end that official support of the State or Federal Government would be placed behind the tenets of one or of all orthodoxies. This the Establishment Clause prohibits. And a further reason for neutrality is found in the Free Exercise Clause, which recognizes the value of religious training, teaching, and observance and, more particularly, the right of every person to freely choose his own course with reference thereto, free of any compulsion from the state. This the Free Exercise Clause guarantees. Thus, as we have seen, the two clauses may overlap. As we have indicated, the Establishment Clause has been directly considered by this Court eight times in the past score of years and, with only one Justice dissenting on the point, it has consistently held that the clause withdrew all legislative power respecting religious belief or the expression thereof. The test may be stated as follows: what are the purpose and the primary effect of the enactment? If either is the advancement or inhibition of religion

then the enactment exceeds the scope of legislative power as circumscribed by the Constitution. That is to say that to withstand the strictures
of the Establishment Clause there must be a secular legislative purpose
and a primary effect that neither advances nor inhibits religion. Everson
v. Board of Education, supra; McGowan v. Maryland, supra, 366 U.S., at
442, 81 S.Ct. at 1113–1114, 6 L.Ed.2d 393. The Free Exercise Clause, likewise considered many times here, withdraws from legislative power, state
and federal, the exertion of any restraint on the free exercise of religion.
Its purpose is to secure religious liberty in the individual by prohibiting
any invasions thereof by civil authority. Hence it is necessary in a free
exercise case for one to show the coercive effect of the enactment as it
operates against him in the practice of his religion. The distinction between the two clauses is apparent—a violation of the Free Exercise Clause
is predicated on coercion while the Establishment Clause violation need
not be so attended.

Applying the Establishment Clause principles to the cases at bar we
find that the states are requiring the selection and reading at the opening
of the school day of verses from the Holy Bible and the recitation of the
Lord's Prayer by the students in unison. These exercises are prescribed
as part of the curricular activities of students who are required by law
to attend school. They are held in the school buildings under the supervision and with the participation of teachers employed in those schools.
None of these factors, other than compulsory school attendance, was
present in the program upheld in Zorach v. Clauson. The trial court in
No. 142 has found that such an opening exercise is a religious ceremony
and was intended by the State to be so. We agree with the trial court's
finding as to the religious character of the exercises. Given that finding
the exercises and the law requiring them are in violation of the Establishment Clause.

There is no such specific finding as to the religious character of the
exercises in No. 119, and the State contends (as does the State in No.
142) that the program is an effort to extend its benefits to all public
school children without regard to their religious belief. Included within
its secular purposes, it says, are the promotion of moral values, the contradiction to the materialistic trends of our times, the perpetuation of
our institutions and the teaching of literature. The case came up on demurrer, of course, to a petition which alleged that the uniform practice
under the rule had been to read from the King James version of the Bible
and that the exercise was sectarian. The short answer, therefore, is that
the religious character of the exercise was admitted by the State. But
even if its purpose is not strictly religious, it is sought to be accomplished
through readings, without comment, from the Bible. Surely the place of
the Bible as an instrument of religion cannot be gainsaid, and the State's
recognition of the pervading religious character of the ceremony is evi-

dent from the rule's specific permission of the alternative use of the Catholic Douay version as well as the recent amendment permitting nonattendance at the exercises. None of these factors is consistent with the contention that the Bible is here used either as an instrument for nonreligious moral inspiration or as a reference for the teaching of secular subjects.

The conclusion follows that in both cases the laws require religious exercises and such exercises are being conducted in direct violation of the rights of the appellees and petitioners. Nor are these required exercises mitigated by the fact that individual students may absent themselves upon parental request, for that fact furnishes no defense to a claim of unconstitutionality under the Establishment Clause. See Engel v. Vitale, supra, 370 U.S., at 430, 82 S.Ct., at 1266–1267, 8 L.Ed.2d 601. Further, it is no defense to urge that the religious practices here may be relatively minor encroachments on the First Amendment. The breach of neutrality that is today a trickling stream may all too soon become a raging torrent and, in the words of Madison, "it is proper to take alarm at the first experiment on our liberties." Memorial and Remonstrance Against Religious Assessments, quoted in Everson, supra, 330 U.S., at 65, 67 S.Ct., at 536, 91 L.Ed. 711.

It is insisted that unless these religious exercises are permitted a "religion of secularism" is established in the schools. We agree, of course, that the State may not establish a "religion of secularism" in the sense of affirmatively opposing or showing hostility to religion, thus "preferring those who believe in no religion over those who do believe." Zorach v. Clauson, supra, 343 U.S., at 314, 72 S.Ct., at 684, 96 L.Ed. 954. We do not agree, however, that this decision in any sense has that effect. In addition, it might well be said that one's education is not complete without a study of comparative religion or the history of religion and its relationship to the advancement of civilization. It certainly may be said that the Bible is worthy of study for its literary and historic qualities. Nothing we have said here indicates that such study of the Bible or of religion, when presented objectively as part of a secular program of education, may not be effected consistent with the First Amendment. But the exercises here do not fall into those categories. They are religious exercises, required by the states in violation of the command of the First Amendment that the Government maintain strict neutrality, neither aiding nor opposing religion.

Finally, we cannot accept that the concept of neutrality, which does not permit a state to require a religious exercise even with the consent of the majority of those affected, collides with the majority's right to free exercise of religion. While the Free Exercise Clause clearly prohibits the use of state action to deny the rights of free exercise to anyone, it has never meant that a majority could use the machinery of the state to practice its beliefs. Such a contention was effectively answered by Mr. Justice Jackson for the Court in West Virginia Board of Education v. Barnette, 319 U.S. 624, 638, 63 S.Ct. 1178, 1185, 87 L.Ed. 1628 (1943):

"The very purpose of a Bill of Rights was to withdraw certain subjects from the vicissitudes of political controversy, to place them beyond the reach of majorities and officials and to establish them as legal principles to be applied by the courts. One's right to . . . freedom of worship . . . and other fundamental rights may not be submitted to vote; they depend on the outcome of no elections."

The place of religion in our society is an exalted one, achieved through a long tradition of reliance on the home, the church, and the inviolable citadel of the individual heart and mind. We have come to recognize through bitter experience that it is not within the power of government to invade that citadel, whether its purpose or effect be to aid or oppose, to advance or retard. In the relationship between man and religion, the State is firmly committed to a position of neutrality. Though the application of that rule requires interpretation of a delicate sort, the rule itself is clearly and concisely stated in the words of the First Amendment. Applying that rule to the facts of these cases, we affirm the judgment in No. 142. In No. 119, the judgment is reversed and the cause remanded to the Maryland Court of Appeals for further proceedings consistent with this opinion.

It is so ordered.

Judgment in No. 142 affirmed; judgment in No. 119 reversed and cause remanded with directions.

Appendixes

A.

Methods to Find the Law

The best way to find what the law may be in reference to a particular problem is to consult a competent attorney who is trained and experienced in the task of researching the law and rendering an opinion. Only from professional experience in researching the law, may come an adequate ability to know where to look for the appropriate law, as well as how to analyze the various court cases or statutory legislation which may properly relate to a particular question. It is appreciated, however, that if education students or practicing school persons are to have some knowledge of school law, they should have, at least, a rudimentary knowledge of the tools that are available to better inform him of such. It is for this reason that we are including the following material.

At the outset, it should be pointed out that when a lawyer has a problem of research into the law, he is ordinarily first concerned with ascertaining what the law of the particular state is in which the matter will be resolved. While a knowledge of the general law of the country is very helpful, particularly in the absence of pertinent law in the particular state in which the problem arises, the indispensable goal is to ascertain the law of the particular state. If a practicing school person has a problem about the correct interpretation of school law as it relates to his specific duties or the school district affairs, he should, be primarily concerned in ascertaining the law of his state. He should, therefore, first ascertain whether or not there is a statutory enactment relating to the particular problem. If there is a statutory enactment in his state that supplies the answer to his problem, together with such court interpretations in his own state as interpret the statute, it does not matter what the law of any other state may be.

Usually, the laws passed by the state legislatures on general assemblies are published in chronological order corresponding to the legislative sessions. Laws enacted each session are contained in bound volumes identified as session laws, containing a subject index as a part of such volumes. These various session laws are compiled into subject or title arrangements and published by private publishing firms as the statutory code of the state. The school code appears as a part of the bound volume or volumes representing the entire code of the state, containing a topical index of the laws, as well as annotations following each code section of court decisions or attorney general opinions in the particular state, construing and interpreting the particular sections. Such bound volumes are usually supplemented on the basis of additional statutory laws enacted, together with court decisions, for the purpose of keeping the bound volumes of the code up to date.

In view of the fact that the state statutory law, as interpreted by the court, is of primary importance in determining what the school law of the particular state may be, it is highly recommended that the school person, in embarking on his research to find the answer to a question of school law, first consult the statutory law of the state with which he is particularly concerned. There he may find the answer to his question, irrespective of what the case law may be in other jurisdictions or irrespective of what the law may be in other states.

If the statutory law of the state is vague or indecisive on the particular point in question, then the school person should next resort to an examination of either one or both of the following resource tools. In many states, the court decisions of the particular state are published and available in law reports or digests. Ordinarily, such digests contain a topical index in reference to subject matter as well as an all-inclusive index. The researcher should examine the particular volumes devoted to the school law of the state, check the topical or all-inclusive index, and attempt to find the subject matter that most specifically relates to his particular problem. Finding then the appropriate subject matter relating to his question, he should analyze the cases that are included within the identical subject. Quite often a key number is used to facilitate the research.

The second research tool that might be exploited to ascertain the state law, would be to refer to any textbook or cyclopedic statement of the law in the particular state. Ordinarily, such publications contain a volume or a portion of a volume containing a textbook statement of what the school law of the particular state may be, together with annotations of appropriate court decisions. A topical index of the school law ordinarily appears at the beginning of the textbook treatment of the school law. The researcher should first examine this topical index and ascertain the topic that most closely relates to his particular question. If he cannot find a topic that seems to be closely associated, he might then refer to the all-inclusive index in the publication relating to matters pertaining to school law, which is ordinarily contained under the general heading of *schools, school districts, public schools,* or *boards of education.* For instance, if his problem relates to teachers, the word, *teachers,* ordinarily appears as a particular index subject.

After the school person has first researched the particular law of the state with which he is primarily concerned, if he has not found an adequate answer to his question, it would then be advisable to research the case law of the United States with the hope of finding what the weight of authority seems to be. It is recommended that the following publications should be consulted as guides to the general law on any school topic of concern to the researcher: such publications *Corpus Juris Secundum* and *American Jurisprudence,* particularly Volumes 78 and 79 of the first publication and Volume 47 of American Jurisprudence. Each publication contains a textual treatment of the school law of the United States, together with copious footnotes of various court decisions from different states, as well as pertinent federal cases. At the beginning of the textbook treatment of the subject matter, there is contained a detailed outline of topics and subtopics, and the researcher should first attempt to apply his question to the particular topic and subtopic which basically deal with the problem. If the researcher cannot find a topic that is closely related to his problem, he might then refer to the all-inclusive index in the appropriate volume appearing as a part of either of the foregoing publications. One particular point of caution. If the researcher has found what apparently is the

answer to his question in the bound volume, it would be well for him to examine the paper supplement found in the pocket at the back of each volume
to ascertain whether there have been any changes in the law or pertinent
court decisions rendered which specifically relate to the topic that was examined
in the bound volume.

Other sources of the law may, likewise, be of importance. It is rather difficult
for a layman to undertake the necessary research with the hope of finding a
specific court case in the United States that may be of pertinent importance to
his problem. This is the area in which the services of a skilled researcher in the
law, as an attorney, is of particular importance. After finding an appropriate
case the researcher, from the standpoint of a lawyer, has not completed his
task until he ascertains whether or not the case has been repealed, amended,
or continues to represent a good statement of the current law. In a subsequent
portion of this article, we shall deal more with such matter.

Two particular publications are of importance in ascertaining the case law
on a particular topic. One is the *American Digest System,* which is a series of
digests of cases from 1658 to date consisting of eight units identified as follows:
Century Digest 1658 to 1896; First Decennial Digest 1896 to 1906; Second
Decennial Digest 1906 to 1916; Third Decennial Digest 1916 to 1926; Fourth
Decennial Digest 1926 to 1936; Fifth Decennial Digest 1936 to 1946; Sixth
Decennial Digest 1946 to 1956; and, the General Digest, Third Series 1956 to
the present time.

In each of these units the cases are arranged according to subject matter by
particular topics. Each topic contains an outline arrangement of the particular
subject matter, and each item in the outline is given a key number. Thus, the
American Digest System represents a method or device to find all the reported
cases on a particular point of law.

The second important publication that reports cases is the *National Reporter
System.* Such system is intended to include all the reported cases from each of
the states, including the opinion of the court in each state. The National
Reporter System is divided into nine geographical sections as follows: The
Northeastern Reporter which covers the states of Rhode Island, Massachusetts,
Ohio, New York, Indiana, and Illinois; the Atlantic Reporter which covers the
states of Maine, Vermont, Connecticut, New Hampshire, Pennsylvania, New
Jersey, Maryland, and Delaware; the Southern Reporter which covers the
states of Alabama, Louisiana, Mississippi, and Florida; the Southeastern Re-
porter which covers the states of West Virginia, North Carolina, Virginia,
South Carolina, and Georgia; the Southwestern Reporter which covers the
states of Tennessee, Kentucky, Missouri, Texas, and Arkansas; the Northwestern
Reporter which covers the states of Wisconsin, Iowa, Michigan, Minnesota,
North Dakota, South Dakota, and Nebraska; and, the Pacific Reporter which
covers the states of Wyoming, Montana, Kansas, Idaho, Colorado, Oklahoma,
Utah, New Mexico, Arizona, Nevada, Oregon, Washington, and California.

The National Reporter System, likewise, covers Federal cases through the
Supreme Court Reporter; the Federal Reporter, which includes cases decided
in the Federal Circuit Court of Appeals; and the Federal Supplement which
includes cases decided in the lower Federal Courts.

The National Reporter System is kept up to date by the publication of
volumes yearly in each series. Before the bound volume is published current
cases are published in weekly bulletins which are called "Advance Sheets."
Through the use of the "Advance Sheets" every recent, reported court decision
from any place within the United States may be examined.

Another publication which is of interest in determining the case law is the

American Law Reports. The intent of this publication is to include only the leading court cases on a particular point of law. The editors of the publication select cases from the various states and also include cases which are new or which represent various conflicts of legal opinion. The editors also include some cases which are outstanding or which particularly review the diverse authorities on a question of law.

The annotations in the American Law Reports consist of condensed cases or statements of principles appearing in connection with most of the reported cases. Such annotations also review the substance of what other courts may have decided on the same point of law. The annotations are very valuable in obtaining a general understanding of what the weight of authority in this country is on a particular point of law. The indexes to the annotated reports included within the American Law Reports (which is ordinarily abbreviated as *A.L.R.*) are very complete, and while the publication contains a numerical system, reference to the complete index is first suggested.

It has been heretofore indicated in this article that when the researcher has found a pertinent case or cases research is not complete unless he finds whether or not such cases have been reversed, disapproved, or modified, or whether or not there are other cases which have followed that law announced in the prior cases. In order to undertake such research, reference should be made to a publication, commonly referred to as *Shepards' Citations,* which indicates the foregoing facts. The researcher may then examine the other indicated cases.

This publication also indicates when any particular case is cited in another court case and shows where the same case may be found in the various publications. There is a separate Shepards' Citations published for each of the respective states, dealing primarily with that state's decisions, as well as a separate publication of volumes devoted to geographical areas corresponding to the National Reporter System.

There is also published *Shepards' Citations* to statutes. Through the use of the publication a person may ascertain the subsequent history of a particular statute since it was first passed, as well as where a particular statutory section of a law has been affected by other or subsequent legislation, including the cases in which the statute has been applied, cited, or construed by the courts.

Still another possible source of school law should be suggested. As heretofore indicated, in some of the states various law firms have published a textbook treatment of the case law of the state, annotated by court decisions, including therein sections devoted to the school law of the particular state. Such publications may be confined in one volume to the school law of the state, volumes embracing a textbook treatment of all the law of the state, or may embrace the law of several states situated in the same geographical area. In each respective state, if the researcher is fortunate enough to have such tools at his disposition, it would be well to examine such volumes dealing with the law of his particular state.

It might be well, also, for the education student or the practicing school person to consult in a local law library any available volumes of the attorney general's opinions for his particular state. As a general rule, while such opinions are generally considered authoritative as representative of the opinion of the chief law officer of the state, they are not to be considered as pronouncements of the law with the same effect as court decisions. The attorney general's opinions should be construed as guides to what the law is, and in the absence of a court pronouncement on the same point, such opinions carry great weight. It should be appreciated that, as a general practice, many state departments and officers of local subdivisions consistently follow the rulings of their attorney generals as a guide to the law on a particular point.

Technically speaking, a particular court case is legally binding only on the litigants involved in the court proceeding. Even in a particular county where various judges sit on the common pleas court bench, or some other court having countywide jurisdiction, each respective judge is not legally required to follow the prior ruling of his fellow judge in another case. Ordinarily, however, all the lower courts of record within a particular judicial jurisdiction follow the rulings of the appellate court within the respective jurisdiction. However, an appellate court within one jurisdiction in a state is not legally bound to follow the rulings of an appellate court in another district. On the other hand, rulings of the State Supreme Court are expected to be binding on all the courts located within the particular state.

Court cases, however, are very valuable as they are commonly cited as precedents in reference to the proper disposal of a pending legal issue. A great portion of the actual law of the United States has been predicated on court decisions. It has been aptly said by many persons, perhaps facetiously, but with a grain of truth, that the law of this country is not what the state legislatures or Federal Congress may provide but rather it is their action as construed, applied, and interpreted by the courts.

In conclusion, it should be said that for the practicing school person, a knowledge of the School Code in the state of his employment is invaluable. He will often find that many of the legal questions that he encounters in his work may be directly answered by reference to the State School Code, as construed by the courts of his state. We do not mean to downgrade, however, the fact that a knowledgeable acquaintanceship with principles of school law, generally, will also be of value to the practicing school person.

The education student, in taking a course in school law, may acquire a good background or foundation for his future career in school work, insofar as legal implications may be involved, by acquiring a knowledge of the general principles of school law. Then when he becomes a practicing school administrator, such knowledge, along with the particular School Code of the state in which he practices, will be of real value to him.

Attitude of Courts

Under our system of government, there are three branches: legislative, executive, and judicial. Courts are very zealous to maintain the principle of separation of powers, and generally a court will refuse to interfere with the administrative act of an administrative agency, unless it finds the act to be unlawful, or that the administrative body abused its discretion in that it acted arbitrarily or unlawfully, or that it exercised its discretion in a fraudulent manner. Courts will also refuse to substitute their judgment for the legislature or for boards of education, because in respect to acts of the legislature, it is not the province of the courts to decide the wisdom of the laws, and insofar as school boards are concerned, it is not for the courts to pass upon the wisdom of their acts, nor attempt in effect to operate the public school system. However, the court may declare an act of the legislature unconstitutional, or it may hold that an act of the board of education is either unlawful, beyond its lawful authority, or the exercise of an arbitrary, unreasonable, or improper discretion.

Courts are not inclined to hold legislation unconstitutional, or to hold actions of boards of education unlawful unless deemed necessary. Every reasonable presumption is to be considered in favor of the constitutionality of the law and in favor of the actions of the boards of education exercised in good faith. It would seem that, insofar as possible, laws relating to education are for the most part liberally construed by courts in order to effectuate the beneficial purpose behind the laws. In substance, to interpret the law liberally is to provide for the proper management and efficiency of the public school structure.

Wherever possible, courts are inclined to follow the principle of *stare decisis* which means to follow precedent. If a court without much thought were to do otherwise, it would result in a destruction of the stabilizing effect of case rule law and it would then become merely a matter of convenience, with little authority and without respect. On the other hand, many courts will not hesitate to ignore or overthrow precedent when they deem it necessary, particularly in view of changed economic or sociological conditions, the trend of established public opinion, the furtherance of justice, or because the principles have become outmoded or unjust. One court has indicated that it does not share the view that a court-made rule, though unjust or outmoded, becomes with age invulnerable to judicial attack and cannot be discarded except by legislative action.

While all courts are bound to follow decisions of the Supreme Court of the United States as the supreme law of the land, they are not bound to follow the decisions of other courts unless they are subordinate to such courts. While courts are not bound to consider precedents in other jurisdictions, they will consider them seriously, at least to a persuasive extent.

As a general rule, a court will not accept jurisdiction in a case where plaintiff has failed to use an available administrative remedy, nor will the court rule on the question that should be properly submitted for decision to an administrative agency. Courts will not decide a case if the factual situation is moot; and if a plaintiff, who has a proper cause of action, waits until after the statute of limitations has expired to bring the action to a court of law, he may lose his right. Even in the absence of a statute of limitations, if a plaintiff has not been diligent in pursuing his legal rights, a court may refuse to grant him any relief on the ground of *laches*.

B.

Glossary of Legal Terms

Ab initio: from the beginning.

Alatere: from the side of; collateral.

Abandum, or *abandun:* any thing abandoned, forfeited, or confiscated.

Abate: to put an end to; to nullify.

Abjudicate: to give away or transfer by judgment.

Abnegation: denial; renunciation.

Abode: a settled place of residence.

Abortive trial: a trial terminated without reaching a verdict.

Abridgement: an orderly abstract or digest of the law.

Abrogate: to annul or repeal a former law by the passage of a new one. Abrogation may be by express words, or by necessary implication.

Absolute: complete; unconditional; not relative or qualified.

Absolution: the dismissal of a charge; declaration of a person's innocence; or remission of sins or penalties.

Abstract: a summary, epitome, or brief statement of essential points.

Abuttals: the boundaries of any piece of land. In old law the ends were said to abut, the sides, to adjoin contiguous tracts.

Accede: to attain an office or position.

Acceleration: the shortening of the time for the vesting in possession of an expectant interest; the performance of a contract; or the payment of a note.

Acceptance: the receipt of a thing, offered by another, with the intention of retaining it.

Accessary, or *Accessory:* one who is not the actual perpetrator of a felony, but is in some way concerned therein. He may be an accessory (a) before the fact, *e.g.,* by inciting or counseling; or (b) after the fact, by relieving or assisting the felon.

Accident: such an unforeseen event, misfortune, act, or omission as is not the result of negligence or misconduct in the party.

Accite: to summon.

Account book: a book in which business transactions are entered, which, if regularly kept as a book of original entry, may be admitted in evidence.

Accrue: to grow to, to be added to, as interest to principal. (2) To arise; to happen or come to pass, as a cause of action.

Accusation: the charge that one has been guilty of a crime or misdemeanor, made to a proper officer.

Acquiescence: silent assent, or neglect to speak when one wishing to object or stand on his rights would naturally speak or act. Conduct from which consent may be implied, as distinguished from express consent.

Acquittal: a release or discharge, especially by verdict of a jury.

Act: something done or established. Laws passed by Congress and the legislatures of the several states are styled Acts. These may be (a) general or public, affecting the whole community; (b) private or special, affecting only particular persons and places and private concerns.

Action: a proceeding taken in a court of law.

Actionable: for which an action will lie; used chiefly of words spoken or written which constitute slander or libel.

Actual: that which is real or existing, as opposed to something merely possible, or to something which is presumptive or constructive.

Ad: at; by; for; near; on account of; to; until; upon.

Ad curiam: at court.

Ad diem: at the day.

Ad hoc: as to this.

Ad infinitum: without limit.

Adequate remedy: one that affords complete relief with reference to the particular matter in controversy, and which is appropriate to the circumstances of the case.

Adjudication: a judgment or decision.

Administrative Procedure Act: an act to establish a uniform system of administering laws by and among the agencies of the government and to provide for administrative and judicial review of the decisions of those agencies. 5 U.S. Code Section 1001, et seq., 60 Stat. 237 (1946).

Adolescence: the period commencing at 12 years in females, and 14 in males, and ending at 21 years of age.

Adoption: the act by which a person takes the child of another into his family and makes him, for all legal purposes, his own.

Adult: of full age. In civil law, a male who has reached the age of 14, a female who has reached the age of 12. In common law, one who has attained to the age of 21.

Advocate: one who conducts or pleads a cause for another.

Affiant: one who makes oath to a statement.

Affidavit: a written statement sworn to before a person having authority to administer an oath, by a person called an affiant, or deponent.

Affirm: to make firm; to establish. (1) To ratify or confirm the judgment of a lower court. (2) To ratify or confirm a voidable contract.

Agent: one authorized by another (the principal) to do an act or transact business for him, and to bind his principal within the limits of that authority.

Allegation: a statement of fact made in a legal proceeding.

Amicable action: an action entered by agreement of parties.

Analytical jurisprudence: a school of juristic thought, founded by John Austin, chiefly characterized by its effort to analyze the law and the legal institutions of the present.

Ancillary: that which is subordinate to, or assists, some other thing, *e.g.*, ancillary administration.

Apostle: a summary statement of a case received by a higher court from a lower one.

Apparent authority: that authority which, although not actually given, the principal knowingly permits his agent to exercise.

Appeal: an application by an appellant to a higher court to rectify the order of the court below.

Appeal bond: an amount required by statute to be filed by an appellant as a requirement for perfecting an appeal.

Appellant: he who makes an appeal from one court to another.

Appellate jurisdiction: the power of a superior court to review the decision of an inferior court.

Appellee: the party in a cause against whom an appeal has been taken.

Arbiter: one bound to decide according to the rules of law and equity.

Arraign: to bring a prisoner to the bar of the court to answer the matter charged upon him in the indictment. The action consists of three parts: (a) calling him by name; (b) reading him the indictment; (c) asking him if he be guilty or not guilty. He may then plead "guilty" or "not guilty," or stand mute, which is, in effect, the same as a plea of "not guilty."

Assault: strictly speaking, is threatening to strike or harm; if a blow be struck, it is battery. Assaults are common or aggravated, the former being those for which no special punishment is prescribed by the law; the latter being made with an intent to commit some additional crime, as rape, murder, or robbery. An assault is in civil law a tort, for which damages are recoverable.

Assent: approval of something done. It may be express, *i.e.,* openly declared; or implied, *i.e.,* presumed by law, as when the thing done is for the person's benefit and he makes no express dissent.

Attested copy: a verified transcript of a document.

Attractive nuisance doctrine: the doctrine that one who maintains instrumentalities or appliances on his premises of a character likely to attract children in play is liable to a child who is injured thereon.

Avoidance: the making of a transaction or instrument void, or of no effect.

Bail: to set at liberty a person arrested or imprisoned, on security (or bail) taken for his appearance on a day and at a place named.

Bail bond: the bond taken with sureties at the time the defendant is released, conditioned for the due appearance of such defendant.

Battery: beating and wounding, including every touching or laying hold, however trifling, of another's person or clothes, in an angry, insolent, or hostile manner.

Bench warrant: an order issued by a court for the attachment or arrest of an individual for contempt, or where an indictment has been found.

Bilateral contract: a contract in which both the contracting parties are bound to fulfill obligations reciprocally toward each other.

Bill of particulars: a statement of a plaintiff's cause of action.

Bona fide: in good faith; honestly; without fraud or unfair dealing.

Bond: a written acknowledgment of a debt or contract to pay, under seal.

Breach: a breaking; either the invasion of a right, or the violation of a duty.

Bribery: the offense of giving or receiving a gift or reward intended to influence a person in the exercise of a judicial or public duty.

Capacity: legal ability to contract, to take hold, and convey property, to sue and be sued, etc. Lunatics are devoid of capacity, and it is more or less limited by statute in the case of infants, married women, and, sometimes, aliens.

Capitulary: a collection of laws and ordinances arranged by divisions.

Case: an abbreviation for Trespass on the case. (2) A statement of facts for counsel's opinion. (3) An action or suit at law, or in equity. (4) A written statement of the facts by an inferior court, for the opinion of the superior court. (5) An agreed statement of the facts made by the parties to a dispute for the purpose of obtaining the opinion of the court thereon.

Case law: a body of law created by judicial decisions, as distinguished from the cases historically.

Case system: a method of teaching or studying the science of the law by a study of the law derived from statutory and other sources.

Caucus: a meeting of the leaders of a party or faction to decide on the candidates or policies to be supported by their followers.

Certificate: a statement, usually in writing, given by a person having some official status, relative to some matter within his official knowledge or authority.

Certiorari: an original writ or action whereby a case is removed from an inferior to a superior court for trial. The record of the proceedings is then transmitted to the superior court.

Cestui que trust: the person who possesses the equitable or beneficial right to property, the legal estate of which is vested in a trustee. Also called a beneficiary.

Circumstantial evidence: evidence of circumstances from which a fact not directly proved, *e.g.,* the commission of a crime by the accused, is to be inferred as a necessary or probable consequence.

Citation: a summons to appear, applied particularly to process in probate courts. (2) Citation *viis et modis,* one posted up in a public place. (3) A reference to authorities in support of an argument.

Cite: to summon; to command the presence of a person; to notify a person of legal proceedings against him and require his appearance thereto.

Citizen: of the United States, any person born in the United States, except an Indian; or born out of the United States, if his parents were citizens; or one of foreign birth and parentage who has become naturalized. A citizen of the United States residing in any of the states is a citizen of that state.

Civil: pertaining to a city or state, and a man in his relations to his fellow citizens.

Civil action: an action which has for its object the recovery of private or civil rights, or compensation for their infraction.

Client: one who employs an attorney or counselor to manage his case in court, or to advise him about legal matters.

Code: a collection or system of laws.

Coercion: constraint; compulsion; compelling a person by physical force, or by threats and the wrongful exercise of authority, to do what he would otherwise not do. Coercion is implied in many cases, as in the commission of a crime by a wife in the presence of her husband.

Cognovit: a defendant's written confession of an action brought against him; *i.e.,* his admission that he has no available defense, and consents to judgment being entered against him.

Collateral: by the side of; indirect.

Collateral attack: an attempt to defeat the operation of a judgment in some proceeding where some new right derived through or from the judgment is involved.

Collateral facts: those not directly connected with the issue or matter in dispute.

Collation: the comparison of a copy with its original to ascertain its correctness.

Collusion: a secret compact between persons apparently hostile, to do some act in order to defraud or prejudice a third person, or for some improper purpose. Judgment obtained by collusion is a nullity.

Color of office: a pretence of official right to do an act made by one who has no such right.

Comity: a term designating the practice by which one court follows the decision of another court on a like question, though not bound by the law of precedents to do so.

Common law: that system of law which does not rest for its authority upon any express statutes, but derives its force and authority from universal consent and immemorial usage, and which is evidenced by the decisions of the courts of law, technically so called, in contradistinction to those of equity and the ecclesiastical courts. It prevails in England and most of the United States except when abrogated or modified by statute.

Community of interest: for the prevention of multiplicity of suits, that which exists where all the parties are interested in the same subject matter and where the same facts and law are applicable to all.

Comparative jurisprudence: a system of jurisprudence based on a comparison of the legal systems of the world.

Compensatory damages: such as measure the actual loss; not exemplary or punitive.

Competency: the legal fitness or capacity of a witness to testify in the trial of a case; also, the quality of evidence offered which makes it proper to be received.

Compos mentis: capable of transacting business.

Concurrent: running along together. Two courts are said to have concurrent jurisdiction when either may entertain a suit relating to the same subject matter at the choice of the plaintiff.

Concurrent negligence: where both the negligence of the plaintiff and that of the defendant contribute directly to produce the injury.

Confession: an admission by a person accused of crime that he has committed the offense charged. It may be judicial, *i.e.,* made before a court or examining magistrate, or extra-judicial, *i.e.,* made outside of court. Voluntary confessions, not made in pursuance of threats or the hope of favor, are admissible in evidence against the persons making them.

Confiscation: the appropriation of property taken from an enemy, or seized for a violation of law, for the use of the state.

Conflict of laws: the variance between the laws of two countries or states, relating to the subject matter of a suit brought in one of them, when the parties to the suit, or some of them, or the subject matter, belong to the other.

Constitution: the fundamental law of a state or nation, establishing the form and limitations of government, securing the rights of the citizen, etc. The Constitution of the United States was adopted in a convention of representatives of the people, at Philadelphia, September 17, 1787, and became the law of the land on the first Wednesday in March 1789. Each of the states composing the United States has a constitution of its own. Constitutions usually prescribe the manner in which they may be amended.

Construction: the interpretation of a statute or written instrument.

Contempt: a wilful disregard or disobedience of public authority. Each house of Congress, and of a state legislature, has power to punish contempt on the part of members or persons properly brought before it by imprisonment, reprimand, or expulsion. Courts may punish one who disobeys the rules, order, or process, or wilfully offends against the dignity and good order of the court, by fine or imprisonment. A person is said to purge or clear his contempt, when he expresses contrition and submits himself to the court.

Contiguous: actual contact or touching, as contiguous lands.

Contra: against; contrary to.

Contract: an agreement between competent parties, upon a legal consideration, to do, or to abstain from doing, some act. In its widest use the term includes agreements of record, judgments, and contracts under seal, or specialties. It is, however, usually applied to simple or parol contracts, not under seal, including written as well as verbal contracts. Contracts may be express, in which the terms are stated in words; or implied, *i.e.,* presumed by law to have been made from the relations of the parties; mutual and dependent, in which the performance by one is dependent upon the performance by the other; independent, when either promise may be performed without reference to the other; entire, in which the complete performance by one is a condition precedent to demanding performance of the other; severable, in which the things to be performed are capable of separation, so that on performance of part, the party performing may demand a proportionate part of the consideration from the other; executed, in which the things each agrees to perform are done at the time the contract is made; executory, in which some act remains to be done by one or both of the parties; personal, *i.e.,* depending on the skill or qualities of one of the parties; or they may be contracts of beneficence, by which only one of the contracting parties is to be benefited, as loans, deposit, and mandate.

Contravention: an act done in violation of a legal obligation.

Contributory negligence: negligence of the plaintiff which, combined with the negligence of the defendant, was the proximate cause of the injury complained of.

Conventio in unum: agreement between two parties upon the sense of the contract proposed.

Copyright: an incorporeal right, being the exclusive privilege of printing, reprinting, selling, and publishing his own original work, which the law allows an author. In England, it lasts for life and seven years longer, or for forty-two years, whichever is the longer period. In the United States, it lasts for twenty-eight years, with a privilege of renewal for twenty-eight more under certain conditions. It extends to maps, prints, engravings, and musical compositions. The right may be assigned by a written instrument duly attested and recorded.

Court: a place where justice is administered.

Court of Record: a court which keeps a permanent record of its proceedings.

Curative act: an act of a legislature having retroactive effect and intended to correct irregularities of a technical nature.

Custom: unwritten law established by long usage.

Damage: an injury to person, property, or reputation, occasioned by the wrongful act or negligence of another, or by accident.

Damages: the amount claimed, or allowed, as compensation for injuries sustained through the wrongful act or negligence of another.

Day in court: the right of a party defendant to have due notice of the claim against him which may result in judgment, and to be given opportunity to defend against it.

De facto; de jure: in fact; by right.

De novo: anew; afresh.

Decision: the conclusion or judgment of the court, as opposed to the reasoning of the court in its opinion.

Declaratory: that which explains or fixes the meaning of something which was before doubtful or uncertain, *e.g.*, a declaratory statute.

Decree: an order made by the court in a suit in equity.

(A) decree nisi: is one which is at first conditional, but becomes absolute, unless within a given time the party against whom it is rendered shows good cause why it should not be.

Dedicate: to devote land to some public use; *e.g.*, to make a private way public; to set apart ground for a public park, etc.

Defamation: scandalous words written or spoken concerning another, tending to the injury of his reputation, for which an action on the case for damages would lie.

Defendant: the person against whom an action is brought, or an indictment found.

Defense: a forcible resistance of an attempt to injure one's self, one's family, or property, or to commit a felony. (2) In pleading, the denial by the defendant of the truth of plaintiff's complaint. (3) The conduct of the trial, on behalf of the defendant, whether he be sued in a civil action or be prosecuted criminally.

Definitive: that which terminates a suit.

Delictum: a crime, tort, or wrong.

Demur: to stay, or abide. To object formally to a pleading, that, admitting the facts to be true as stated, no cause is shown why the party demurring should go further. It imports that the party demurring will stay, and not proceed, until the court decides whether he is bound to do so.

Deponent: a person who makes an affidavit, or gives testimony under oath, which is reduced to writing for use in the trial of a cause, called a deposition.

Dictum: the expression by a judge of an opinion on a point of law arising during the hearing of a case, which, however, is not necessary for the decision of that case. A dictum is not, therefore, binding on other judges.

Digest: an abridged and methodically arranged compilation of decisions or statutes intended to aid one in finding out what the law is on a given subject. The principal digests now in use are the *United States Digest,* the digests of the various states, and United States reports.

Directory statute: is opposed (1) to declaratory, *i.e.*, a statute which merely declares what the law is; and (2) to imperative. When a statute directs that an act should be done in a specific manner, or authorizes it upon certain conditions, if a strict compliance with its provisions is not essential to the validity of the act, it is said to be directory, although the performance may be enforced by mandamus; but if such compliance is essential, it is said to be imperative.

Discretion: the use of private and independent judgment.

Dismiss: to send out of court, as a defendant, or an action.

Dissenting opinion: an opinion disagreeing with that of the majority, handed down by one or more of the members of the court.

Divisible: susceptible of being divided or separated into component parts.

Doctrine: a principle of law developed through court decisions.

Due process of law: law in the regular course of administration through courts of justice, according to those rules and forms which have been established for the protection of private rights.

Ex necessitate legis; rei: from the necessity of the law; the thing.

Ex officio: by virtue of his office.

Ex parte: of the one part. An action is ex parte when it is not an adverse proceeding against anyone else.

Ex post facto: made after the occurrence, *e.g.,* legislation, which has, or would have if passed, a retrospective application.

Ex relatione: on the relation of information.

Edict: a law ordained by a sovereign.

Ejusdem generis: of the same kind or nature.

Eminent domain: the right which a government retains over the estates of individuals to resume them for public use.

Enabling statute: one which removes a restriction or disability.

Enact: to establish by law; to decree.

Equal protection of the laws: a right the denial of which by the states is prohibited by the Fourteenth Amendment to the Federal Constitution; a guaranty that no person or class of persons shall be denied the same protection of the laws which is enjoyed by other persons or other classes in like circumstances, in their lives, their liberty, their property, and in pursuit of happiness.

Equity: fairness. That system of jurisprudence which grew up in and was first administered by the English Courts of Chancery.

Error: a mistake in judgment. An incorrect ruling or charge on the trial of a case. Contracts and settlements made under error of fact will in some cases be avoided; those made under error of law will not, as a matter of public policy.

Estoppel: an admission or declaration, by which a person is concluded, *i.e.,* prevented from bringing evidence to controvert it, or prove the contrary.

Executed contract: one which has been wholly performed, as opposed to an executory one.

Executory: that which is not completed; which requires something to be done, or to happen, before it is perfect or assured.

Expert: one who has acquired by special study, practice, and experience, peculiar skill and knowledge in relation to some particular science, art, or trade. (2) A witness who, because of such special knowledge, is called to testify in cases depending on questions peculiar to such science, art, or trade.

Express: that which is stated in direct words, and not left to implication.

Fait accompli: an accomplished fact.

Feasance: a performance.

Fee simple: a freehold estate of inheritance, absolute and unqualified. This is the highest and most ample estate known to the law, out of which all others are taken or "carved." An owner in fee has absolute power of disposition.

Felony: signifies any indictable offense which is greater than a misdemeanor.

Fiat: a decree; an order or warrant by a judge or other constituted authority.

Fiduciary relation: that which exists in all cases in which influence has been acquired and abused, in which confidence has been reposed and betrayed.

Final order: an order or judgment which determines the cause and prevents further litigation upon the point in the court which gives it.

Finding: the conclusion of a court or jury as to a question of fact or law at issue.

First instance, court of: that before which an action is first brought for trial, as contrasted with a court of appeal.

Forfeiture: the loss of some right or property as a penalty for some illegal act, negligence, or breach of contract.

Franchise: a special privilege or liberty, conferred by government, and vested in particular individuals.

Fraud: the gain of an advantage to another's detriment by deceitful or unfair means.

Fuero: Spanish statute law.

Full faith and credit: the requirement, under Article IV, section 1, that the public acts, records, and judicial proceedings of every state shall be given the same effect by the courts of another state that they have by law and usage in the state of litigation.

Gross negligence: such want of care as not even inattentive and thoughtless men are guilty of with respect to their own property.

Habeas corpus: words used in various writs, commanding one who detains another to "have," or bring him before the court issuing the same.

Hearing: the trial of a suit. (2) The examination of a person charged with a crime or misdemeanor and of the witnesses for the accused.

Hearsay evidence: statements made by a witness on the authority of another, and not from personal knowledge or observation.

Historical jurisprudence: a theory of jurisprudence characterized by the idea that law is best understood by studying its historical development, and that the growth of law is determined by the customs and habits of the people.

Implied power: such power as may be reasonably necessary to make an express power effective.

In loco parentis: in the place of a parent.

In pari causa; delicto materia: in an equal case; in equal fault; upon the same matter or subject.

In statu quo: in the same situation as.

Indictment: a written accusation against one or more persons, of a crime of a public nature, preferred to and presented upon oath by a grand jury.

Information: communicated knowledge. (2) A formal accusation or complaint, charging a person or corporation with some crime or violation of law.

Initiative: a procedure frequently authorized by statute whereby, upon the petition of a certain number of electors, laws may be adopted by popular vote.

Injunction: this was originally the Court of Chancery's discretionary process of preventive and remedial justice. Injunctions are (a) preventive, restraining a person from doing something, or mandatory, commanding something to be done; (b) preliminary, provisional interlocutory, granted on the filing of a bill, or while the suit is pending or continuing to do the acts complained of until final hearing or the further order of the court; or (c) final, perpetual, awarded after full hearing on the merits, and as a final determination of the rights of the parties.

Imputed negligence: negligence chargeable to a person by reason of his relation to the negligent party, *i.e.,* as master of a negligent servant.

Instanter: immediately; at once.

Instrument: a formal legal writing.

Interim: in the meantime; meanwhile.

Interim order: one made in the meantime, and until something is done.

Interlocutory: Incident to a suit still pending. An order or decree, made during the progress of a case, which does not amount to a final decision, is termed interlocutory.

Interpolate: to insert words in a complete document.

Interpretation: the discovery and declaration of the meaning of words or signs employed in a statute or instrument.

Intra vires: the opposite of ultra vires.

Inure or *Enure:* to take effect.

Ipse dixit: a bare assertion, resting on the authority of an individual.

Ipso facto: as the necessary consequence of the act.

Ipso jure: by the mere operation of law.

Judgment: the decision of a court; the expression by a judge of the reasons for his decision. Judgments may be final, putting an end to the case; interlocutory, given in the progress of a case upon some matter which does not finally determine the case. They may be rendered on confession by the defendant; on default, when the defendant fails to appear to answer or demur within the allotted time; or on the merits, after a full trial on the pleadings and evidence.

Juris: of law; of right.

Juris et de jure: A conclusive presumption, which can not be rebutted.

Jurisdiction: the power of a court to entertain and decide any action or matter.

Jurisprudence: the science of law. (2) A body of law.

Jus: law; right; equity; authority.

Laches: negligence or unreasonable delay in pursuing a legal remedy, whereby a person forfeits his right.

Law: a rule of action to which men are obliged to conform. The statutes are called the written law, as opposed to the unwritten law founded on precedents and custom.

Legal: according or relating to law.

Legally competent: one who is of legal age, of sound mind, and who has not been convicted of a crime rendering him infamous.

Lex: a law; the law; sometimes used as synonymous with jus, right.

Lex communis: the common law.

Lex contractus: the law of the contract.

Liability: a debt or responsibility.

License: a permission or authority to do something which would otherwise be inoperative, wrongful, or illegal. It may be either written, or verbal; but all licenses under statutes are written.

Liquidated: fixed; ascertained, *e.g.,* damages, the exact amount of which must be paid, or may be collected, upon a default or breach of contract.

Litigation: contest in court.

Locus: a place.

Lowest responsible bidder: a term referring not only to the bidder's financial responsibility but also to such characteristics as his general ability and capacity to carry on the work, his equipment and facilities, his promptness, and the quality of work previously done by him.

Mal: a prefix, meaning bad; wrong; fraudulent.

Mala: bad; wrong; fraudulent.

Mala in se: acts which are wrong in themselves.

Mala prohibita: acts which are prohibited by human laws, but not necessarily mala in se, or wrong in themselves.

Malfeasance: the commission of an unlawful act.

Malice: hatred; ill will; a formed design of doing an unlawful act, whether another may be prejudiced by it or not. If the known and necessary consequence of the act done is injury to another, the law implies malice; but express malice, *i.e.,* actual ill feeling toward the person injured, may also be proved to exist.

Malicious: implying malice; wrongful; wanton; without just cause.

Malicious injuries: such as are inflicted on person or property wantonly and without just cause, *e.g.,* arson, destruction of property, etc.

Mandamus: a prerogative writ of a remedial nature, addressed to a person, sole or corporate, and not to the sheriff, as are ordinary writs, requiring the person to whom it is addressed to do some act therein specified, which is generally one connected with his duty as a public official, or as a corporation exercising public franchises. The writ may be alternative, *i.e.,* granted on ex parte affidavits, and requiring the person to do the thing or show cause why he should not be compelled to do it; or peremptory, *i.e.,* after final hearing, when there is nothing for the defendant to do but obey.

Mandatory: he to whom a mandate or charge is given. (2) He that obtains a benefice by mandamus.

Mandate: a judicial command. (2) A charge or commission. (3) A bailment of goods without reward to have something done to them, not merely for safe custody.

Market value: the price which property will bring when it is offered for sale by one who desires, but is not obliged to sell it, and is bought by one who is under no necessity to buy it.

Measure of damage: the test which determines the amount of damages to be given.

Mechanic's lien: a statutory lien allowed one who furnishes labor or material toward the making of an improvement, either upon the fund in the owner's hands or upon the land improved.

Merits, judgment upon: is one rendered, after a hearing of the case upon the pleadings and evidence, upon the justice of the cause, and not upon technical grounds alone.

Ministerial: belonging to a minister or subordinate who is bound to follow instructions; opposed to judicial or discretionary.

Misdemeanor: any crime or indictable offense not amounting to a felony.

Misfeasance: a wrongful act. (2) The improper performance of some lawful act. (3) Negligence.

Modus: manner; means; way.

Moral turpitude: an act of baseness, vileness, or depravity, contrary to the accepted and customary rule of right and duty between men.

Negligence: want of care.

Negligence, contributory: is where a person, by his own want of care, has contributed to bring about a loss or accident, and cannot, therefore, recover damages against the defendant.

Negligence per se: negligence of itself or as a matter of law; the violation of a statute passed for the protection of the public.

Nisi: unless.

Nolens volens: whether willing or unwilling.

Non compos mentis: one not of sound mind; a lunatic, idiot, or drunken person.

Non-suit: a judgment against the plaintiff when he fails to prove his case or neglects to appear at the trial.

Nudum pactum: a bare contract, *i.e.,* one not under seal and made without any consideration upon which, therefore, no action will lie.

Nuisance: something noxious or offensive. Anything not authorized by law which causes hurt, inconvenience, or damage. It may be (a) private, as where one so uses his property as to damage another's or disturb his quiet enjoyment of it; (b) public, or common, where the whole community is annoyed or inconvenienced by the offensive acts, as where one obstructs a highway, or carries on a trade that fills the air with noxious and offensive fumes.

Oath: a solemn affirmation, declaration, or promise made under a sense of responsibility to God for the truth of what is stated or the faithful performance of what is undertaken.

Offense: an open violation of law; a crime or misdemeanor.

Opening statement: a statement and appraisal, by counsel for plaintiff, of his case and of the facts which he intends to establish in support thereof, given before any evidence is offered in the trial of such case.

Ordinance: a law; statute; decree. The term is generally applied to the laws of a municipal corporation.

Original jurisdiction: the jurisdiction of a court to entertain a case in its inception, as contrasted with the appellate jurisdiction.

Overt: open, public.

Pares: a person's peers or equals.

Parliamentary law: that body of regulations which governs parliamentary procedure.

Parol: by word of mouth; not under seal. Pleadings when made viva voce are called the parol; to pray that "the parol might demur," is to ask that the pleadings might be stayed until a certain date.

Pecuniary: relating to money.

Per capita: by the head.

Per se: by itself; alone.

Peremptory: absolute; final; admitting of no excuse for non-performance, *e.g.,* an order; mandamus.

Perjury: a false statement under oath, or affirmation, wilfully made in regard to a material matter, in judicial proceedings.

Perpetual injunction: an injunction which finally disposes of the matter in dispute, and is indefinite in point of time.

Petition: a supplication made by an inferior to a superior, and especially to one having jurisdiction. The right to petition the government for a redress of grievances is secured to the people by the Constitution of the United States. The written statement of the plaintiff's case in an action is commonly called a petition.

Philosophical jurisprudence: a theory of jurisprudence which seeks to explain and test law by reference to certain philosophical tenets.

Plaintiff: one who brings an action.

Plea: the formal answer of a defendant to the plaintiff's declaration in an action.

Pleadings: the alternate and opposing statements of the parties to an action from the declaration, petition, or bill of complaint, until issue is joined.

Plenary: full, conclusive.

Plenary suits: those in which the proceedings must be full and formal, as opposed to summary, in which the proceedings are brief and informal.

Plurality: a greater number. A plurality of votes is a larger number of votes cast for one candidate than any other has received. It may be less than a majority, which is more than half of all votes cast.

Police power: the power of legislatures to pass laws regulating and restraining private rights and occupations for the general welfare and security.

Poll: the head; whence poll-tax, a capitation tax; to poll a jury, *i.e.,* to question them one by one as to their verdict; to poll, *i.e.,* to take votes, etc.

Power: an authority to act which one person gives to another.

Practice: that part of the law which regulates the conduct of legal proceedings. (2) The conduct of legal proceedings in the courts through all their various stages.

Prayer: that part of a bill which asks for relief. It may be general, asking for any relief the court is authorized to grant; or special, asking for a particular form of relief.

Precedents: previous decisions of the court, which should always be followed in similar cases by courts of co-ordinate authority. (2) Forms of procedure which have been sanctioned by the courts, or long usage, and are therefore to be followed.

Prejudice: a forejudgment, or bias, which interferes with a man's impartiality and sense of justice.

Prejudicial error: An error committed during a trial, of sufficient importance that it will be ground for a new trial or for reversal on appeal.

Premeditation: a design or intention formed to commit a crime or do an act, before it is done.

Prescribed by law: authorized by actual legislative enactment.

Prima facie: at first view; on the first aspect. Prima facie evidence, presumptions, etc., are such as will prevail, if not rebutted, or disproved.

Pro tanto: for so much; to that extent.

Procedure: the mode in which the successive steps in a litigation are taken.

Process: the means whereby a court enforces obedience to its orders.

Proximate cause: that which produces an event, and, without which the event could not have occurred.

Punitive statute: one creating a forfeiture or imposing a penalty.

Purge: to clear one's self of a criminal charge.

Quantum meruit: a form of action brought by one party to a contract against the other, not founded on the contract itself, but on an implied promise to pay for so much as the party suing has done. If one party refuses to perform his part, the other may rescind and sue on a quantum meruit.

Quash: to annul or discharge, *e.g.,* an indictment, a conviction, or order.

Quasi: as if; almost.

Quasi contract: one which arises without express agreement between the parties; an implied contract.

Quid pro quo: a consideration.

Quit-claim: to release a claim or right of action.

Quo warranto: a writ or proceeding, by which the government inquires into the right of a person, or corporation, to hold an office, or exercise a franchise, which was never lawfully held, or which has been forfeited by neglect or abuse.

Quorum: the minimum number, *e.g.*, of directors or legislators, necessary to be present in order to constitute a formal meeting capable of transacting business.

Ratification: the act of adopting, or confirming, a thing done or contract made, by another without authority, or by the person himself at a time when he was legally incompetent.

Reasonable doubt: that state of the case which after the entire comparison and consideration of all the evidence leaves the minds of the jurors in that condition that they can not say they feel an abiding conviction to a moral certainty of the truth of the charge.

Recital: the rehearsal or making mention in an instrument of something which has been done before. Recitals lead up to and explain the operative part, and are either introductory or narrative. Recitals in a deed are binding upon the party making them and his privies.

Reductio ad absurdum: the method of disproving an argument by showing that it leads to an absurd consequence.

Referee: one to whom anything is referred for arbitration, inquiry and report, or trial.

Referendum: the practice of referring to the voters measures passed by the legislative body for their approval or rejection.

Relevancy: the degree of connection between a fact tendered in evidence and the issue to be proved. An irrelevant fact is one which has no applicability to the issue joined, and is therefore inadmissible in evidence.

Relief: legal remedy for wrongs.

Remand: to re-commit a person to prison. (2) To send back a cause to the same court out of which it came, for trial or some further action on it there.

Remedy: the legal means to recover a right or redress a wrong.

Replevin: a form of action which lies to recover possession of specific chattels which have been taken from the plaintiff unlawfully. It may be brought by a general owner, who has the right to immediate possession, or by one who has a special property and possession at the time the goods are taken.

Res judicata: a point already judicially decided; it is conclusive until the judgment is reversed.

Rescission: the rescinding or putting an end to a contract by the parties, or one of them, *e.g.*, on the ground of fraud.

Respondeat superior: the responsibility of a master for the acts of his servants.

Respondent: the party who makes answer to a bill in chancery. (2) One who is security for another.

Restraining order: an injunction.

Restraining statute: one which narrows and restricts the operation of the common law.

Right: a well-founded claim; the correlative of obligation.

Sanction: of a law, is the power of enforcing it, or inflicting a penalty for its violation. (2) Consent.

Sans recours: without recourse.

Scienter: an allegation in the pleading that the defendant, etc., did the thing in question wilfully.

Semper paratus: a plea that the defendant has been always ready to perform what is demanded of him.

Simple: plain; unconditional; not under seal, nor of record; not combined with anything else.

Simple negligence: that which is neither gross nor wanton, but merely a failure to exercise ordinary care.

Slander: the malicious defamation of a person in his reputation, profession, or business, by words.

Sociological jurisprudence: a theory of jurisprudence which regards law as one of the agencies of social welfare, and holds that by study and conscious effort it may be molded to meet social needs.

Stare decisis: to stand by decided cases. The name of a doctrine giving to precedent the authority of established law; not, however, always regarded.

Status: the condition of a person in the eye of the law. (2) By analogy, a thing is said to have a status.

Status quo: the existing state of things at any given date. To leave in status quo, is to leave unaltered.

Statute: a law enacted by the legislative power in a country or state. It may be (a) declaratory, *i.e.,* one which does not alter the existing law, as opposed to remedial or amending; (b) enabling, *i.e.,* removing restrictions, as opposed to disabling. Statutes may also be either public or private, the latter including those which have a special application to particular persons or places. The public, general statutes are called the Statutes at Large.

Statutory: created by or depending upon express statute, and not upon equitable or common-law rules.

Stipulation: a bargain, proviso, or condition.

Strictissimi juris: to be most strictly applied.

Subpoena: a writ commanding attendance in a court under a penalty.

Subrogation: substitution of one person for another, the person substituted acquiring the other's rights in respect to a debt or claim, which he has paid.

Substantial evidence: more than a mere scintilla; such relevant evidence as a reasonable mind might accept as adequate to support a conclusion.

Substantive law: the positive law of duties and rights.

Sue: to bring a civil action.

Suit: a civil action.

Summary: short; speedy; as opposed to plenary or regular summary jurisdiction is the power of the court to give judgment, or to make an order forthwith without further preliminaries, such as committing for trial.

Summing up: the argument made by counsel at the close of the evidence. (2) The concise review of the evidence made by a judge in charging the jury.

Summons: a writ commanding the sheriff to notify a party therein named to appear in court on or before a specified date, and to answer the complaint in an action commenced against him.

Sumptuary laws: those in restraint of luxury and excessive expenditure.

Supersedas: a writ by which proceedings are stayed.

Supra: This word occurring by itself in a book, etc., refers the reader to a previous part, like ante.

Supra protest: after protest.

Surety: one who makes himself responsible for the due fulfillment of another's obligation, in case the latter, who is called the principal, fails himself to fulfill it.

Syllabus rule: a rule peculiar to the supreme court of Ohio providing that the syllabus of a case, as printed in the official state reports, alone constitutes the law of the case.

Symbolic delivery: the delivery of something as a representative of another thing, of which actual delivery can not be conveniently made, because of its bulk or situation.

Tacit: silent, implied from silence.

Tales: jurors summoned to fill up any vacancies existing in the regular panel.

Tales, de circumstantibus: such jurors selected from the bystanders.

Talmud: the body of Jewish civil and canonical law.

Tangible: that which may be felt or touched; corporeal.

Tariff: a schedule or tabulated list of import duties or rates.

Tax: a sum assessed against and collected from a citizen for the support of the government.

Temporary injunction: an injunction somewhat in the nature of a restraining order, effective only until the trial of the action in which it was issued.

Tenor: the purport and effect of a document, as opposed to its actual words. (2) It is sometimes opposed to "effect," to signify a correct copy.

Tenure: the mode of holding property or office.

Third party: one who is a stranger to a contract, or proceeding, not being plaintiff or defendant.

Tort: injury or wrong.

To wit: to know; that is to say; namely.

Town: a civil division less than a county; a small collection of houses, or a village.

(A)township: i.e., a division of the public lands of the United States into tracts of six miles square, containing thirty-six sections, of six hundred and forty acres each.

Transaction: an act by one party which affects another, out of which an action might arise and judgment be taken.

Transcript: a copy, especially an official copy.

Traumatic injury: a bodily injury produced by violence.

Trial: the examination of a cause, civil or criminal, by a competent tribunal; the decision of the issues of law or fact in an action. It may be by a judge or judges, with or without a jury.

Tripartite: divided into three parts; a deed or contract to which there are three distinct parties.

True bill: the indorsement which the grand jury makes upon a bill of indictment when, having heard the evidence, it is satisfied that there is a prima facie case against the accused.

Ultra vires: A company or corporation is said to act ultra vires, when it exceeds the authority imparted to it by its charter, articles of association, etc.

Umpire: one who decides a question in dispute; a referee, especially one who is chosen by arbitrators to determine finally a point on which they are unable to agree.

Unilateral contract: when the party to whom an engagement is made makes no express agreement on his part, the contract is called unilateral, even in cases where the law attaches certain obligations to his acceptance of the engagement. A loan for use is of this kind.

Unlawful: contrary to law.

Ure: custom.

Usage: practice long continued. The habit, mode, or uniform course of dealing in a particular trade.

Usurpatio: a taking and holding of a thing without right.

Valid: good; effectual; of binding force.

Venue: the neighborhood; the county in which an act is done, or a cause of action arises, from which the jury is taken for the trial of the case. A change of venue is the sending of a case to be tried before a jury of another county, when circumstances render it impossible to have an impartial trial in the county where the cause of action arose.

Verbal: made by word of mouth, oral.

Verdict: the decision of a jury reported to the court on the matters submitted in the trial of a case.

Vested: established; which ought to be maintained. A right or estate is said to be vested in a person when he becomes entitled to it. It may be vested in possession when he has a right to present enjoyment, or vested in interest when he has a present fixed right of future enjoyment, *i.e.*, a right to an estate, the possession of which is postponed to a fixed time, or the happening of a certain event.

Veto: the refusal of an executive officer, whose assent is necessary to the validity of an act passed by a legislative body, to concur therein. The veto power is given to the President of the United States and the governors of many of the states.

Violation: an act contrary to another's right, committed with force.

Void: of no force or effect; absolutely null.

Voidable: of imperfect obligation, so that it may be legally annulled, or, on the other hand, cured or confirmed at the option of one of the parties, *e.g.*, the contract of an infant with an adult.

Voluntary: acting without compulsion; done by design.

Voucher: a document which evidences a transaction; a receipt.

Waive: to forego, to decline to take advantage of, *e.g.*, a legal right or an omission or irregularity of another person. By waiver, a legal right is lost.

Want of consideration: the total lack of any valid consideration for a contract.

Warrant: an authority. (2) A precept under hand and seal to some officer to arrest an offender. (3) A writ of summons.

Warrant of attorney: a written authority addressed to a solicitor of the court in which it is intended that a judgment shall be entered up, authorizing him to appear on behalf of the person giving the authority and to confess judgment. The instrument is usually given to secure payment of a debt, and is defeasible on payment by a certain day.

Whereas: a word which introduces a recital of a fact.

Wilful: intentional; deliberate.

Without day: indefinitely. A defendant was formerly said to go without day when he was successful, the action not being adjourned to any future date.

Witness: one who sees an act performed, *e.g.*, the execution of a deed. (2) One who gives evidence in a cause. The attendance of a witness on the trial of a case in court is secured by the issuing of a subpoena.

Writ: a judicial process, by which a person is summoned to appear. (2) A legal instrument to enforce obedience to the orders and sentences of the courts. It is issued by authority of a court or other competent tribunal, and directed to the sheriff, or other officer, authorized by law to execute the same. He must return it with a brief statement of what he has done in pursuance of it to the court or officer authorizing its issue.

Writ of error: an original writ, directing an inferior court to send the record of proceedings before it to a superior court for review.

Wrong: the infringement of a right.

The primary source of material for the foregoing glossary is *Cochran's Law Lexicon, Fourth Ed.,* published by the W. H. Anderson Company, 646 Main Street, Cincinnati, Ohio.

C.

Code of Professional Ethics

Preamble

We, professional educators of the United States of America, affirm our belief in the worth and dignity of man. We recognize the supreme importance of the pursuit of truth, the encouragement of scholarship, and the promotion of democratic citizenship. We regard as essential to these goals the protection of freedom to learn and to teach and the guarantee of equal educational opportunity for all. We affirm and accept our responsibility to practice our profession according to the highest ethical standards.

We acknowledge the magnitude of the profession we have chosen, and engage ourselves, individually and collectively, to judge our colleagues and to be judged by them in accordance with the applicable provisions of this code.

Principle I

Commitment to the Student. We measure success by the progress of each student toward achievement of his maximum potential. We therefore work to stimulate the spirit of inquiry, the acquisition of knowledge and understanding, and the thoughtful formulation of worthy goals. We recognize the importance of cooperative relationships with other community institutions, especially the home.

In fulfilling our obligations to the student, we—

1. Deal justly and considerately with each student.
2. Encourage the student to study varying points of view and respect his right to form his own judgment.
3. Withhold confidential information about a student or his home unless we deem that its release serves professional purposes, benefits the student, or is required by law.
4. Make discreet use of available information about the student.
5. Conduct conferences with or concerning students in an appropriate place and manner.
6. Refrain from commenting unprofessionally about a student or his home.
7. Avoid exploiting our professional relationship with any student.
8. Tutor only in accordance with officially approved policies.

9. Inform appropriate individuals and agencies of the student's educational needs and assist in providing an understanding of his educational experiences.
10. Seek constantly to improve learning facilities and opportunities.

Principle II

Commitment to the Community. We believe that patriotism in its highest form requires dedication to the principles of our democratic heritage. We share with all other citizens the responsibility for the development of sound public policy. As educators, we are particularly accountable for participating in the development of educational programs and policies and for interpreting them to the public.

In fulfilling our obligations to the community, we—
1. Share the responsibility for improving the educational opportunities for all.
2. Recognize that each educational institution may have a person authorized to interpret its official policies.
3. Acknowledge the right and responsibility of the public to participate in the formulation of educational policy.
4. Evaluate through appropriate professional procedures conditions within a district or institution of learning, make known serious deficiencies, and take any action deemed necessary and proper.
5. Use educational facilities for intended purposes consistent with applicable policy, law, and regulation.
6. Assume full political and citizenship responsibilities, but refrain from exploiting the institutional privileges of our professional positions to promote political candidates or partisan activities.
7. Protect the educational program against undesirable infringement.

Principle III

Commitment to the Profession. We believe that the quality of the services of the education profession directly influences the future of the nation and its citizens. We therefore exert every effort to raise educational standards, to improve our service, to promote a climate in which the exercise of professional judgment is encouraged, and to achieve conditions which attract persons worthy of the trust to careers in education. Aware of the value of united effort, we contribute actively to the support, planning, and programs of our professional organizations.

In fulfilling our obligations to the profession, we—
1. Recognize that a profession must accept responsibility for the conduct of its members and understand that our own conduct may be regarded as representative.
2. Participate and conduct ourselves in a responsible manner in the development and implementation of policies affecting education.
3. Cooperate in the selective recruitment of prospective teachers and in the orientation of student teachers, interns, and those colleagues new in their positions.
4. Accord just and equitable treatment to all members of the profession in the exercise of their professional rights and responsibilities, and support them when unjustly accused or mistreated.

5. Refrain from assigning professional duties to non-professional personnel when such assignment is not in the best interest of the student.
6. Provide, upon request, a statement of specific reason for administrative recommendations that lead to the denial of increments, significant changes in employment, or termination of employment.
7. Refrain from exerting undue influence based on the authority of our positions in the determination of professional decisions by colleagues.
8. Keep the trust under which confidential information is exchanged.
9. Make appropriate use of time granted for professional purposes.
10. Interpret and use the writings of others and the findings of educational research with intellectual honesty.
11. Maintain our integrity when dissenting by basing our public criticism of education on valid assumptions as established by careful evaluation of facts or hypotheses.
12. Represent honestly our professional qualifications and identify ourselves only with reputable educational institutions.
13. Respond accurately to requests for evaluations of colleagues seeking professional positions.
14. Provide applicants seeking information about a position with an honest description of the assignment, the conditions of work, and related matters.

Principle IV

Commitment to Professional Employment Practices. We regard the employment agreement as a solemn pledge to be executed both in spirit and in fact in a manner consistent with the highest ideals of professional service. Sound professional personnel relationships with governing boards are built upon personal integrity, dignity, and mutual respect.

In fulfilling our obligations to professional employment practices, we—

1. Apply for or offer a position on the basis of professional and legal qualifications.
2. Apply for a specific position only when it is known to be vacant and refrain from such practices as underbidding or commenting adversely about other candidates.
3. Fill no vacancy except where the terms, conditions, policies, and practices permit the exercise of our professional judgment and skill, and where a climate conducive to professional service exists.
4. Adhere to the conditions of a contract or to the terms of an appointment until either has been terminated legally or by mutual consent.
5. Give prompt notice of any change in availability of service, in status of applications, or in change in position.
6. Conduct professional business through the recognized educational and professional channels.
7. Accept no gratuities or gifts of significance that might influence our judgment in the exercise of our professional duties.
8. Engage in no outside employment that will impair the effectiveness of our professional service and permit no commercial exploitation of our professional position.

Index